"What a novel but powerful and essential concept: that art is a way of listening. In this book—international in scope and wide-ranging in its understanding of the arts—the authors present inspiring portraits of using the arts to affirm languages that are suppressed or that may soon disappear unless they are reclaimed and revitalized. They remind us that if we just listen to our students, and work respectfully and collaboratively with their families and communities, then the education of all students—monolingual, bilingual, multilingual, and emergent—will inevitably be enriched."

—**Sonia Nieto,** *Professor Emerita,*
*University of Massachusetts, USA*

"In this important new book, the contributors demonstrate how art can be incorporated into the educational experiences of emergent bilinguals. They also explain why we should use art to inspire and motivate students to dream and excel."

—**Pedro A. Noguera,** *Dean, Rossier School of Education,*
*University of Southern California, USA*

"The book provides educators with rigorous research and stories of inspiring practice to lead us into collaborative, meaningful and transformative action in our teaching and learning environments. Arts-infused strategies equip educators with examples that vigorously combat anti-Blackness; authentically welcome immigrant families; decolonize Indigenous communities; refute the violence of displacement; disrupt discrimination of cultural identity and challenge hierarchical frameworks on what counts as knowledge."

—**From the Foreword by Patty Bode,**
*Southern Connecticut State University, USA*

*Always listening*
*Amanda*

# ART AS A WAY OF LISTENING

Offering a wealth of art-based practices, this volume invites readers to reimagine the joyful possibility and power of language and culture in language and literacy learning. Understanding art as a tool that can be used for decolonizing minds, the contributors explore new methods and strategies for supporting the language and literacy learning skills of multilingual students. Contributors are artists, educators, and researchers who bring together cutting-edge theory and practice to present a broad range of traditional and innovative art forms and media that spotlight the roles of artful resistance and multilingual activism. Featuring questions for reflection and curricular applications, chapters address theoretical issues and pedagogical strategies related to arts and language learning, including narrative inquiry, journaling, social media, oral storytelling, and advocacy projects.

The innovative methods and strategies in this book demonstrate how arts-based, decolonizing practices are essential in fostering inclusive educational environments and supporting multilingual students' cultural and linguistic repertoires. Transformative and engaging, this text is a key resource for educators, scholars, and researchers in literacy and language education.

**Amanda Claudia Wager** is Canada Research Chair in Community-Engaged Research and Professor of Education at Vancouver Island University, Canada.

**Berta Rosa Berriz** is Professor Emerita of Creative Arts and Learning at the Graduate School of Education at Lesley University, USA.

**Laura Ann Cranmer** is a Professor of Indigenous/Xwulmuxw Studies at Vancouver Island University, Canada.

**Vivian Maria Poey** is Professor of Photography and Integrated Studies at Lesley University, USA.

# ART AS A WAY OF LISTENING

Centering Student and Community Voices in Language Learning and Cultural Revitalization

*Edited by Amanda Claudia Wager,*
*Berta Rosa Berriz, Laura Ann Cranmer,*
*and Vivian Maria Poey*

Routledge
Taylor & Francis Group
NEW YORK AND LONDON

Designed cover image: Vivian Maria Poey

First published 2023
by Routledge
605 Third Avenue, New York, NY 10158

and by Routledge
4 Park Square, Milton Park, Abingdon, Oxon, OX14 4RN

*Routledge is an imprint of the Taylor & Francis Group, an informa business*

*Library of Congress Cataloging-in-Publication Data*
Names: Wager, Amanda Claudia, editor. | Berriz, Berta Rosa, editor. |
Cranmer, Laura Ann, editor. | Poey, Vivian, editor.
Title: Art as a way of listening : centering student and community voices in
language learning and cultural revitalization / edited by Amanda Claudia Wager,
Berta Rosa Berriz, Laura Ann Cranmer and Vivian Maria Poey.
Description: First Edition. | New York : Routledge, 2023. |
Includes bibliographical references and index.
Identifiers: LCCN 2022042166 (print) | LCCN 2022042167 (ebook) |
ISBN 9781032298160 (Hardback) | ISBN 9781032275468 (Paperback) |
ISBN 9781003302186 (eBook)
Subjects: LCSH: Language arts–Correlation with content subjects. |
Art–Study and teaching. | Literacy–Study and teaching. |
Education, Bilingual. | English language–Study and teaching–Foreign speakers. |
Indigenous peoples. | Intergenerational communication.
Classification: LCC LB1575.8 .A735 2023 (print) |
LCC LB1575.8 (ebook) | DDC 372.6–dc23/eng/20221230
LC record available at https://lccn.loc.gov/2022042166
LC ebook record available at https://lccn.loc.gov/2022042167

ISBN: 978-1-032-29816-0 (hbk)
ISBN: 978-1-032-27546-8 (pbk)
ISBN: 978-1-003-30218-6 (ebk)

DOI: 10.4324/9781003302186

Typeset in Bembo
by Newgen Publishing UK

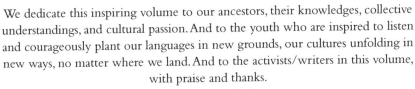

We dedicate this inspiring volume to our ancestors, their knowledges, collective understandings, and cultural passion. And to the youth who are inspired to listen and courageously plant our languages in new grounds, our cultures unfolding in new ways, no matter where we land. And to the activists/writers in this volume, with praise and thanks.

¡La Lucha Continúa!

Write On!

# CONTENTS

# Table of Contents

# A NOTE ON THE COVER AND TABLE OF CONTENTS

The cover and table of contents depict the (de)construction and re-imagining of a map of the world that provides fertile ground for multiple ways of being. We consciously deconstruct the map to place emphasis on the upheavals of linguistic dispossession and the diasporic transformation of language across the planet through time and space, and as represented by the journey of languages in this book. We also put the world upside down to resist the Westernized map we normally see and to re-imagine the world from a different perspective.

Locations of the chapters of the book are highlighted by flowers across the map and connected via lines and arcs. These connections show the journey that the chapters take you through, *Roots* and *Routes*, as well as the many spaces and places that the authors of each chapter are connected to (their ancestries, the places they were born, current locations, etc.). The images on the cover and table of contents reflect a map-making workshop where language work is always and everywhere a work-in-progress.

# FOREWORD

*Patty Bode*

Educators are called to reckoning. Globally, nationally and locally we are propelled to reflect inward on our perspectives and simultaneously outward to take responsibility for justice and passionately affirm diversity. We seek solidarity and assert courage to sustain emergent multilingual learners in our intersectional, dynamic worlds. This can be a daunting commitment amid great need in an inequitable society and the multiple goals that justice-minded educators hope to attain. This text, *Art as a Way of Listening: Centering Student and Community Voices in Language Learning and Cultural Revitalization*, edited by Amanda Claudia Wager, Berta Rosa Berriz, Laura Ann Cranmer, and Vivian Maria Poey provides more than hope.

The book provides educators with rigorous research and stories of inspiring practice to lead us into collaborative, meaningful and transformative action in our teaching and learning environments. Arts-infused strategies equip educators with examples that vigorously combat anti-Blackness; authentically welcome immigrant families; decolonize Indigenous communities; refute the violence of displacement; disrupt discrimination of cultural identity and challenge hierarchical frameworks on what counts as knowledge. In a range of contexts from PK-12 schools, community settings, and intergenerational learning environments across regions, nations and hemispheres, *Art as a Way of Listening* amplifies the voices, languages and artistic engagements of the participants and the reflections of educators who are collaborating among them.

This widened view on linguistic spaces highlights the elegant complexity and sometimes messy complications of diversity and the requirement for layered, multidimensional approaches to teaching and learning. The many places and ways learning happens presented in the two book sections, *Roots* and *Routes*, are illuminated with case studies, arts-interventions, narratives, art-installations, and performance projects in diverse languages/locations including: Kreole/Haiti;

N|uu/South Africa; Hawaiian/Hawai'i; Zapotec/Spanish/Oaxaca, Mexico; Arabic/Palestine and the "global mediasphere" (as advanced in Joshua Schwab Cartas's example). The global reach of this work demonstrates that advocating for the arts in learning, especially in public schools is essential and critical for both policy *and* practice. Engagement in the arts is a cultural right that must be upheld, and we are beginning to witness such rights being advanced at the policy level with dedication to cultural revitalization. For example, in the United States Congress in October 2021, *The Arts Education for All Act* was introduced by Congresswoman Suzanne Bonamici from Oregon to support arts educators and expand arts programming for children of all ages, including those in PK-12 schools and youth involved in the juvenile justice system. As this book goes to press, this initiative remains at the level of a bill, but its hopeful passage includes provisions which would further arts and arts education research, support professional development for elementary and secondary educators, and encourage partnerships to increase arts education and development in afterschool and summer learning programs (NAEA, 2021; H.R.5581 — 117th Congress, 2021–2022). *Art as a Way of Listening* provides distinctive examples of excellence for such approaches.

This kind of political will and structural support illustrates the promise of determined and dedicated activist teaching exemplified in these chapters. The text illuminates multifaceted learning which amplifies youth voice and highlights the flourishing of emergent multilingual learners when sociocultural perspectives guide our teaching with and through the arts. Home languages and academic languages are not viewed as separate entities by teachers or students. Both languages—or *multiple languages* as is the case for many students— thrive when the arts sustain the seeds, roots, stems, and flowering of community linguistic power. "Cultural ways of knowing must be understood as complex practices rather than simple notions of student assets," explain Ling Hao and Sally Brown in a chapter describing their case study with students who are Chinese-American emergent bilinguals. They turn our attention to view translanguaging as an art form. In this case, the children use drawing and talking to express understandings of picturebooks. These examples bring to life the assertion by the President of the National Art Education Association, James Haywood Rolling Jr. that, "The arts offer a complete integration of word, image, and life experience as data; information is thus networked for common points of reference" (2011, p. 9).

The modes, media, and models of arts-based infusion in *Art as a Way of Listening* are as diverse as the languages and regions. The authors invite us into critical reflection on their imaginative methods of engagement, which include: *cellphilms* (short videos shot entirely on a cellphone, smart device, or tablet) to enable intergenerational learning; improvisation as communication; Hip-Hop as Black Linguistic Brilliance; weaving *lauhala* as a space for historical, relational, and cultural learning; and Twitter-based pedagogical possibilities as *language kinscapes*, to name just a few. Furthermore, Khitam Edelbi and Yamila Hussein-Shannan point out that in addition to the verbal, oral home language of Arabic, the pedagogy of Playback Theater opens avenues for "colorful language we remember, resist, and lean towards healing, nurturing our humanity and envisioning our liberation." The perspectives from each chapter layer a new lens over the next, as regions and arts-based practices emphasize the intricacies of place and culture. For example, the complexity of language revitalization and reclamation is vividly vibrant in Maria Cecilia Schwedhelm Ramirez's essay about a language teacher education program in Oaxaca, Mexico in which she asserts there is a "great need to expand the work of language reclamation to spaces deemed non-Indigenous, like this University, and among both, Indigenous and non-Indigenous identifying youth." The research, stories and art compiled by Amanda, Berta, Laura, and Vivian verify that teachers and students can co-create spaces that decolonize, disrupt and challenge dominant cultural perspectives to cultivate a sense of belonging and thriving. As Rocky Cotard told us in the introduction to the *Routes* section, written collaboratively with his high school art teacher, Guy Michel Telemaque, "This led to a sort of awakening to reclaim my identity through my art."

I started this foreword by stating that *Art as Way of Listening* gives more than hope, but that *does not diminish the essential role of hope* in justice work and arts-based teaching in our homes, schools, community sites, and societies. The editors and authors of this book make me hopeful for the forthcoming generation of youth on a global scale and from an intimately personal perspective. I consider the case of my 8-year-old granddaughter, Anju, who is the child of my eldest foster son, Keo. Keo arrived in the United States thirty-seven years ago as a toddler with his parents and baby brother, all with refugee status from Cambodia. Now in his forties, he has his own family, which includes a daughter, Anju and his spouse, my daughter-in-law, Maya, who was born in Peru to a white-American mother and Peruvian father. The roots and branches of my granddaughter's family intertwine around our shared love. Anju calls me "Grammy Patty." She affectionately refers to her father's mother as "Yeay," which is "grandmother" in Cambodian Khmer. She names her mother's parents in Spanish, as "Abuelo and Abuela." She speaks English at school in Brooklyn, New York and attends after-school Spanish classes to reenforce the Spanish her mother speaks to her at home. Much of Anju's world is dominated by monolingual English-speaking cultures, but simultaneously many of the landscapes of her life in school, neighborhood, dance class, summer camp, and grandparent visits are layered with multilingual dialogue, multiracial families, multiethnic scents and tastes, along with paintings of glitter-rainbow unicorns and enjoying multi-colored ice cream cones with grandparents of all backgrounds. In many ways, her multi-hemispheric diasporic roots, multilingual familial ties, and love of chocolate sprinkled cupcakes make her a quintessential student in US public schools. I hope her languages will continue to be affirmed and awakened through the arts by her current and future educators. Art *is* a way of talking, listening, making, and knowing in Anju's multiple worlds, as I hope it will be for the youth of every community cited in this book and far beyond.

Collectively, this book brings readers to peer through the viewfinder of a kaleidoscope in our collective call to reckoning. Each author overlaps a lens of various emergent multilingual learners and turns the scope to layer the range of possible arts-based practices in our view. Each chapter alters our vision with the rotation of each shifting lens, reflecting inward on our perspectives while simultaneously holding the viewfinder upward and outward to bring in external light that illuminates our responsibility for justice. *Art as a Way of Listening* ultimately shapes a more colorful, spherical, and evolving hopeful vision of the possibilities of arts-based practices to truly reawaken language and activism with young people.

Patty Bode

## References

Haywood Rolling, J. (2011). *What High Quality Art Education Provides: Art Education as a Network for Curriculum Innovation and Adaptable Learning.* Advocacy White Papers for Art Education. [Advocacy White Papers for Art Education. Section 1]. NAEA White Paper. (pp. 8–11).

National Art Education Association. (2021). *Advocacy & Policy: Legislation to support the arts.* The Arts Education for all act. www.arteducators.org/advocacy-policy/articles/832-arts-education-for-all-act

*The Arts Education for All Act* (2021) H.R.5581 — 117th Congress, 2021–2022. www.congress.gov/bill/117th-congress/house-bill/5581?s=1&r=3

# CONTRIBUTORS

**Jeffrey Ansloos** is the Canada Research Chair in Critical Studies in Indigenous Health and Social Action on Suicide and Associate Professor at the Ontario Institute for Studies in Education at the University of Toronto. He completed his doctoral residency in Clinical Health Psychology at the University of Manitoba; a PhD and MA in Clinical Psychology and MAT in Ethics from Fuller Graduate School of Psychology, and a BA in Counseling from Trinity Western University. His research concerns social and environmental determinants of Indigenous peoples health, particularly in the areas of suicide, housing, and community mental health, as well as research on Indigenous social media, and cultural and language revitalization. Jeffrey is Nehiyaw (Cree) and English. He is a band member of Fisher River Cree Nation (Ochekwi-Sipi; Treaty 5). He was born and raised in the heart of Treaty 1 territory in Winnipeg, Manitoba and currently resides in Toronto, Canada.

**José Barreiro** is Smithsonian Scholar Emeritus, author and activist on behalf of Indigenous causes. A member of the Taino Nation of the Antilles, Barreiro is a pioneering contributor to Native American journalism and publishing and an award-winning author. He received the Doctor of Philosophy degree in American Studies from the State University of New York, Buffalo, in 1992. He co-edited, with John Mohawk, the national Native journal, *Akwesasne Notes*, from 1975 to 1984. In 1984, he co-founded the Native American Journalists Association. At Cornell University from 1984 to 2002, he served as an associate director and an editor-in-chief of Akwe:kon Press and the journal Native Americas. His program at Akwe:kon developed communications and community development networks among Indigenous peoples of the Americas. His significant publications include: *Indian Roots of American Democracy* (1988); *Indian Corn of* *the Americas: Gift to the World* (1989); *Indigenous Economics: Toward a Natural World Order* (1990), *View from the Shore: American Indian Perspectives on the Columbus Quincentenary* (1990), *Chiapas: Challenging History* (1994). His recent titles on American Indian topics include: *Taino*, (2012, novel); *Thinking in Indian: A John Mohawk Reader* (2011), *America is Indian Country* (2006), and *Panchito: Mountain Cacique* (2001, 2016).

**Berta Rosa Berriz** concluded her doctoral research at the Harvard Graduate School of Education (HGSE) investigating the relationship between the cultural identity of Puerto Rican and Dominican second-generation third-grade students and their teachers' assessment of their academic performance. She concluded her 33 years in Boston Public Schools as a Founding Co-lead teacher of the Boston Teachers' Union School (2008–2013). Including distinctions such as National Board Certification (2006), Doctoral studies HGSE (2005), Massachusetts Teacher Scholar (1992), faculty at Lesley University (1990 to 2018), Berriz was awarded a Lucretia Crocker Fellowship—TEAMSTREAM (1990)—for integrating bilingual students with special needs and gifted students through a collaborative arts approach. Recent publications include *Art as a Way of Talking for Emergent Bilingual Youth: A Foundation for Literacy in K-12 Schools* (2018), *Art as Voice: Creating Access for Emergent Bilingual Families and Communities* in the Journal of Pedagogy, Pluralism, and Practice (2017), both with co-editors Amanda Claudia Wager and Vivian Maria Poey. "Looking Forward Backwards: Teaching Freedom and Democracy in the Classroom" in Why Teach Now? Sonia Nieto, Editor (2015); "Multicultural Teaching Story: Boston Teachers Union School: Teacher Leadership and Student Achievement" in (2013) Affirming Diversity: Sociopolitical Context of Multicultural Education.

**Patty Bode** (pattybode.com) holds an EdD and MEd in Language, Literacy & Culture with a focus on critical multicultural education and curriculum reform, and a BFA in Art Education from the University of Massachusetts Amherst. She advances curriculum transformation, racial literacy and community-embedded practices through visual arts in PK-12 schools and higher education. Publications include "Visual Culture Art Education to Cultivate Critical Racial Consciousness" in *Art Education* (2022), and her co-authored book with Sonic Nieto, the 7th edition of *Affirming Diversity: The Sociopolitical Context of Multicultural Education* (2018). She is Associate Professor and Coordinator of Art Education at Southern Connecticut State University. She is a founder of the arts activism and community-engaged practice, the *Remember Love Recovery Project* which aims to destigmatize addiction disorder though art-making as human connection. (see rememberloverecovery.org) xx List of Contributors

**Sally Brown** is Professor of Literacy Education at Georgia Southern University where she teaches undergraduate and graduate literacy courses. Prior to working in higher education, she taught K-3rd grade in South Carolina public schools. Her research interests focus on supporting the literacy development of emergent bilinguals using technology, multimodal literacies, and culturally sustaining pedagogies in diverse early childhood classrooms. She is the former co-editor of *Talking Points*, a sub-affiliate of the National Council of Teachers of English and is currently a Literacies and Languages for All executive board member. Her work has been published in journals such as *The Reading Teacher*, the *European Early Childhood Research Journal*, and the *Journal of Research in Childhood Education*.

**Joshua Schwab Cartas** is a mixed race Indigenous Binnizá-Austrian, father, filmmaker, and Indigenous language scholar activist born outside his ancestral community on the traditional and unceded territory of Musqueam, Squamish, and Tsleil-Waututh Nations (Vancouver). He has a PhD in Integrated Studies in Education with a focus on Arts-based approaches to Indigenous language revitalization from McGill University and is presently Assistant Professor in Art Education in the Department of Art and Contemporary Culture at Novia Scotia College of Art and Design (NSCAD). Also, for the last 18 years he has been an active member of a Zapotec media and cultural collective known as Binni Cubi based in his grandfather's community of Ranchu Gubiña, Mexico. During that time, he has successfully worked on many community-based initiatives aimed at celebrating and perpetuating the Zapotec language and culture, such as documentary films, urban murals, and establishing a community radio station. His research seeks to explore how best to combine mobile technology, specifically cellphilms, into Indigenous practice and land-based education as means to fostering intergenerational knowledge transmission and language reclamation. He also uses a cellphilm method as a means to unpack and examine the emotional work involved in the journey of language reclamation.

**Rocky Cotard** born in Mirebalais Haiti and raised in Boston, Massachusetts, United States, places himself between two cultures as a bridge for artistic international connections. He draws inspiration from artists like Gontran Durocher, Phillipe Dodard, and Ronald Mevs. He returns to Haiti on a yearly basis informing his work on experiential research. His body of illustrations depict the perspective of the Haitian Diaspora in defiance to the narrow representation of it through media. Cotard's paintings, prints, and illustrations dig into his identity and lineage to collect his history, to reclaim his narrative, and to build cultural pride. His work portrays a wide range of color, the use of bold figures that demand attention, and improvisation. Conceptually, the work fights the unbalanced power by raising the people who have been generalized and making them into icons whose power is present and staring back.

**Laura Ann Cranmer** is Professor in Indigenous/Xwulmuxw Studies and Honorary Research Associate at Vancouver Island University, Canada. Born to David Cranmer of the 'Namgis, and Pearl Weir of the Haida, Laura was raised by her grandparents Chief Dan Cranmer and Agnes Cranmer. Mother to four children, Jake, Nan, Josh, and Ems, and grandmother to five grandsons (Seth, Josh, Patrick, Marcus, and Weston) and one granddaughter (Margo). On reflection, Laura's post-secondary journey with her BA in English, MA in Curriculum Studies, and her PhD in Language and Literacy Education was a halting two steps forward, one step back journey to self-empowerment. The development of her writing voice to a theatrical expression of her voice led her back to where she began, the language of her paternal lineage in which she was first raised—Kwak'wala. Along the way, she combined her therapy with her creative writing to help her navigate the complicated transformational journey necessitated by confronting her internalized colonial consciousness. As a residential school survivor, she is interested in how the literary and performing arts create a transformational space of autoethnographic inquiry for all those engaged in Indigenous language reawakening.

**Marit Dewhurst** is a Michigander-turned-Brooklynite who fell into weaving by accident. She has worked as an arts educator and program coordinator in multiple arts contexts including community centers, museums, juvenile detention centers, and international development projects. She is currently the Director of Art Education and Associate Professor of Art and Museum Education at The City College of New York. Her research and teaching interests include social justice education, community-based art, youth empowerment, and the role of the arts in community development. She writes often. In addition to journal articles and chapters, her first book, *Social Justice Art: A Framework for Activist Art Pedagogy* highlights young activist artists. Her second book, *Teachers Bridging Difference: Exploring Identity Through Art* describes how to use art as a tool to connect people across different sociocultural identities. She is a printmaker, weaver, textile artist, and maker of things.

**Khitam Edelbi** (PhD, Lesley University) is a specialist in Expressive Art Therapies, with over 25 years of extensive experience in drama, story-telling, theater production and art therapy. She founded the "Mobile Expressing Therapies Program" to promote empowerment, resilience, and opportunities for healing among Palestinian youth living under colonial rule. In addition to diplomas on Early Childhood from the Hebrew University, Jerusalem, and Teenage Leadership from Beit Rotenberg, Haifa, she holds a BA in Drama and Education, an MA in Expressive Arts Therapies and a PhD in Expressive Therapies from Lesley University, Cambridge, MA, United States. Dr. Edelbi is a TV show and talks presenter, narrator, and actor. Her publications include *Handbook of Drama Activities,*

*The Drama Handbook for Kindergarten Teachers*, and regular contributions in educational journals. She is fluent in Arabic, English, and Hebrew.

**Lina Maria Giraldo** is a Colombian-born, Boston-based designer, interactive media artist, and storyteller with a Co-design, Civic Media, Art, and Technology background. She is currently Assistant Professor of Data Visualization in the Journalism Department at Emerson College. Her work focuses on interactive storytelling for social change through data visualization, grassroots storytelling, public installations, and computer-generated work. She holds a Master of Professional Studies in Interactive Telecommunications from Tisch School of the Arts at New York University and a Bachelor of Fine Arts from Studio of Interrelated Media at Massachusetts College of Art and Design.

**Ling Hao** is a PhD candidate in the Teaching and Learning program at the University of South Carolina. She works as a graduate assistant and helps organize family–school partnership workshops for supporting bilingual families. She also works with English language learners and Chinese immigrant families. She received her master's degree from the University of Florida with a specialization in English/Reading Education. Her research interests include literacies in families, multimodal literacies, and reading assessment. Her research focuses on exploring emergent bilingual children's multimodal meaning-making process and promoting the literacy development of students with diverse cultural and linguistic backgrounds. She is the co-editor of the book *Multimodal Literacies in Young Emergent Bilinguals: Beyond Print-Centric Practices*.

**Yamila Hussein-Shannan** (EdD, Harvard University) is a scholar, educator, activist and public speaker dedicated to socio-economic and political justice. She teaches at the graduate level on the intricate relationship between language, power and (in)justice, and how matrices of oppression and liberation operate in the context of settler colonialism and anti-Black racism. She has designed, directed and taught academic programs for teachers in Boston (Harvard University, Boston College, Goddard College, Lesley University, BTR/UMass Boston), and internationally (Morocco, Jordan, Spain, Palestine, Mexico, and the Balkans). She holds an EdD in Politics of Education, and an MA in Community Education from Harvard University, Cambridge, MA, United States, and a BA in English Literature from AlQuds University, Palestine. A Palestinian born in Colombia and raised in Jerusalem, she is fluent in Spanish, Arabic, and English.

**Terry Jenoure** is a musician, visual artist, writer, and educator who grew up in New York City's *Bronx River Housing Projects* and began studying violin in elementary school. A self-taught visual artist who works with assemblage fiber figures and watercolor illustrations, her hand-stitched dolls are carried by the Smithsonian

Institute Museum shop and in private collections. Her poetry, essays, and arts-based research have appeared in numerous publications. She has been on the graduate faculty of the University of Massachusetts Amherst (UMass), Antioch College, Lesley University, and Goddard College, and has lead arts activism projects in India, South Africa, and Mexico. She was the Director of Augusta Savage Art Gallery at UMass for three decades and has earned numerous awards for music composition. Her book, *Navigators: African American Musicians, Dancers, and Visual Artists in Academe* (2000) has been referenced by numerous scholars. She has a masters degree and a doctorate in Education, and a bachelor's degree in Philosophy. She continues to perform, exhibit, and publish the many projects that come to her imagination.

**Chelsea Jimenez** is a certified elementary teacher in the state of South Carolina. She is currently a PhD student in the Urban Education program, as well as an educational researcher for the University of Pittsburgh. Within her undergraduate education at the University of South Carolina Columbia, she studied early childhood education with a focus in Urban Education and Research. Chelsea credits much of her research interests to her experience with living in city settings and majority Black areas, such as New York, Pennsylvania, and South Carolina. She identifies as a Black and Hispanic queer woman. She was raised by immigrant multilingual parents and was an ESOL pull-out teacher for much of her K-12 education. In relation to her diverse background and her own personal experiences, much of her research focuses on language, culture, race, power, access (or lack thereof) to mainstream society, education curriculum, instruction, and policy in relation to AAL and other Black languages. She hopes to continue to work alongside educators, yet through a new lens of shifting curriculum and teaching practices through education policy work.

**Bokyoung (Devin) Jo** is an international graduate student from South Korea studying a PhD in Arts Education at the University of Georgia. She received her bachelor's and master's degrees in arts education and art studies in Korea. She focuses on her research interests, encompassing art appreciation for higher education, artful inquiry, international (graduate) student studies, and Asian feminism studies, especially art-based learning to integrate and expand various knowledge.

**Charlot Lucien** is a Haitian storyteller, poet, and visual artist and the founder of the Haitian Artists Assembly of Massachusetts. He uses his art to promote Haitian culture and advocate for various humanitarian, civil rights and public health issues through his work with Haitian Diaspora cultural and civic organizations. A former high school teacher in Haiti, Lucien currently works in the public health field for the State of Massachusetts. He became interested in the United States–Haiti historical connections, after surveying the relevant historiography in the United

States. He is currently pursuing a master's degree in international relations at the University of Massachusetts where he is also a lecturer in the Gerontology OLLI Program of the McCormack Graduate School of Global Studies. His work has been published in *La Tentation de l'autre rive,* "*The Boston Haitian Reporter*".

**Samantha McCormick** is a PhD student in the School and Clinical Child Psychology program at the Ontario Institute for Studies in Education at the University of Toronto. She completed her MA in the same program. She also holds an Honours BA in Psychology from Algoma University and Advanced Diploma in Child and Youth Work from Sault College. She has Anishinaabe and Settler ancestry and hails from Baawaating, in Northern Ontario. She is an Indigenous language learner and dedicated to supporting Indigenous language revitalization in her work. Further, she is passionate about Indigenous feminisms and queer studies. Her doctoral research aims to understand the mental health needs of young Indigenous women, queer, trans, and two-spirit youth. She is proud to have co-authored the recent publication: Ansloos, J., Zantingh, D., Ward, K., McCormick, S., & Bloom Siriwattakanon, C. (2021). Radical Care and Decolonial Futures: Conversations on Identity, Health, and Spirituality with Indigenous, Queer, Trans, and Two-Spirit Youth. *International Journal of Child, Youth and Family Studies,* 12(3–4), 74–103.

**Ashley Caranto Morford** is Assistant Professor of Writing and Literature in the Department of Liberal Arts at the Pennsylvania Academy of the Fine Arts in Lenapehoking, the ongoing and unsurrendered homelands of the Lenape Peoples (colonially called Philadelphia). She is a diasporic Filipina-British settler scholar and educator whose work is accountable to and in relationship with Indigenous studies, Filipinx/a/o studies, critical race studies, anti-colonial methods and praxis, and digital humanities. She has a PhD in Literature from the University of Toronto, Canada, an MA in Literature from Simon Fraser University, Canada, and a BA in Literature and Indigenous Studies from Simon Fraser University, Canada. Her current scholarly and community work reflects on how settler Filipinx/a/os can be better kin and relations to Indigenous lands and life within so-called North America.

**Cherie Okada-Carlson** is a wannabe farmgirl in South Kona, on the Big Island of Hawaii. In 1996, she started teaching high school for the Hawaii Department of Education and in 2001 left the classroom to become a middle school Student Services Coordinator. She started weaving *lauhala* hats in 2003 at the *Ka Ulu Lauhala O Kona* annual weaving conference and has attended every year since then. Her website, lauhalahats.com, sells and makes *pāpale lauhala Hawai'i* available to those who live outside *Hawai'i nei.* She is interested in food security and sustainability, sketching with fountain pens, and vintage *mu'umu'u.* She is also venturing into the world of Risograph printmaking.

**Vivian Maria Poey** is Professor of Photography and Integrative Studies at Lesley University. She served as Director of the MEd in Community Arts and Education and taught graduate courses to teachers across the country on integrating the arts into the curriculum. As an artist and educator, she engages the arts as a process of investigation both in and out of the classroom. Her photographic work examines a number of issues ranging from history, migration, and cultural assimilation. She is American, born in Mexico of Cuban parents and lived in Guatemala and Colombia before moving to the United States. This complicated trajectory informs all of her work. She has exhibited her work widely and has published on integrated arts and inclusive pedagogy. Vivian is co-editor of *Art as a Way of Talking for Emergent Bilingual Youth: A Foundation for Literacy in PreK-12 Schools* and is the recipient of the Massachusetts Art Education Association Higher-Educator of the Year Award.

**Maria Cecilia Schwedhelm Ramirez** holds a PhD in Second Language Education from the University of Minnesota. Her research interests touch on the intersections of emotion, identity and language learning in contexts of Indigenous and heritage language education and revitalization. She comes from the Valley of Mexico and from stories of wandering ancestors. She is a writer and theater artist and has worked as a language teacher and curriculum developer in the field of educational technology. Her current work explores the possibilities of embodied, arts-based pedagogies to (re)imagine equitable multilingual spaces, and create and enact processes and practices of language and culture reclamation. She is active in community-based organizations in Mexico and in Minnesota helping develop projects that promote the teaching and learning of students' home languages through the integration of academic and artistic activities.

**Patricia A. Shaw** is Professor Emerita at the University of British Columbia, dedicated to the interdisciplinary application of Linguistics, Anthropology, and Language and Literacy Education. She has worked for many decades within academia and in close collaboration with several Indigenous scholars and language communities to develop locally based expertise in the documentation of linguistic and cultural heritage, in research and archiving methodologies, and in the co-development of pedagogical materials for Indigenous language reawakening and sustainability. At UBC, she was the Founding Director (1996–2014) of the UBC First Nations and Endangered Languages Program, Founding Editor of the UBC Press First Nations Languages Series, Director of the Aboriginal Languages and Literacies Institute (2006, where she and her co-author Laura first met), and Director of the BC Breath of Life Archival Institute (2017). She served as President of SSILA, is on the Endangered Languages Fund Board of Directors, and frequently collaborates as a faculty mentor at CoLang/InField Institutes, at the California/AICLS-Berkeley and the National Breath of Life Archival Institutes. Centered in all things by her two daughters and two grandchildren, she and they work towards enhancing the vital role of the arts in nurturing inclusivity, cultural and bio-diversity, and social justice.

**Guy Michel Telemaque** is a Visual Arts Faculty Member and Director of the Sandra and Philip Gordon Art Gallery at the Boston Arts Academy (BAA). He received his Bachelor of Arts in Fine Art from Flagler College and his Master of Fine Arts in Photography from the Massachusetts College of Art and Design. Prior to BAA, he has been an instructor at the Southeast Center for Photographic Studies, the Southeast Museum of Photography, and at the Massachusetts College of Art. His work has been exhibited nationally and collected by the Southeast Museum of Photography. His awards include an artist's fellowship from the Surdna Foundation, a Power of Art Fellowship from the Robert Rauschenberg Foundation, a Distinguished Educator of the Year from the Massachusetts College of Art and Design, and a fellowship with the Perrone-Sizer Institute for Creative Leadership.

**Becky Thiessen** after almost 18 years in Winnipeg, MB, has settled once again in her birth province of British Columbia and is calling Nanaimo home. As a graduate of the Master of Community Planning program at Vancouver Island University (VIU) she hopes to encompass all that she has learned to help create and design places that inspire creativity and community. Twenty years of dynamic community development work as an Artist and Arts Educator, and now a Planner, she has compiled a unique set of leadership, facilitation, art and design skills. Her experience ranges from women's advocacy, accessibility planning, family and community outreach, and child and youth arts education. Her work has taken her across Canada to the high Arctic and in various rural, coastal, northern and inner city communities. Currently she works at VIU as a Campus Planner with a specific focus on Universal Access and as the Research Centre Coordinator for arc: A Centre for Art, Research and Community. She is constantly planning and envisioning ways where she can incorporate more art into her community.

**Lorato Trok** is an early literacy consultant and expert in developing reading for pleasure books for young children. She has more than 20 years' experience in publishing, writing, editing, translation, and story development. Her career highlights include being a Project Coordinator at the Centre for the Book, a specialist unit of the National Library of South Africa for the award winning (IBBY 2004) First Words in Print project. She was also a Publishing Programme Manager at Room to Read South Africa, an American International NGO. She was a South Africa, Lesotho and Zambia Country Coordinator for the African Storybook Initiative, a digital publishing platform for children's stories across Africa. She is a creative writing facilitator and has facilitated multilingual writing workshops in Southern and East Africa and the United States of America. She is also an award-winning translator and editor. In 2020 she won an IBBY award for best translation.

**Amanda Claudia Wager** is a Tier II Canada Research Chair in Community-Engaged Research and Professor in the Faculty of Education at Vancouver Island University in Canada. Of Jewish Ashkenazi ancestry, born in Los Angeles and having grown up in Amsterdam, she embraced learning and hearing languages everywhere. As a trilingual/literate/cultural (English/Spanish/Dutch) educator, she views language learning and teaching as a cultural art form and as an interdisciplinary scholar, she practices community-engaged research and pedagogy that encompasses literacies, languages, and the arts with local youth, families, and communities. Amanda is the founding Director of the *arc: A Centre for Art, Research and Community* that works together with many communities across Vancouver Island using the arts as a form of bridging communities, language reawakening and literacy learning. She has published multiple journal articles and co-edited/authored three books using art as a form of advocacy, *Engaging Youth in Critical Arts Pedagogies and Creative Research for Social Justice, Art as a Way of Talking for Emergent Bilingual Youth,* and *The Reading Turn-Around with Emergent Bilinguals.* https://research.viu.ca/dr-amanda-wager#.

**Yixuan Wang** is currently a doctoral student and graduate teaching assistant in the Department of Language and Literacy Education with a concentration on TESOL and World Language Education at the University of Georgia. She earned her bachelor's degree in English Language and Literature in China and her Master's from the same program at the University of Georgia. Yixuan's research interests include arts-based educational research, arts-based teaching and learning, poetic inquiry in qualitative research, multilingual and multicultural education, Chinese heritage language education, justice-oriented language teacher education, and Asian Critical Race Theory. Her recent single-authored and co-authored publications appear in *GATESOL Journal* and *Critical Issues in Education.*

# PREFACE

## Language Reawakening, Diaspora, and Activism with Young People

*As an educator, this book offers me several examples of how to decolonize my classroom linguistically and culturally, whether in K-12 schools or at the university.*

Foulis, 2020, p. 149

This quote is from a book review about the first co-edited book, *Art as a Way of Talking* (Berriz et al., 2018). It reflects how the book garnered considerable interest from our readers, primarily multilingual educators, who have been moved by it. We believe the main reason for the book's appeal is that it challenges notions of what it means to engage students through the arts in bringing their cultural knowledges and languages as resources for learning. This current volume, *Art as a Way of Listening: Centering Student and Community Voices in Language Learning and Cultural Revitalization*, focuses on how artistic practices, both traditional and innovative, can be used to increase literacy and language abilities with multilingual learners, as well as students with limited access to academic English and those working on reawakening their language. Student voices and leadership are centered—especially voices from Indigenous, African American, and international communities engaged in language and cultural revitalization. We have included artists, educators, and researchers that exemplify how the arts and language-learning intersect with sociocultural ways of knowing, pedagogical strategies and advocacy while promoting multilingual educational practices. As a complement to our first book *Art as a Way of Talking* this volume, *Art as a Way of Listening*, focuses on language reawakening, the global diaspora and activism with young people.

## How the Book is Organized

The content is organized and presented in two major sections: *Roots* and *Routes*. Each section begins with an opening example, is followed by six chapters, and concludes with questions for reflection and further applications for practice. The first section of the book, *Roots*, opens the volume with an emphasis on art as a tool for decolonizing minds and the revitalization of languages. Researcher and educator Becky Thiessen highlights an artistic collaboration among an intergenerational group of respected Elders, community members, artists, teachers, facilitators, and researchers and describes their process of using local languages to disseminate their findings. Khitam Edelbi and Yamila Hussein-Shannan then discuss the use of Playback Theater to create spaces for Palestinian adolescents to practice intentional listening as they narrate and enact their and others' stories, expressing how they make sense of the world around them while cultivating inner and collective strength. From South Africa, Lorato Trok emphasizes the importance of Indigenous knowledge systems and how its application can be used to attain the same outcomes as mainstream teaching practices. Maria Schwedhelm Ramirez illustrates and analyzes the work of a university class through an ethnodrama, underscoring the value of the arts and performance pedagogies to foster critical ideological awareness, advocacy, and activism for language reclamation in Oaxaca, Mexico. Cherie Okada-Carlson and Marit Dewhurst reflect on how both Hawaiian language and weaving-specific terminology can be a space for historical, relational, and cultural learning. Joshua Schwab Cartas, through a participatory and visual use of cellphilms (short videos shot on a cellphone) grounded in Zapotec ancestral traditions, demonstrates how youth reawaken their relationship with their ancestral language of diidxazá. Closing the *Roots* section, Ashley Caranto Morford, Samantha McCormick, and Jeffrey Ansloos examine how Indigenous communities transform the social media platform, Twitter, into a learning environment for their ancestral languages.

The second section, *Routes*, follows diasporic journeys while honoring peoples' perspectives as languages unfold in new lands. In the opening example Guy Michel Telemaque and Rocky Cotard create visible stories of migration from Haiti to the US through the convergence of student and teacher at the Boston Arts Academy. Chelsea Jimenez features African American Language (AAL) and Hip-Hop music as tools to improve academic performance and affirm her students' linguistic and cultural identities. Ling Hao and Sally Brown highlight the voices of Chinese learners to show the power of art, multilingual talk, and culture in learning about the world. Charlot Lucien chronicles his journey as a storyteller rooted in the Haitian oral tradition while negotiating the cultural and linguistic challenges of storytelling in a new environment. Through their relationship as graduate students, Bokyoung Jo and Yixuan Wang use visual journaling as a collective and artistic voice exposing anti-Asian discrimination, while encouraging researchers and educators to include arts, translanguaging, and Critical Race Theory in future pedagogies and methodologies. From work at the Boston Community Center for Youth and Family, Lina Maria Giraldo discusses how ITS (Identity, Technology and Storytelling) encourages critical thinking with an intergenerational and multilingual cohort. Closing the *Routes* section, multidisciplinary artist Terry Jenoure exposes artistic, linguistic, ethnic, racial, familial, and educational factors that give perspective to her artmaking.

## An Invitation

The chapters included in this volume accentuate the power of community to further language reawakening, and how artists, teachers and researchers can be advocates for language and literacy education and cultural reawakening through the arts. Throughout these pages, we hope you may discover innovative ways to engage learners, and all that they represent, in their language learning journeys, and understand how what we teach should be connected to their communities and everyday lives. Enjoy!

## References

Berriz, B. B, Wager, A. C., & Poey, V. M. (Eds.). (2018). *Art as a way of talking for emergent bilingual youth: A foundation for literacy in prek-12 schools.* Routledge. https://doi.org/10.4324/9781351204231.

Foulis, E. (2020). *Journal of Folklore and Education* Reviews [Review of the book Art as a way of talking for emergent bilingual youth: A foundation for literacy in prek-12 schools. by Eds. B.R. Berriz, A.C. Wager & V.M. Poey]. *Journal of Folklore and Education,* 7, pp. 147–152.

# ACKNOWLEDGMENTS

We begin by thanking the authors of this magnificent volume, for sharing their stories, their research, their relations, their knowledges with us and all of you. This book is only possible because of their contributions and gifts that further the field and practice of arts-based learning for language reawakening and acquisition. We could not have navigated this journey without the fine editors at Routledge, particularly Karen Adler for reaching out to us and encouraging us to create *Art as a Way of Listening* after the international success of *Art as a Way of Talking* (Berriz et al., 2018). Thank you Karen for all of your support and patience along this second journey together. Sending much gratitude to our community of exceptional friends and colleagues who served as *our* listeners through out the process and shared their reflections with us: Amy Bebergal, Marit Dewhurst, Kristen Goessling, Sharon Karsten, Noreen McHale, Sonia Nieto, Prilly Sanville, Patricia A. Shaw, Becky Thiessen. We are especially grateful to all of the young people, their families, and communities that we work with; we learn more from and with you everyday. Thank you for these humbling, reciprocal and beautiful relationships. And most importantly, special thanks to our families who generously gave up time with us as we worked through endless evenings and who served as encouragers, listeners, mappers, readers, political discussers, and editors with embracing enthusiasm:

Berta's husband, Ty dePass, for his wordsmithing and critical eye; Tristan Karl Weinkle, Berta's son who at the age of two, delighted in looking at the world upside down.

Amanda's partner, Drew Smith, for his thoughtful map-making skills, and her wee girl, Sedara, born during the making of this book, and her not-so-wee-boys Sylvain and Eric, who demand she stop typing and *just listen* to them.

Laura's husband Bill Holdom who keeps me grounded, my children, Jake, Nan, Josh and Ems and my grandchildren, Seth, Josh, Margo, Patrick, Marcus, and Weston who are all precious gifts from gigami laxa iki. My beloved Yotu for her strength and guidance, my cousin Myrna Cranmer for teaching me not to sugarcoat our colonial history, and finally our ancestors who continue to inspire our work today.

Vivian's husband Guy Michel for sharing his story, and teen daughter Camila for teaching us all about language in the next generation. They are my anchors.

xxxiv    Acknowledgments

# OPENING CALL: INDIGENOUS CREATION—LITERATURE AS HISTORICAL/CULTURAL RECOVERY

*José Barreiro*

Begins with Taino song: Sacred Earth

> (He né guakéya yá, He né guakéya /
> He né guakéya yá, He né guakéya /
> He né guakéya ya / He né guakéya /
> He né guakéya /guahoúpia héh héh
> guahoúpia héh héh, nowéh)

Tau ti, fellow writers, scholars, and communicators, guatiaos all: thank you for your invitation and your time.[1]

I am a writer and communicator, a campaigner; I value creativity and belong like you to the clan of the creative workers, trying to help vision and imagination, knowledge and learning blend together and create something that might be useful.

I came here representing three elements of my life: a literary work, an institution, and a people. The literary work is "Taino, the Indian Chronicles," my own novel that recounts the story of the conquest of the Caribbean and gives a Taino point of view about the encounter that changed our peoples, our islands, our hemisphere, forever.[2] The institution is the American Indian Program at Cornell University, where for nearly 20 years, we published a hemispheric magazine for Indigenous peoples, *Native Americas*, as well as books, and coordinated forums and international projects with communities and academics, on Native topics. The people I represent are the Taino Nation of the Antilles, to whom I belong, and who sometimes request my at-large representation of its cultural and literary interests in international events.

## Taino Nation: A people sustains

The Taino Nation represents a cultural revitalization movement presently asserting itself in the Greater Antilles (Cuba, Puerto Rico, Dominican Republic, Jamaica, Haiti) and in the North American diaspora. It reflects a conscious people and it is made up of groupings (yukayeke) reflecting thousands of people (several thousand families) in the diaspora and several enclaves or communities of population in the islands. Taino is one of several groupings of people who identify as Native people of the Caribbean, some specifically as Taino, or as related Ciboney, Guajiro, Jibaro, Indio or Montuno, Maroon (Jamaica). In the smaller islands, it extends to the Kalinago (Caribs) of Dominica and the Garifuna and its diaspora in Central America. The crucial challenge facing this movement is to give the lie to the notion that our culture and continuous identity as a land-based, indigenous people became extinct and can never reassert its value, much less revitalize or reconstruct.

I will be showing a video production, "Taino: Indigenous Survival in the Caribbean," which is an initial graphic report about the early outreach of Taino people and the effort to thread together the various communities of Native ancestry, in Cuba, Puerto Rico, Dominican Republic, and the North American diaspora. Centrally important, within it you meet the Taino-descendant Indio people of Cuba and the leaders and people of the Taino Nation in Boriken (Puerto Rico/ NY) rebuilding indigeneity and reconnecting our people. You can see that the application of the term "extinction" is misguided when examining the cultures and identities of peoples.

Our Taino culture and our Taino people persist; we are reorganizing and deepening our presence. Within communities, within families and within individuals, the impetus to reconnect with each other is a very strong social reality in the indigenous Caribbean. Our Taino language, much studied and much forgotten, is scrutinized, deciphered, and reapplied by various Taino groups, working with empathic linguists, and the enthusiasm of many of our people. This is now ongoing and is not likely to be stymied by denials from academic circles or by governmental dictums. Thus I am honored to represent the Taino cultural recovery movement at this first international congress on Indigenous literature; I bring you greetings from the family Elders, from the councils of men and women Elders, increasingly identified as nitainos, and most specifically from our head Elder of the Cuban mountains, our beloved Cacique Panchito Ramirez Rojas and from the matriarch of the mountain, Reina Ramirez.[3]

## Akwe:kon Press Cornell University

My professional base is at the American Indian Program at Cornell University (1984–2002), where I direct a communications and Native community empowerment project called Akwe:kon Press, which publishes a journal, *Native Americas.*[4] Akwe:kon is an active program that existed primarily to bridge understanding and collaboration between cultures and worldviews. We are established as an independent Indian forum at a major North American university and we greatly value Native knowledge. We work in documentation, culture preservation, and community development with culture-bearing people from dozens of Native nations. We celebrate the functions of both oral and written traditions and assist shared endeavors among Indigenous communities from Central, South, and North America. Our commitment is to value the culture-bearing Elders of Indigenous nations and to consider the oral traditional knowledge for verities on a par with the documentary tradition of the doctorate and academia.

At Cornell University, the American Indian Program, and the Akwe:kon center, guides over 100 Native college students in higher education every year. Nationally and internationally, we communicate with several thousand more Native students and community leaders via a network of Internet site links, publications, and conferences. Planned for an Indigenous constituency and for a general public, these dialogues among and about Indigenous issues have often transcended to the American body politic, with the purpose of educating the public and opening space of Native perspectives in national life.

An appreciable teaching from the AIP at Cornell was its founding in consultation with many families and several councils among traditional Native communities in New York State. In responding particularly to the Haudenosaune Elders' instruction to the university at that time, the program committed and hopefully will always endeavor to reconnect our Native students with their home communities and homelands, and when possible, provide a return or "full circle" higher education experience that assists community generational cohesion, growth, and culture.

The high energy of Native people at this time is palpable. We are seeing the creators, the artists, writers, community leaders emerging everywhere. We see many travelling Indigenous delegations these days, south and north, with always persistent activity at the United Nations, now in its International Decade of Indigenous Peoples. There is good networking, and increasing protagonism in many spheres of work, and we also see that here in Guatemala the Maya thinking and tradition is being recognized more, and hopefully will be applied more and more to community development, to ecological interaction. Across the Western Hemisphere, we see increased Indian-to-Indian understanding and mutual work: Crees from Ontario helping Ye'kuanas in Venezuela to demarcate their lands using the latest GIS (Geological Information Survey) technology; Iroquois partnering up with Mayas to market coffee; Athabascans meeting with Mapuche over ecological issues in Chile; Kunas hosting a major international bio-diversity congress in their comarca of San Blas; United States American Indians actually running the major new Smithsonian museum on the Americas, running some Native 32 tribal in-community colleges and universities; Maya writers hosting a major international literary congress and enlisting the support of embassies, ministries, universities, and foundations. To paraphrase José Martí's words upon the death of Benito Juarez, "Until now there was no America, until now that its royalty cries for the Indian." So we might say, "Until now there is no America, until its governmental institutions pay homage and support its Native creators!"

It is a privilege and it gives tremendous hope to be a part of this work, to have seen this process emerge from the days in the darkness just twenty years ago and grow to its present maturity and strength; it is uplifting to contemplate its potential for the positive recovery of Native identity, for the health of Native communities, and for the future of our youth.

Akwe:kon means "all of us," in the Mohawk language. It is a phrase used extensively in the major oration of the Haudenosaune culture, the "Thanksgiving Address." It directs human minds to think about "all of us," in the same context as the Lakota, "mitakuye oyasin," (we are all related) and instructs that we "put our minds together," to thank the natural gifts of the Creator. We labored in that principle during the founding of the now American Indian and Indigenous Program, at Cornell University, back in the 1980s, to guide Native students in higher education, but to be a place which, as well, extended good offices, publication pages, classes and all of our hearts to the intelligence of Native communities—which is all of you. Stay strong, let's share information, regular reports, strengthen the links.

## Novel As Historical Recovery

I promised to talk about the creative act, about writing and about how our art might be of use to our various peoples. Writing a novel, at least in my case, is solitary work. Mine actually began as a historical work based in part in a retelling of my own stories, what I relished of our Cuban guajiro culture from my childhood in the eastern Cuban provinces of Camagüey and Oriente in the 1950s and early 1960s. The history was to be about the conquest of the Caribbean islands, the response and various fates of the Taino chiefs and their peoples to Spanish domination in the first five decades after the landfall of Columbus. For that I conducted research in the early chronicles and histories, the six or seven basic treatises and works of documentation (Columbus, Las Casas, Oviedo, Martyr de Angleria, Hernandes, Friar Roman Pané), comparing different accounts of the same incidents and adding all I could from the combing of secondary and tertiary documents.

I conducted more primary research during a conference invitation to Spain, at the Archive of Indies, in Seville. I got very lucky at the voluminous archives in that venerable institution, finding important, direct references to a particular historical character, a young Taino boy, Diego Colón, the adopted son of the Admiral. This character, Diego Colón, surfaced in more and more places. I found him in my mind's eye and his voice grew in me to the point that I dreamed of Diego twice. This happened as I was nearing the end of my historical research and the second dream was the impetus to move the narrative directly from a history to a novel in the form of a journal, Diego's journal, set in the island of Santo Domingo of 1532–33.

My personal stories and influences of childhood provided background to perspective. In the part of Cuba where I grew up, and certainly among older members of my family, the story of the Taino rebel chief, Hatuey, his message to our Cuban Indian ancestors and his resistance to Spanish rule had saliency as a story that belonged to us. My people, via the history of resistance to Spain, fully identified with Hatuey and the story of his message as ancestor bases to our rebellious Cuban consciousness. The Hatuey story contained spiritual as well as historic-patriotic layers. I heard it many times and from various people during my childhood, and one current of it, represented in "the Light of Yara," which names the place where Hatuey was burned at the stake, I learned particularly at the lap of my Tia Lilina, my father's sister.

In our guajiro country culture of eastern Cuba, from Camagüey into the mountains of the Sierra Maestra, the ways of the medicinal plants, the most indigenous uses of the yucca, maize and other endemic plants, and indeed, medicinal healing and protection ceremonies such as the "tracking cure" (cura del rastro) and planting of endemic root crops by the lunar phases were commonplace into the 1950s and early 1960s. In recent trips home, I have seen that this is still alive today. Particularly the traditions of the conuco or small family food plot, as well as the use of many indigenous plants for medicine and as spiritual guides, are widespread in all three Spanish-speaking islands among guajiro, jibaro, and indio campesino populations. In Cuba, at least one continuously inherited cacique lineage has represented itself publicly in recent years.

So, the narrative that grew in me and the voice that I carried one morning from my dream to the writing table, offered a line of storytelling that did not abandon me for over two years as, sometimes in the middle of the winter of Northern New York, surrounded by deep snows, I would drift in my imagination to the Caribbean shores of the early 1500s, savoring anew those early encounters from the time when our old people, those deeply indigenous ancestors of our people, were whole. I consciously fashioned into Diego's tapestry the best of my perception on the various lines of research I had undertaken, but the voice was a gift throughout until the narrative came to its natural conclusion.

One thought from our Caribbean experience and also the research on the encounter: the deepest discernable messages of the Taino chiefs to the Spanish at that early moment of contact were to be repeated over and over across the Caribbean and via the expansion south and west of European colonization. Among those early Taino messages were these:

- The land as provider and equalizer. Guarionex, cacique of the Magua region of Hispaniola (Santo Domingo/Haiti), goes to the Columbus brothers in 1494 to plead against the imposition of the gold tribute by the Spanish. The gold tribute dictated that every Taino man over 14 years of age must wear a wooden medallion on his chest to prove that he has provided his tribute of a gold every three months to the Spanish governor. Failure to display the medallion brought on punishment at will by any Spanish soldier, usually by amputation of hands, cut-off noses and ears and other mutilations that generally resulted in death. Guarionex brought over one thousand men and women with digging sticks (*coas*) and seeds and cuttings of every crop, from yucca to maize. The cacique offered to plant a field of massive proportions to feed "the Castilla," on the island and across the water, if only the tribute of gold could be taken off, since it was resulting in widespread tragedy for his people.

The Columbus brothers refused the offer and the slaughter continued, but the gesture by native chiefs of offering the bounty of the earth and its knowledge as a gift that could be shared, and could equalize human beings, this would happen again and again. Alas, it was not to be even recognized by westerners until very recent times.

It has been noted by contemporary historians that the Taino refused to plant crops in the late season of 1494 in what the conquistadors called a "diabolical" plan to starve out the heroic Spanish soldiers setting up forts on their lands. It seems Guarionex had a reason for not wanting to plant that season, since his generous offer had been refused and the gold tribute continued that ultimately martyred him and decimated his people.[5]

- The notion of gold as the real god of the Spanish. To this day, many Native people suspect money and the "whiteman's" violent lust of it. "The love of possessions is a disease with them," said Chief Red Cloud, of the Lakota in the 1880s. From Cuba in 1513 comes the example of Hatuey, as resistance hero and as critical thinker. The cacique Hatuey traveled by canoe to Cuba as a Taino, or relative, from Haiti to warn the Cuban caciques of the impending Spanish invasion. He assured them that gold is the actual god of the Spanish; it is what they seek and will brutalize them for.

Hatuey's thinking is also clear in a second respect that carries across many histories of contact:

- We have a religion of our own. After capture by the forces of conquistador Diego Velazquez, Hatuey is about to be burned at the stake. A Franciscan friar approaches. "Would the cacique now accept baptism and thus enter the Kingdom of Heaven?" he asks. "And if I don't?" replies Hatuey, "where do I go?" In that case, straight to hell, the friar assures him, in so many words. And the Spanish, where do they go? Hatuey insists. They are baptized, so they go to heaven, replies the friar. "Then don't baptize me," responds Hatuey. "I prefer to go to hell, to be not with such cruel people as they."

Thus the three main and often repeated themes of Indian thinking as the conquest travels in place and time can be found in just these two Taino stories: the land and the sun as source of life, equalizer of the human; Gold as God in the eye of the conquistador, and; we have a spirituality of our own. Lesson: there must be resistance to a religious system that sides with brutality.

There is more, both from the chronicles, and in the persistence of culture and Native ways among campesino, including the Native guajiro, and other people in Cuba, Boriken and Quisquella, who still practice traditional natural indigenous ways.

As I approached the often-hidden pieces of information, I found that being consistent in my own *guajiro* point of view paid off. Caciques in the chronicles, for instance, who kept telling Columbus about numerous women and much gold to be found on other islands. They even named fictitious places that later lived in European myths of the Americas (about an island of exclusively Amazon women, for example). These my Diego identified mostly as the cleverness of scandalized elders trying to get the lusty, bearded louts to move on and out of their territories.

That novel and of course the parallel work of spiritually aligning in the cultural recuperation efforts of the Taino Nation, and particularly standing with the elders of Cacique Panchito, signaled for me the actual depth required to understand the ongoing Caribbean Indian history that does not end in 1519, or in 1550 or in 1900 or in the year 2000.

Our common interest is profound and evidence of the long-term saturation of Taino knowledge, Spiritual and material culture that threads into our national identities. Even though the focus of the early history shifted to the mainland and away from the Caribbean for two hundred years after Hernan Cortés invaded México and the wealth-laden mainland, in fact, for Cuba and the other Spanish-speaking Caribbean islands, this meant a diminished Spanish population and a slower, long-term Native survival, mostly blended in the *mestizaje* with both African and Iberian people, in the monte and campo, areas largely inaccessible to colonial governments, sometimes for centuries.

There we survived, and there emerged in the grass-roots Caribbean a synthesis of the indigenous land-based culture, which was foundational built upon, often brutally but also side by side in many contexts, with Iberian and African, to create our layered national culture. In the Americas, the first human-nature nexus was the indigenous. This was what Martí meant when he said that the "intelligence of our America is an Indian headdress," to which he added that new branches may be from Rome, Greece or Paris, [or even New York], however, "the trunk must be our own."[6] Most deeply rooted are our communities and caserios of related Native families in the mountains of Cuba, Boriken, and Quisquella, treasures of cultural indigeneity knowledge for our fragmented and blended populations, and which are all presently, serendipitously, revitalizing and re-linking.

The act of creation opens new spaces, where discourse flows, where dream narratives are woven and our traditions reinvent themselves and survive. The vision is ancient and profoundly contemporary. It's the times we live in.

I have had the good fortune to have my novel read as a contribution to this larger and real-life quest and see it used by researchers and Taino cultural activists as a point of reference, sometimes a point of departure, in their own search for authenticity. This has been my most pleasant and humbling reward.

## Notes

1 "Guatiao" is the Taino equivalent to the Nahuatl, "In lak'ech," or you are my other self. Guatiao is grounded in the exchange of names ceremony.
2 Jose Barreiro, "Taino, a novel," Fulcrum Press, Boulder, 2012
3 See, Jose Barreiro, "Dreaming Mother Earth: Life and Wisdom of a Native Cuban Cacique Francisco (Panchito) Ramirez," Ediciones Campana/Casa de las Americas, Havana-New York, 2018
4 Note: these remarks are from over twenty years ago. The author left Cornell University in 2002, to direct Culture and History Research at the Smithsonian National Museum of the American Indian until 2017. He is presently Smithsonian Scholar Emeritus and resides at the Mohawk community of Akwesasne.
5 Carl O. Sauer, "The Early Spanish Main," University of California Press, Berkeley and Los Angeles, 1966, Pp. 62, 87. Sauer cites Oviedo's charge on Taino refusal to plant and Guarinex's earlier offer.
6 José Barreiro, "The Indian In Martí," The Americas Review, Houston, Fall, 1995

# INTRODUCTION

## Language Reawakening as Pilgrimage— Stepping Back and Stitching Hope

*Amanda Claudia Wager, Berta Rosa Berriz, Laura Ann Cranmer, and Vivian Maria Poey*

> *"Who is to say that robbing a people of its language is less violent than war?"*
> – Ray Gwyn Smith (Anzaldúa, 1987, p. 53)

Close your eyes and just listen for a moment …

Walk outside, barefoot. Sit on the ground. Feel the pulse of the earth beneath you. Listen to it …

This is where the stories of this book come from. This is where the languages live, sleep, breathe. Language is rooted in the soil where we stand, where we sit, and deep within the waters that flow beneathe us. The languages were here before us. And it is our hope, through the stories that the authors and others share, they will remain here. Language reawakening and diaspora create new routes to flow through, like water forging its way through new soil to find its way to the ocean, metamorphosing into different shapes and sounds, dancing and singing through the ages of technology and beyond, while still being connected by their roots.

José Barreiro, Smithsonian Scholar Emeritus, writes a passionate Opening Call: Indigenous Creation: Literature as Historical/Cultural Recovery. In this address to the "First International Congress of Indigenous Literatures," held in Guatemala City, Guatemala, August 15, 1998, he asserts that in the context of securing educational opportunities for Indigenous peoples the arts function as an anti-colonial tool in healing and community-building processes. More than two decades later, his words are still heard. Within these pages, our authors respond. The Call sheds light on the roots of this book—to explore the places where language was born prior to colonization. It reminds us to listen; to listen to our ancestors, to listen to our creative spirit, to listen to our dreams.

DOI: 10.4324/9781003302186-1

## Art as a Way of Listening versus Talking

*Art as a way of listening: Centering student and community voices in language learning and cultural revitalization*, is the sister book to *Art as a way of talking for emergent bilingual youth: A foundation for literacy in PreK-12 schools* (Berriz et al., 2018). In this new volume, the emphasis on emergent bilinguals shifts to a focus on reawakening/ reclaiming dormant or suppressed languages, highlighting diasporic languages. The authors—language warriors, some being immigrants, and others oppressed by colonialism in their own homelands—discuss how they use the arts to further language learning in their communities. Language warriors center learners' voices and leadership—especially members of Indigenous,[1] African American and international communities—engaged in language and cultural revitalization initiatives. Included are a broad range of artistic forms, both traditional and innovative, ranging from embodied performance to multimedia, highlighting arts-fueled resistance and multilingual activism as applied to language and literacy education.

The editors offer this volume as a resource for educators, community youth workers, arts teachers, activists, researchers, and undergraduate and graduate students interested in understanding the complexities of arts and language learning as a sociocultural way of knowing. Chapters address theoretical issues, pedagogical strategies, and stories related to arts and language learning, including discussions of arts-based work and advocacy projects.

We now focus on listening because so much about language and cultural learning is rooted in listening. We listened from the womb—to words, songs, beats, and rhythms. We listened before we had speech. And from listening as babies, speech was born. There are many different stories, Indigenous to many cultures world-wide, about the importance of listening. Indeed, it's been said that the Creator gave us two eyes, two ears and one mouth so that we can listen and observe twice as much as we speak. In a similar vein, Playwright Eugene O'Neill noted that, "God gave us mouths that close and ears that don't."

Quelshemut, the xwulmuxw name for the late Ray Peter, a Quw'utsun' Elder in the Indigenous / Xwulmuxw Studies Department at Vancouver Island University, Canada, often spoke about the method of "sit-watch-listen" (SWL) (Meijer Drees et al., 2012). He described SWL as a method of learning that represents what the Coast Salish peoples value in learners. In academia, learners are expected to listen and then walk away with what they needed or absorbed. In a Coast Salish context, the responsibility is to act on what the learner takes in, and to give back, as a gift. It is a cycle of teaching and learning that involves practicing the values of love, respect, and discipline. Learners need to love the teachers, who are the Elders that represent their ancestors. This respect for the teachers and the subject helps them gain discipline to come, learn, and then act responsibly with the gifts they are given. Orality is a powerful learning tool. The teachings speak to swallowing the words; like food and drink they nourish and keep us alive. The land is the library, the teacher and the communities are its librarians. Elders teach that growing takes time, we are not alone, we are family, we learn and grow and teach one another. We also co-exist with many others. We are told to sit with the tree or water and notice our ego, what makes us human, and see what the land will show us. Remembering is reconnecting. SWL is a critical window into understanding and transformation.

## Sociocultural Ways of Knowing, in the Time of COVID

The global pandemic brought academic instruction into our homes, thus creating bridges between family, language, culture, and traditional schooling; families were essential to the learning project. The language of home became a resource for multilingualism. The new communication technologies of Zoom meetings, cell-phone videos, and similar online media became tools for cultural exchange. The Elders learned from youth, even as youth included the voices and stories of the Elders in the process of enlivening their language and cultures.

We, the editors, are also working in remote relationships with one another from our homes across Turtle Island. We write this introduction in the western lands of the K'omoks (Amanda) and Qualicum (Laura) peoples, the eastern shores of the Pawtucket (Vivian), and south to the lands of the Saluda (Berta) peoples.

Each contributor to *Art as a Way of Listening* is woven into this virtual tapestry of relationships, each manifesting a passion for honoring family language and constructing literacy that embraces family culture, both rooted in our land and along the routes of diaspora. The chapters cover a range of languages and arts from present day locations: Taino novel-writing from Cuba; Hul'q'umin'um', Nuu-Chah-Nulth, and Kwak'wala media creation from Vancouver Island; embodied meaning through Playback Theatre in Palestine; N|uu in children's books from South Africa; Zapotec scripting and improvising language stories virtually in Oaxaca, Mexico; traditional Hawaiʻian weaving; diidxazá cellphilms from Oaxaca; Native languages on Twitter from Turtle Island; Kreyol visual arts from Haiti; African American Language (AAL) through Hip-Hop; and stories from a multidisciplinary and cultural artist.

These are but a few samples of the many ways language is learned through the arts around the world. At the time of a global pandemic, when many artists, academics and teachers were overwhelmed with balancing home and work life in one place, it was challenging to forge new relationships for this book. We relied on past and current relationships with many individuals throughout our years as teachers, professors, researchers, students, artists, advocates, language learners, and mothers (to name just a few of our identities). We had deeply rooted friendship and collegial relationships with some of our contributors, while others were reached through newer routes—such as watching a conference presentation or introductions through other colleagues. Therefore, even though there are many voices/languages/arts missing, we hope that this book will encourage and facilitate future journeys furthering relationships and broadening our knowledges.

## *Weaving our Perspectives as Artists, Academics & Activist*

The four of us—Berta, Laura, Amanda, and Vivian—come from distinct walks of life, with many overlaps and similarities, yet with more than a few contrasts. We each specialize in one of the four areas of language learning, literacies, arts, and Indigenous studies; however, we are all passionate about all of these subjects and the education of language learners. In this section we explore the perspectives we bring to the text; what motivated us to form this collaborative and seek other voices in the field. We offer our lived experiences as a tool for transparency as we introduce the text.

## Berta's Language Story: The Language of the Lizards

It was sunrise, just in time to avoid adult oversight. Jump into my shorts quietly. Tiptoe out the front door. I lay low and still in the grass between the two small palms. My eyes at grass level. The lizards in our yard had a language. I could see it; each move signaled an event—fight, love, fear, play. From my own stillness I could discern meaning. "The Language of the Lizards" (see Figure I.1) I created this stained-glass piece as it opens doors to my language story.

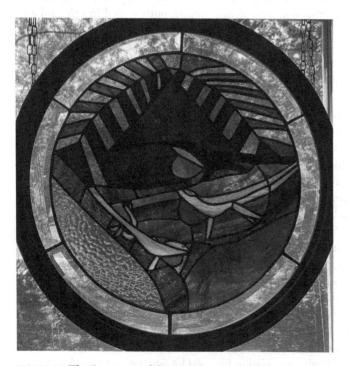

FIGURE I.1 The Language of the Lizards.

This awareness served me well when my family moved from Cuba to the United States. In our house in Philadelphia mostly my mom, Abuelita, and my little brother and I shared everyday life. It seemed difficult for the Elders to learn English quickly. I felt an obligation to help. Remembering my lizard friends, I understood that watching bodies and facial expressions was key to puzzling out meaning in this strange new language. In three months' time—the family story goes—I learned English well enough to serve as interpreter during everyday events. I was eight years old and repeating third grade, this time in English.

My mother chose to live near the school run by the same order of nuns as my school in Cuba. There English became the sole focus of my education. Though one of my favorite teachers from Cuba was at the school, I was prohibited from speaking with her. They changed my name to *Bertha*, the *th* sound I could not yet pronounce. This imposed isolation from my past sent a clear signal to me: Those in control of my education let me know that the English language was a priority in my acculturation. I could see that my friends, my home, my culture were moved into a second tier and was compelled to dance to a new English beat.

Growing up in Miami in the sixties, Spanish was the language of home, not the language of school. I remember going with my mom to a clandestine reading group studying Betty Friedan's Feminine Mystique—with shades drawn down. Watching the hush among the women, I understood this underground book club as central to their own process of liberation. Juxtaposing the intensity in the room with the conformity to women's role in the *machista* everyday life of the same women, led me to question this power dynamic in my emerging bilingual identity.

The example of the civil rights movement compelled me to reflect my awareness of power, race, and cultural erasure. As a result, I reclaimed my name—Berta. At the University of Miami campus, I participated in demonstrations for the peace movement, environmental justice, and student rights with my little brother, Alberto, as chaperone. The deeper my involvement in these social justice efforts, the more I needed to learn about affirming my own bicultural identity (Darder, 2016).

At age forty I took two giant steps to embrace both my family language and Cuban culture through dance. It was a painful step, but I took Spanish language lessons from a Colombian teacher who was part of a community literacy project. That same year, I returned to Cuba for the first time in 32 years. As a dancer, I joined a summer course on Afro-Cuban dance in La Habana, the city of my birth. There I sang and danced to songs from the Yoruba and Congolese traditions. The dances taught me stories, traditions, and yes, I could hear the meaning of my people in my own body.

Closing my language story with eyes wide open to the images that stay with me from my long career as a bilingual teacher in Boston Public Schools: The day, November 2002, that white suburban voters eliminated bilingual education across the state. This ballot initiative overruled the educational rights of immigrants established by the Supreme Court in Lau v. Nichols (1974). The vote affirmed the wishes of people with no actual stake in the outcome, while denying a voice to the families directly affected.

Words of my fourth-grade bilingual students capture their anxiety and insecurities on the day after: "¿Maestra? Does this mean that I can't speak Spanish with my family?" "Why do they hate us because we speak Spanish?" (Berriz, 2003). This history includes repression of culture and language of Native Americans, denial of literacy to African Americans, and the history of bilingual education that springs from the work of Chinese families (Spring, 1997). This history of language oppression colonizes our minds to value less or sometimes even reject our family languages, cultural knowledge, and wisdom. The process of listening to the courageous stories contained in this volume has served me, in the ongoing battle to decolonize my own mind.

## Laura's Language Story: The Language of Dreams

Gilakasdaxw'la natnamwayut! Nugwadi KixÃ…ala. GayuÃ…an laxida'Yalis. GayuÅ‚amxa'an laxida Haida laxan abaskutamε. GayuÃ…an laxida'Namgis laxan oskutamε. Hεman gagampwaÅ‚a Gwanti'lakw 'i'axsila gaxan. Greetings to those with whom I am one. My name is Laura Ann Cranmer. K'ixÃ…ala is my feast name, which loosely translates to a large fire to feed many people. On my father's side,

FIGURE I.2 The Language of Dreams.

David Cranmer, I am 'Namgis from Alert Bay and on my mother's side, Pearl Weir, I am Haida from Old Masset. My paternal grandmother Gwanti'lakw took care of me when I was a child.

As a Professor of the Indigenous/Xwulmuxw Studies Department at Vancouver Island University (formerly called the First Nations Studies Department) I have taught in the Arts One First Nations program (2000–2017) where first year students encounter the promulgators of destructive colonial policy and laws that simultaneously enforced familial separation by sending Indigenous children to residential schools, suppressed cultural traditions and practices, and stole land and resources. An abiding subject of study in the Arts One First Nations program was how Canadian colonial laws impact Indigenous communities and families and continue to shape Indigenous identities. One of the assignments in the Arts One First Nations program was to have students create a plaster mask to express their conception of their unique identities. The mask above is one of the first ones I made. My cousin, Kevin Cranmer, painted the image of our ancestor 'Namxxalagayu on my mask. The backdrop of my mask is a dream fragment. Asleep in the crook of the lowest branch of a Western Fir, I feel a sense of communion with the tree as if with an intelligent, compassionate consciousness. I view in my mind's eye the inky blue horizon broken by the white frothy waves washing up on shore.

Decades of therapy combined with my creative writing not only made possible an extended psychological work (in the current parlance of Indigenous Studies—decolonial work) to expunge my false colonial consciousness, expand my energetic container not only to accommodate new learnings, but also to reawaken Kwak'wala bound up with my earliest years. Dreams, when combined with my therapy and art, have long been a feature of my healing journey. The image above, a compilation of two benchmarks in my journey, shows that art has formed a third language that draws on my lived experience as a 'Namgis/Haida woman born in the early fifties—who has endured a life-long separation from my maternal Haida roots. Literary art, particularly the playwriting genre helps me to create a third, delimited space to attempt to express the inexpressible. Using various generative strategies for my writing, particularly free writing along with developing skills in various genres—such as playwriting, poetry, creative nonfiction—has allowed me to create and shape commentary on the socio-economic conditions that have brought Indigenous peoples to this point in our collective history. Combining my literacy with my memories of the sounds and rhythms of Kwak'wala speech is my main route to increasing my proficiency and fluency.

At the start of my auto-ethnographic study of Kwak'wala (re)learning, in "Reclaiming Kwak'wala through Co-constructing Gwanti'lakw's Vision" (Cranmer, 2016) I recorded another dream fragment that symbolically speaks about linguistic suppression. What does language learning have to do with dreams? Our images are our ancestors and my images can be simultaneously empowering, and bewildering, and yet show me the way forward when it feels like there is no earthly way forward. I dreamt I was trapped under thick ice. Looking up I could see people walking over me busy getting ready for a gathering. The ice suddenly melts and I am in the middle of the crowd. Alongside this note are the following questions I was contemplating: how might features of Second Language Acquisition theory, Language Socialization, and Socio-cultural theory assist in building an Indigenous theoretical framework to expand understanding the challenges of Heritage Language Acquisition—applying these theories to my own Kwak'wala learning experience. These disparate notes confirm for me that Kwak'wala is embodied, dynamic, and alive and that with consistent patient effort—the good memories of those who peopled my childhood immersed in Kwak'wala rhythms—continually unfolds. In another one of my dreams, a few of the Green College residents (a graduate residential college on the University of British Columbia [UBC] campus in Vancouver, BC) swoop down on a rambling mansion, known in a previous life, now transformed into a rambling pawn shop chock-a-block with furniture. Someone loudly proclaims, also known in a previous life, about how she didn't need any of her treasures anymore and please just pick up whatever we would like. Falling into my old pattern with people who have been abusive toward me, I hang back. Wandering along the dark aisles full of junky furniture I poke here and there, and spot a desk the right size for an eight year old child. The owner appears, and asks if I am interested. The day of my dream was the second day of our historic Kwak'wala class offered for the first time at UBC, co-instructed by fluent Kwak'wala speaker Dr. Robert Joseph, and Dr. Patricia Shaw. Dr. Shaw had posed the question, "what, ultimately, do you want to save of your language?" Analyzing my dream within the framework of Dr. Shaw's question, Kwak'wala for me is symbolized by the mansion-now-turned-pawn-shop where folks arrive to hive off what treasures they find. The owner of the mansion-turned-pawn-shop and my former tormenter, now long dead, holds a give-away. Our psychic lives, as invisible as ephemeral, remind us through our dreams that symbolic communication is important to pay attention to especially in circumstances of uncertainty, deep disruption or crisis as my dream reminds me of the necessary work to dissolve the stubborn structures of English to make room for Kwak'wala to grow in my heart's mind.

## Amanda's Language Story: Humbling Relationships

My name is Amanda Claudia Wager and I was born in Los Angeles. My Hebrew name is צְבִיָּה (Tzviah). It means doe, like the deer, after my late Grandma Pinky. My late father is Peter Polland Wager of Chicago and my mother is Marilyn Dee Pincus of Los Angeles. Both sides of my biological family stem from Jewish Ashkenazi ancestry. In the beginning of the 20th Century all four of my great-grandparents emigrated to the United States from Poland, Belarus, and Lithuania to find a safer place, fleeing the Jewish genocide of the Russian Army. My Great-Zayde Jake Blackman was a Cantor. Cantors lead worship, officiate at lifecycle

**FIGURE I.3** Relationship.

events, teach adults and children, run synagogue music programs, and offer pastoral care. In some ways I followed in his footsteps, as I grew into a teacher, professor, and a director of theatre. I wrote my language story in *Art as a Way of Talking* (Berriz et al., 2018) and here I reflect more on how language is embodied and cultivates community and relationship through the arts, similar to how authors Yamila Hussein-Shannan and Khitam Edelbi express this in their chapter about Playback Theatre in Palestine. As a former bilingual elementary and ESL teacher, and now as a teacher educator and researcher, I question pedagogy that asks students to become engrossed in texts but limits the modes to strictly English text-based options through which students can express that engagement (Enriquez & Wager, 2018).

These two pictures (Figures I.3 and I.4) were taken from a theatre performance created with youth who were or had been living on the streets and were advocating for the reopening of safe houses (Wager, 2014). Together, we co-scripted their experiences of living in safe houses and the unsafe spaces they ended up in, such as squats and adult shelters, when they were closed by the government. At the beginning of the production, the young people wanted little to do with me because I was an elementary school teacher. But through 6 months of rehearsal, relationships and bonds formed. The strength of those relationships can be seen in the pre-performance circle (Figure I.3). In post-production interviews, the young people commented on how the community that they formed was so important that they would continue to do productions unpaid.

Figure I.4 below is the final scene in the youth performance when they no longer are willing to be a statistic, as seen by the number on their shirts while they each lift their masks and proudly show their faces. I consider the research

**FIGURE I.4** Resisting Becoming a Statistic.

that I do with community, especially in consideration of language reawakening, a "formal pedagogy of resistance" (Cammarota & Fine, 2008) where community members have the ability to provoke ripples of social change, beginning with themselves.

Our family story is that the Russian Army burnt the fields in Poland the night my maternal great grandparents got married while hiding in a barn. They then fled to Hamburg to sail to Turtle Island, colonially known as the United States. My grandparents spoke Yiddish at home and we spoke English and eventually Dutch in our house after being adopted by my stepfather Paul Logchies of Amsterdam. As a descendant of ancestors who were religiously persecuted I consider myself a 'fellow resister' or a 'compatriot of conscience' (Cranmer, 2016, p. ix). Being a multi-lingual, -literate and -cultural (English, Dutch, and Spanish) educator and a life-long language learner, I use critical pedagogies, including the use of drama in the classroom partnered with discussions regarding local political and school issues to impact and progress literacy and language education.

The values that guide my work are that of humility and holding a deep respect for humanity, nature, and myself. These have guided me through my life as an educator, a student, a researcher, an artist, a colleague, a collaborator, a friend, a daughter, a granddaughter, a sister, a partner, and now a mother of three beauti-fully wild children. I come to this work from a humble place, a space of being in between cultures. Having lived as an immigrant in multiple cities around the world, I understand that each community has certain protocols. My first respon-sibility is to learn their protocols before even entering the community. And then I actively listen … for a very long time. Relationships are rooted and grow from listening.

## Vivian's Language Story: Un Pedacito de Mar

As a child in Mexico I used to say my name was Vivian Maria Poey Alcazar Diago Valdez Muñoz Díaz. In my U.S. passport and official documents I am just Vivian Maria Poey. Our names tell stories. The long list of names, invisible in my current official identity, reminds me that my story began long before my birth.

Beyond the history of migration inherent in my name, French, Arabic and Spanish all converging in Cuba, I continued to move after my birth. I was born in Mexico from Cuban parents who were U.S. American citizens. By the time I came to live in the United States at 14, I had lived in Mexico, Guatemala, and Colombia, sung multiple national anthems, and learned as many histories.

Even as we moved around, my understanding of language and identity was tethered, through stories, food, and ways of being, to Cuba, an island I had never physically been to. As we moved from country to country I brought all that with me as my sense of self evolved and transformed, gathering new cultural sediment in each place. In spite of having attended bilingual schools and being fluent in English, when I arrived in Miami, my high school education rendered much of my understanding of the world invisible and either irrelevant or inaccurate. Nobody knew or cared about Benito Juarez or Simon Bolivar, and even the world was divided differently, into five continents instead of seven.

**FIGURE I.5** Un Pedacito de Mar/A Little Piece of the Sea.

I understood then that our understanding of the world and its borders is constructed, told through stories that hold and reproduce particular perspectives. I could also see that language was alive and dynamic. Languages grow and transform both over time and over borders. As we moved across borders through Latin America, I learned to listen to the many accents, words and histories reflected in the various *Spanishes* (Spanish did not seem like a singular language). Listening was key to understanding a new place and finding a sense of belonging; listening helped me find my own space in each new context with new ways of speaking and being.

I don't remember learning English, I learned it slowly through years of bilingual schooling, but it was for me a foreign and academic language, not a social or familial one. In Miami I felt like a foreigner among my Cuban American peers for whom Spanish was the language of grandparents, and English the language of the moment. For me Spanish is the thread that connects both time and space, always relevant. I remember being surprised when I started to dream in English, then sprinkling Spanish at home with English words, until English became my dominant language. Still, Spanish is central to who I am, the language of childhood, nursery rhymes, prayers, the language of that island and the other countries and cultures that I still carry with me and work hard to pass on to my daughter, connecting generations.

In a photography class in community college I discovered that art could hold my worlds across all its borders. Photography allowed me to document and represent my experience, and most importantly, it engaged me in investigating, imagining, creating, and communicating in new ways. Art helped me make sense of the world and gave me a sense of possibility. This is the gift I tried to share with my high school students in Pittsburgh, the young kids in Washington D.C., and eventually, with teachers across the country.

As a teacher and parent, I have learned how difficult it is to maintain a language other than English, even one as widely spoken as Spanish, in a country where every space seems to scream "English only." I recall one of my 5 year old Salvadoran students yelling in distress "ENGLISH, only ENGLISH!" as I translated his homework into Spanish for his mother. And I was heartbroken when my own three-year-old daughter insisted "ENGLISH ONLY" as I read the Spanish part of Sandra Cisneros' bilingual book *Pelitos* (1994).

My daughter's last names, Telemaque Poey DuRocher Alcazar, tell a new hybrid story, like rivers meeting and new water flowing. She is now 14, the age I was when I arrived in the United States. She does not (yet) speak Creole or French (from her father's Haitian roots) but she is proud of her Spanish and working hard to keep it from slipping away. Language is a journey and it encompasses much more than what we speak. The authors in this book have opened my eyes to new/old worlds, they have made visible the "sediment of texts" inherent in the land and flowing across oceans, and most importantly they have reminded me to listen ever more carefully for what is not visible.

## Recent Context and Unfolding Pedagogy

Elder Gary Manson of the Snuneymuxw Nation observed the following about his Indigenous language of Hul'qumi'num': "Fluency is probably non-existent in my village now. There are maybe a handful of Elders that can do it if they had somebody to speak to" (Cunningham, 2018). Manson amplifies the calls for continued research for language reawakening, often referred to as language reclamation and revitalization (these terms are described in detail by author Joshua Schwab Cartas in his chapter in the *Roots* section). Demographic trends of language learning and revitalization call for authentic ways of honoring and engaging communities by educators and activists today. Below are demographics that reflect the dire need for reawakening Indigenous languages and lifting diasporic languages today, yesterday, and tomorrow.

## Facts about Languages Spoken in Our World Today

- There are around 7,000 languages spoken in the world today (Lane & Mikihara, 2017).
- More than half of the world's languages have no written form.
- Half of the languages spoken in the world today are predicted to disappear during this century.
- There are 2,000 languages spoken in Africa.
- 80% of African languages have no written form.
- Fewer than 10% of the world's languages can be considered entirely safe from endangerment.
- Most people in the world are bilingual or multilingual (as compared to the majority of the United States being monolingual English-speakers).
- The 2018 American Community Survey (ACS) found that more than sixty-seven million inhabitants spoke a language other than English at home. Among those people, some sixty-three million also knew and used English and hence were bilingual. This represents 20.55 percent of the population (Grosjean, 2021).
- A language dies every 14 days.
- There are over 100 languages spoken in the United States today.
- Over 80% of the languages spoken in the United States are endangered.
- Half of the world's languages are spoken in Asia and the Pacific Islands.
- Only 4% of the world's languages come from Europe.
- There are over 200 endangered or recently extinct languages in Australia.
- Native American languages are distinct in political status and history, and are the object of school- and community-based reclamation and retention efforts aligned with the Native American Languages Act of 1990 (NALA) (Commission on Language Learning, 2017, p. ix).

- One of the biggest obstacles in the United States to improved language learning is a national shortage of qualified teachers. Forty-four states and Washington, D.C., report that they cannot find enough qualified teachers to meet current needs (Commission on Language Learning, 2017, p. ix).
- In a world of around 250 nations, there are over 6000 languages. This means that there are very few languages with a country of their own. A language that is not a language of government, nor a language of education, nor a language of commerce or of wider communication is a language whose very existence is threatened in the modern world. (Hinton & Hale, 2001, p. 3)

## Objectives of Art as a Way of Listening

We have two main objectives in writing this book. *The first objective is to affirm family languages and cultures through the arts in everyday life.* Culture is coddled in the way we speak each day. Languages give voice to our history and knowledges (González et al., 2013; Gutiérrez et al., 1999; Moll, 1992). Artfully, we create language anew in the process of proclaiming our sounds. Listening and retelling are tools for decolonizing our minds (Wa Thiong'o, 2005).

The way we make things, our disciplines in music, poetry, dance, weaving, molding, drawing, and singing are tools for grounding, healing, and action. The arts, as cultural production, engage young people in exploration of critical local issues and heritage languages, making meaning of challenging concepts and weaving in cultural knowledges (Dewhurst, 2014; Goessling et al., 2020). *Languaging* through the arts gives voice to anticolonial activism and social justice healing. In listening to and embracing our own roots and routes we gain insight and courage to combat racism and embrace solidarity (Delpit, 2006).

*Our second objective is to bring to light innovative approaches by opening windows to artists in action, both traditional and innovative, who are educators and culture bearers.* Language warriors champion dialogic education, emphasizing listening to the knowledges that learners, families and communities bring to learning and teaching projects and elevates the possibilities for new learning for all (Treuer, 2020). Creative, artful voices challenge us to reimagine educational practices that engage all of us in the context of the current moment. Entering into artful cultural processes creates a bridge for the transmission of multiliteracies (Janks, 2010; Jewitt & Kress, 2008; Kalantzis & Cope, 2012) and brings new possibilities to document and contextualize the past as well as to imagine what could be in the future. Culturally responsive teaching values youth, families, and community as sources of cultural knowledge and learning in the traditions of their home communities (Joo & Keehn, 2011; Zhang-Wu, 2017) while bringing them into the present and preparing the soil for them to thrive into the future. Creating access lifts cultural pride through community-arts and language initiatives that inspire a sense of belonging. Creative, artful voices challenge us to reimagine educational practices that engage all of us in the context of the current moment (Gallagher &

Ntelioglou, 2011; hooks, 2003). As readers and writers we can listen to language learning in many places and ways learning happens.

## Language Reawakening through the Arts

Given that western education, historically, was the main vehicle for assimilative policies and practices by which Indigenous languages and cultural practices were suppressed, there is a current estrangement and distrust by Indigenous communities toward Western education and academia. Clearly, the work of language reawakening occurs at a deeply personal level, as well as moving outward to expand efforts to the community. Alfred and Corntassel (2005) argue that shifts in thinking stem from the level of the self rather than from institutional processes. Daniels-Fiss (2008) documents her own Cree language reclamation process and cites Battiste's (1986) phrase "cognitive imperialism" to describe how her own Cree cognitive map had been obscured by settler education (p. 611). Also known as decolonial work, Indigenous language revitalization of necessity occurs within, by and for the community (Sadeghi-Yekta, 2020). In the arts we create a community of like-minded players encouraged to be present and introspective in order to reach deep down into one's core to pull out new awareness of old learnings. Indeed, Indigenous language reawakening creates shifts in thinking.

## Indigenous and Creative Community-Engaged Research Methodologies

The community-engaged methodological framework that informs the research chapters in this volume promotes humanizing inquiry and fosters in-depth dialogic interaction, negotiation, and action, leading to a consciousness-raising research approach that develops humble relationships of respect between the researchers and participants. Indigenous and community-engaged research builds relationships through respect, care, reciprocity, and humility with participants (community members) and the researcher via researcher reflexivity (Kirkness & Barnhardt, 2001; Smith et al., 2019; Tuck, 2009). This researcher-reflexive methodological approach to research with communities challenges the traditional positivist colonizing approaches to research, practice, and policy, and moves toward one that is participatory and community-engaged. Many of the authors see their roles as multiple; as mentors, reflexive researchers, and as relationship-builders, as people who can mediate tensions and further collaborations between the multiple partners involved.

Creative research methodologies have also proven effective for engaging with and empowering participants (Wilson et al., 2007). Arts-based approaches to learning languages may be particularly powerful for fostering meaningful insight into the nuanced experiences and interpretations among participants while simultaneously encouraging self-empowerment and self-expression (Conrad, 2004;

Goldstein, 2002; Mitchell, Jonas-Simpson, & Ivonoffski, 2006; Wager & Ansloos, 2021; Winn, 2010). Researchers have demonstrated the power of arts-based research for empowering communities to share their experiences and ideas and make meaning of difficult topics.

### Storytelling as Healing Practices

Along with these research chapters there are interwoven narratives of lived experience using the arts for language learning. These short narratives are stories gifted to us from the authors; many of the stories were gifted to the authors through intergenerational routes of learning from family and community. These stories come from their hearts. Listening to stories as children is one of our first instances of learning to listen. For generations of Indigenous children, not only the intergenerational transmission of language was interrupted, but also the requisite internalized social skills born out of familial bonds. Indigenous peoples ask: how do we know how to be in a good relationship, how can we heal through telling our stories? As a healing practice, storytelling through artistic channels has the power to heal by first expressing and then learning to shape one's own narrative. Group settings with the objective of language revitalization through the arts, ideally and practically will establish ground rules for sensitivity, confidentiality, and boundaried group interaction.

In her ground-breaking book *Indigenous Storywork: Educating the Heart, Mind, Body and Spirit* Jo-Ann Archibald (2008) develops a framework for a storytelling method rooted in her Sto:lo story-telling traditions. Based on this framework, Archibald acknowledges the diverse First Nations in Canada with their multiple languages that are unified by the underlying principles and practices of respect and reciprocity, among others, that serves as a healing and humanizing antidote to a history of oppression. Employing a Coyote story to serve as a metaphor for the difficult but necessary confrontation of how Canadian history has resulted in the distorted perception of contemporary Indigenous-settler relations in the modern era, Archibald takes her reading audience on a journey to discover how educators and students alike may rebalance these misperceptions.

### Democratizing and Revitalizing Teacher Education: Indigenous, Feminist, and Critical Race Critiques

We are concerned by the ways in which "whiteness" is constructed and reinforced in education and in teacher education programs (Schroeter, 2019; Wager et al., 2022; Wager & Schroeter, 2021; Zeichner et al., 2015); how a dominant lens is applied to curriculum and educational scholarship. White teachers are overrepresented in classrooms and teacher education programs (Souto-Manning & Emdin, 2020) in many countries, especially in Canada and the United States. The field of education is a workforce dominated by women and, while statistics on race and employment are difficult to obtain, white educators are estimated to make up between 71–96% of teachers across Canada (Ryan, Pollock, & Antonelli, 2009), and 85% of the teaching force in the United States (Howard, 2016). For decades, research has demonstrated that white educators are not always well-equipped to teach students from different racial backgrounds (Delpit, 2006; Dei, 1994; Evans-Williams & Hines, 2020; Howard, 2016) because Black, Indigenous, and other students of colour drop-out and are pushed-out of schools that fail to meet their needs in alarming numbers (Codjoe, 2001; Fine, 1991; Morris, 2016). Growing out of the multicultural education movement of the 1970s and 80s, calls for culturally relevant, affirming, and sustaining pedagogies (Ladson-Billings, 2014; Nieto, 2013), as well as anti-racist (Dei, 2006), decolonizing (Battiste, 2013), and abolitionist education (Love, 2019) have grown louder.

One factor that undeniably shapes educators' worldviews and life experiences is their race and ethnicity. To listen to and grasp the experiences of their students from diverse cultures, teachers must engage in critical dialogue with their students that honors the knowledge that each student brings to the learning project (Motha, 2014; Nieto, 2013; Noguera, 2008). Additionally, teachers must become aware of the institutional factors that influence their students' academic identities (Darder, Mayo & Paraskeva, 2017). For example, segregated programing, ability grouping, and similar hierarchies shape access to educational resources and how students see themselves as capable learners (Kitchin, 2013). Souto-Manning and Emdin note that although teacher education programs have begun to integrate multicultural materials, they often do so in ways that uphold Eurocentric values while also citing "good intentions."

Caragarajanah (2002) deconstructs the processes by which western academe generates knowledge based on Eurocentric assumptions while simultaneously devaluing and marginalizing already suppressed local knowledges (LK) as fairy tales and myth. He also posits that, "The assumption that one's knowledge is of sole universal relevance does not encourage conversation" (p. 257) in his systematic deconstruction of the Eurocentric paradigm. While Caragarajanah defines LK as "context bound, community specific, and non-systematic" he also argues for the engagement of conversations across cultures, languages, and borders to encourage a "pluralistic mode of thinking" with an attitude of humility (p. 244). Archibald's (2008) principles for Indigenous storywork seem to parallel the democratizing process of knowledge systems with respect, reciprocity that Caragarajanah concludes with, "Breaking away from the history of constructing a globalized totality with uniform knowledge and hierarchical community, we should envision building networks of multiple centers that develop diversity as a universal project and encourage an actively negotiated epistemological tradition" (p. 257). Archibald's (2008) storywork principles may facilitate breaking open as yet unimagined horizons of possibility for language learners. Further, applying Caragarajanah's exhortation to visioning networks of multiple centers, promoting diversity applied to Indigenous languages can or may yield powerful results in reversing endangered languages.

Our research and practice in and out of schools affirms that significant changes to curriculum, including arts throughout, are needed to meet the needs of all students. Ernest Morrell (2004) proposes that popular culture engaged critically is a potential bridge to academic literacy for young people,

> ... critical pedagogy and popular culture form a powerful combination that allow students to draw upon their personal experiences to better learn literacy skills needed to navigate the literacies of power associated with schooling while also learning the literacy skills needed to deconstruct schooling and society.

*p. 420*

In this volume, Chelsea Jimenez documents the power of Hip-Hop and Rap pedagogy. By centering African American Language away from the margins (Bakhtin, 1982) young scholars gain an essential sense of belonging as intellectuals and influencers of future liberation.

We invite you now to listen with open hearts to the courageous and creative voices in *Art as a Way of Listening*.

*Welcome, Bienvenidos, Mabrika (Taino), أهلا بك (ahlaan bik), 欢迎 (huanying), Welkom, Welina, haere mai (Maori), ulihelisdi (Cherokee), hay ch qa'(hul'qumi'num), תודה (shalom)*

Are you listening?

## Note

1 There is no one official definition of Indigenous peoples worldwide (World Health Organization, 2007). For the purposes of this book, "Indigenous" is used to refer to peoples with roots in ancestral lands predating colonial invasion and the resulting nation-state boundaries. In Canada, Indigenous peoples are defined by the constitution as First Nations, Métis peoples, and Inuit (Government of Canada, 1982).

## References

Alfred, T. & Corntassel, J. (2005). Being Indigenous: Resurgences against contemporary colonialism. *Government and Opposition*, 40(4), 597–614.
Anzaldúa, G. (1987). *Borderlands: La frontera* (Vol. 3). Aunt Lute.
Archibald, J. A. (2008). *Indigenous storywork: Educating the heart, mind, body, and spirit.* UBC press.
Bakhtin, M. (1982). *The dialogic imagination.* University of Chicago Press.
Battiste, M. (2013). *Decolonizing education: Nourishing the learning spirit.* Purich Publishing.
Battiste, M. (1986). Micmac literacy and cognitive assimilation. In J. Barman, Y. Hebert, & D. McCaskill (Eds.), *Indian education in Canada Volume 1: The legacy* (pp. 23–45). University of British Columbia Press.
Berriz, B. (2003). La Revuelta. *Journal of Pedagogy, Pluralism, and Practice*, 2(3), 41.

Berriz, B., Wager, A., & Poey, V. (Eds.) (2018). *Art as a way of talking for emergent bilingual youth: A foundation for literacy in PreK-12 schools*. Routledge/Taylor and Francis.

Cammarota, J. & Fine, M. (Eds.). (2008). *Revolutionizing education: Youth participatory action research in motion*. Routledge.

Caragarajanah, S. (2002). Reconstructing local knowledge. *Journal of Language, Identity, and Education*, 1(4), 243–259.

Cisneros, S. (1994). *Hairs= Pelitos*. Random House.

Codjoe, H. M. (2001). Fighting a "Public Enemy" of Black academic achievement—the persistence of racism and the schooling experiences of Black students in Canada. *Race Ethnicity and Education*, 4(4), 343–375.

Commission on Language Learning. (2017). *America's languages: Investing in language education for the 21st century*. American Academy of Arts & Sciences.

Conrad, D. (2004). Exploring risky youth experiences: Popular Theatre as a participatory, performative research method. *International Journal of Qualitative Methods*, 3(1), 12–25. https://doi.org/10.1177/160940690400300102

Cranmer, L. (2016). Reclaiming Kwak'wala through co-constructing G̱wa̱nti'lakw's vision. [Unpublished dissertation], University of British Columbia.

Cunningham, T. (2018). Revitalizing Indigenous language at heart of islands first symposium. *Vancouver Island Free Daily Paper*. Retrieved June 1, 2022, from https://www.vancouverislandfreedaily.com/news/revitalizing-indigenous-language-at-heart-of-islands-first-symposium/

Daniels-Fiss, B. (2008). Learning to be a Nehiyaw (Cree) through language. *Diaspora, Indigenous, and Minority Education, 2*, 233–245.

Darder, A. (2016). *Culture and power in the classroom: Educational foundations for the schooling of bicultural students*. Routlledge/Taylor and Francis.

Darder, A., Mayo, P., & Paraskeva, J. (Eds.). (2017). *International critical pedagogy reader*. Routledge.

Dei, G. J. S. (1994). Afrocentricity: A cornerstone of pedagogy. *Anthropology and Education Quarterly, 25*, 3–28.

Dei, G. J. S. (2006). "We cannot be color-blind": Race, antiracism, and the subversion of dominant thinking. In E. W. Ross (Ed.), *Racism and antiracism in education* (pp. 25–42). Praeger.

Delpit, L. (2006). *Other people's children: Cultural conflict in the classroom*. The New Press.

Dewhurst, M. (2014). *Social justice art: A framework for activist art pedagogy*. Harvard Education Press.

Enriquez, G., & Wager, A. C. (2018). The Reader, the text, the performance: Opening spaces for the performing arts as Reader Response. *Voices from the Middle. 26*(1), 21–25.

Evans-Winters, V. E., & Hines, D. E. (2020). Unmasking white fragility: How whiteness and white student resistance impacts anti-racist education. *Whiteness and Education, 5*(1), 1–16.

Fine, M. (1991). *Framing dropouts: Notes on the politics of an urban high school*. Suny Press.

Gallagher, K., & Ntelioglou, B.Y. (2011). Which new literacies? Dialogue and performance in youth writing. *Journal of Adolescent and Adult Literacy, 5*(54), 322–330.

Goessling, K.P., Wright, D., Wager, A. C., & Dewhurst, M. (Eds). (2020). A critical mixtape for the movement: Reflecting on creative and critical youth practices in research [Special Issue]. *International Journal of Qualitative Studies in Education, 33*(1), 1–7. https://doi.org/10.1080/09518398.2019.1678791

Goldstein, T. (2002). No pain, no gain: Student playwriting as critical ethnographic language research. *Canadian Modern Language Review, 59*(1), 53–76. https://doi.org/10.3138/cmlr.59.1.53

González, N., Moll, L. C., & Amanti, C. (Eds.). (2013). *Funds of knowledge: Theorizing practices in households, communities, and classrooms.* Routledge.

Government of Canada (1982). *Constitution act.*

Grosjean, F. (2021). *Life as a bilingual.* Cambridge University Press.

Gutierrez K.D., Baquedano-Lopez P., Alvarez H. & Chiu M.M. (1999). Building a culture of collaboration through hybrid language practices. *Theory into Practice 38*, 87–93.

Hinton, L. & Hale, K. (2001). *The green book of language revitalization in practice.* Brill Press.

hooks, b. (2003). *Teaching community: A pedagogy of hope.* Routledge.

Howard, G. R. (2016). *We can't teach what we don't know: White teachers, multiracial schools.* Teachers College Press.

Janks, H. (2010). *Literacy and power.* Routledge.

Jewitt, C. & Kress, G. (Eds.). (2008). *Multimodal literacy.* Peter Lang.

Joo, E. & Keehn, J. (Eds.). (2011). *Rethinking contemporary art and multicultural education.* Routledge.

Kalantzis, M. & Cope, B. (2012). *Literacies.* Cambridge University Press.

Kirkness, V. J. & Barnhardt, R. (2001). First Nations and higher education: The four R's - respect, relevance, reciprocity, responsibility. Knowledge across cultures: A contribution to dialogue among civilizations. *Comparative Education Research Centre, The University of Hong Kong.*

Kitchin, K. (2013). Official literacy practices co-construct racialized bodies: Three key ideas to further integrate cultural and racially literate research. In K. Hall, T. Cremin, B. Comber & L. Moll (Eds.), *International handbook of research on children literacy learning and culture.* Wilely-Blackwell.

Ladson-Billings, G. (2014). Culturally relevant pedagogy 2.0: aka the remix. *Harvard Educational Review, 84*(1), 74–84.

Lane, P., & Makihara, M. (2017). Indigenous peoples and their languages. In O. Garcia, N. Flores & M. Spotti (Eds.), *The Oxford handbook of language and society.* (pp. 299–230) Oxford University Press.

Lau v. Nichols, 414 US 563 (1974) U.S. Supreme Court. No. 72-6520. Pp. 414 U. S. 565–569.

Love, B. L. (2019). *We want to do more than survive: Abolitionist teaching and the pursuit of educational freedom.* Beacon Press.

Meijer Drees, L., Martin, M., & McFarland, D. (2012). *Sit, Watch, Listen: Collaboratively Creating Indigenous Knowledge Protocols*, IFLA Presidential Programme Spring Meeting: Indigenous Knowledges, Local Priorities, Global Contexts. https://viurrspace.ca/bitstream/handle/10613/405/IFLA2012_SitWatchListen.jpg?sequence=1&isAllowed=y

Mitchell, G. J., Jonas-Simpson, C., & Ivonoffski, V. (2006). Research-Based theatre: The making of *I'm Still Here! Nursing Science Quarterly, 19*(3), 198–206. https://doi.org/10.1177/0894318406289878

Moll, L. C. (1992). Literacy research in community and classrooms: A sociocultural approach. In R. Beach et al. (Eds.), *Multidisciplinary perspectives on literacy research* (pp. 211–244). National Council of Teachers of English.

Morrell, E. (2004). *Linking literacy and popular culture: Finding connections for lifelong learning.* Christopher-Gordon.

Morris, M. W. (2016). *Pushout: The criminalization of Black girls in school.* The New Press.

Motha, S. (2014). *Race, empire, and English language teaching: Creating responsible and ethical anti-racist practice.* Teachers College Press.

Nieto, S. (2013). *Finding joy in teaching students of diverse backgrounds: Culturally and socially just practices in U.S. classrooms.* Heineman.

Noguera, P. (2008). *The trouble with Black boys and other reflections on race, equity, and the future of public education.* Jossey-Bass.

Ryan, J., Pollock, K., & Antonelli, F. (2009). Teacher diversity in Canada: Leaky pipelines, bottlenecks, and glass ceilings. *Canadian Journal of Education, 32*(3), 591–617.

Sadeghi-Yekta, K. (2020). Drama as methodology for Coast Salish language revitalization. *Canadian Theatre Review, 181*(Winter), 41–45.

Schroeter, S. (2019). Embodying difference: A case for anti-racist and decolonizing approaches to multiliteracies. *Studies in Social Justice, 13*(1), 142–158.

Smith, L. T., Tuck, E., Yang, K. (Eds.). (2019). *Indigenous and decolonizing studies in education.* Routledge. https://doi.org/10.4324/9780429505010

Souto-Manning, M., & Emdin, C. (2020). On the harm inflicted by urban teacher education programs: Learning from the historical trauma experienced by teachers of color. *Urban Education, 0*(0). https://doi.org/10.1177/0042085920926249.

Spring, Joel. (1997). *Deculturalization and the struggle for equality: Brief history of the education of dominated cultures in the United States.* McGraw Hill.

Treuer, A. (2020). *Language warrior's manifesto: How to keep our languages alive no matter the odds.* Historical Society Press.

Tuck, E. (2009). Suspending damage: A letter to communities. *Harvard Educational Review, 79*(3), 409–428. https://doi.org/10. 17763/haer.79.3.n0016675661t3n15

Wa Thiong'o, N. (1992). *Decolonising the mind: The politics of language in African literature.* East African Publishers.

Wager, A. (2014). *Applied drama as engaging pedagogy: Critical multimodal literacies with street youth* [Unpublished doctoral dissertation]. University of British Columbia.

Wager, A. C., Ansloos, J. P., & Thorburn, R. (2022). Addressing structural violence and systemic inequities in education: A qualitative study on Indigenous youth schooling experiences in Canada. *Power and Education, 14*(3), 228–246.

Wager, A. C., & Ansloos, J. P. (2021). Street wisdom: A critical study on youth homelessness and decolonizing arts-based research. In K.P. Goessling, D.E. Wright, A.C. Wager & M. Dewhurst (Eds.), *Engaging youth in critical arts pedagogies and creative research for social justice* (pp. 84–105). Routledge.

Wager, A.C. & Schroeter, S. (2021). Critical inquiry through the arts: Ethical limitations of teaching process drama to educators. *ArtPraxis, 8*(1), 115–135.

Wilson, N., Dasho, S., Martin, A. C., Wallerstein, N., Wang, C. C., & Minkler, M. (2007). Engaging young adolescents in social action through photovoice. *The Journal of Early Adolescence, 27*(2), 241–261. https://doi.org/10.1177/0272431606294834

Winn, M. T. (2010). "Our side of the story": Moving incarcerated youth voices from margins to center. *Race Ethnicity and Education, 13*(3), 313–325.

World Health Organization (2007). Fact Sheet: The Health of Indigenous Peoples. Retrieved Feb 26 from: www.who.int/gender-equity-rights/knowledge/factsheet-ind igenous-healthn-nov2007-eng.pdf?ua=1

Zeichner, K., Payne, K. A., & Brayko, K. (2015). Democratizing teacher education. *Journal of Teacher Education, 66*(2), 122–135.

Zhang-Wu, Q. (2017). Culturally and linguistically responsive teaching in practice: A case study of a fourth-grade mainstream classroom teacher. *Journal of Education, 197*(1), 33–40.

# PART I
# Roots

PART I

BOOK

# THEY ARE LISTENING

*Becky Thiessen with Youth Researchers MJ,*
*Charlie, Jaydin and Junior*

Sally, a Kwakw̲a̲ka̲'wakw Elder, spoke to us in Kwak'wala every day in Circle before we began. It was always a prayer, and never words that I could recognize, yet at times I could understand what she was conveying. I could understand the love, dedication, and compassion that she was offering to the youth and to all who wanted to listen. But I think I also understood that there was a sense of urgency. Our time together was precious.

As fluent language speakers diminish, there are great efforts, intergenerationally, to reawaken Indigenous languages. There are three Indigenous languages that come from what we now call Vancouver Island: Kwak'wala[1], Hul'q'umi'num[2], and Nuu-chah-nulth[3] and each language has regional dialects.

Every Tuesday for four months, in early 2021, we met at Tsawalk Learning Centre – an Indigenous community-based learning program in Nanaimo, B.C. Our project was a collaboration between Tsawalk Learning Centre, The Nanaimo Aboriginal Centre, myself-Becky Thiessen, and Dr. Amanda Wager, both of us, community-engaged facilitators from the Centre for Art, Research, and Community (arc) at Vancouver Island University. Sally joined us all in Circle as we began our weekly sessions. Together, the group consisted of respected Edlers, young researchers, teachers, facilitators, community members, and artists who collaboratively created the project *Youth Language Warriors: Reclaiming Culture through Intergenerational Relationships and the Arts* (funded by the Vancouver Foundation and Artstarts). We were all learning to research using art techniques and language to explore, gather, and disseminate our findings – we were learning across generations from one another.

It is fitting that the name of the learning centre, the Nuu-chah-nulth word, *tsawalk*, means "one." Tsawalk is an Indigenous worldview that recognizes the relationship between the physical and spiritual as an entwined whole. Indigenous, non-Indigenous, all species, the natural and built environment and all matter are

DOI: 10.4324/9781003302186-3

integrated as one (Atleo, 2004). As our local and global communities consider how to sustainably, ethically, and responsibly make decisions for future generations, I see the understanding of this worldview critical to healthy communities globally.

The aforementioned group convened face-to-face during the heightened time of Covid-19, thus we needed to follow the British Columbia Ministry of Health guidelines. Masked, sanitized and feeling a little anxious to be in close proximity, we were committed to our precious time together. Bracken Hanuse Corlett and Amanda Strong, artists from across the Salish Sea, remotely taught us digital art techniques. Dr. Amanda Wager, 7 months pregnant and doubled up on Kn95s, bravely led us through research methodologies. The late Elder Sally Williams, who was quite ill at the time, prayed and guided us weekly while navigating Zoom from the comfort of her bed. Globally, Earthlings were adjusting to new digital techniques and ways to remain connected; we were adapting together with the rest of the world.

Within the first few weeks, the youth researchers created the following research questions:

- What is love?
- Why are we the Salmon's problem? (see Figures I1.1 and I1.2)
- Where did all the fish go? (see Figure I1.3)
- Why don't we matter? (Missing and Murdered Indigenous Women and Girls) (see Figures I1.4 and I1.5)

**FIGURE I1.1** Jaydin and Junior use Nuu-chah-nulth language to demonstrate the salmon cycle.

**FIGURE 11.2** Jaydin and Junior's stop motion animation response to the degradation of the local salmon, a primary resource that has given life to their communities for thousands of years.

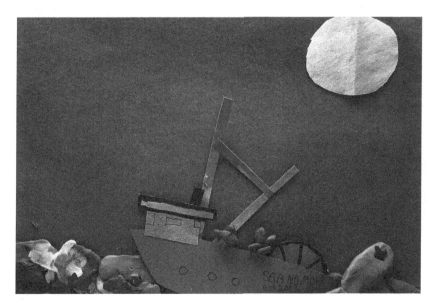

**FIGURE 11.3** As youth researcher activists, Jaydin and Junior asked the question: "Where did all the fish go?"

**FIGURE I1.4** MJ's initial drawing about the Missing and Murdered Indigenous Women and Girls in Canada.

**FIGURE 11.5** MJ and Charlie's video performance activism asking, "Why don't we matter?" in response to the Missing and Murdered Indigenous Women and Girls in Canada.

- Why aren't they [Missing and Murdered Indigenous Women and Girls] found?; Why don't the police help?

They worked their way through themes of systemic racism, misogyny, environmental degradation, and philosophical angst. As young people these deep complexities and anxieties were intertwined with teenage rebellion, strong wills, indulgence, and tendencies to withdraw. It is an age to not take lightly; it is an age where we, as adults, have a responsibility to listen. Elder Sally knew this. She knew we needed to listen to them. There was a sense of urgency in her words, not only to share, but to listen to the youth. Elder Sally was with us for her last days, opening our meetings every time with a Sharing Circle and guiding us through prayer in Kwak'wala. She told the youth that their work was historic.

We kept her close and carried on after she passed to the spirit world.

One afternoon when we were together in Circle, the youth were present... but the adults were missing. Elder Sally had passed on by this time, another Elder-in-Training was away fishing, another got a job teaching on the West Coast of the Island. One teacher was on leave for surgery and Amanda had started her maternity leave. There was no Kwak'wala, no Hul'q'umi'num, no Nuu-chah-nulth to open the Circle. We paused. I asked the youth: "What should we do? How do we start our Circle?" One of the youth, a young woman stood up, timid and bold, and holding her cedar paddle she welcomed us in song, wavering and strong in Hul'q'umi'num. She was listening. They ARE listening.

The final work from the youth researchers is a video that showcases their exploration through activism, performance, stop-motion animation, language, art, and design.

## Note

1 **Kwak'wala** – An Indigenous language of northern Vancouver Island, nearby islands, and along the adjacent coast of mainland British Columbia, spoken by the Kwakwaka'wakw.
2 **Hul'q'umi'num** – An Indigenous language of southeastern Vancouver Island spoken by the Snuneymuxw, Stz'uminus, and Snaw-Naw-As people.
3 **Nuu-chah-nulth** – An Indigenous language on the west coast of Vancouver Island spoken by the Nuu-chah-nulth people.

## Reference

Atleo, E. R. (2004; 2000). Tsawalk: A Nuu-chah-nulth worldview. UBC Press.

# 1

# A COLORFUL LANGUAGE

## Playback Theater as a Way of Listening with Youth in Palestine

*Khitam Edelbi and Yamila Hussein-Shannan*

## Our Story

Dr. Khitam Edelbi and Dr. Yamila Hussein-Shannan (the authors) explain how their involvement in and understanding of Playback Theater (PT) is grounded in their commitment to the liberation of their Palestinian land and people.

**Dr. Edelbi** (A Palestinian woman living in her homeland as a second-class citizen)

Escaping Zionist militias invading Palestine in 1948, my parents ran for their lives, barefoot, through villages, mountains, and valleys, in the middle of the night. Except for their children, they lost everything overnight: the house they had in Al-Birwa, their land and social fabric. Everything. Or so they thought. They had also lost two of their seven children. My mother and older sisters incessantly tell the story of how, for two days, my devastated mother could not eat, sleep, or move until she was reunited with her two missing children. Although I was not yet born, their experience of exile, loss, and devastation, in all its details, has become part of me and informs how I view and interact with the world.

I feel moved by a sense of responsibility to tell my family's story. In that retelling, I feel as if I have lived through it. In a Playback Theater space and with an engaged audience, I had the opportunity to watch it performed on stage. For the first time, I could witness it, experience it, hear it, and feel it. I saw my parents with my siblings on stage. I saw the village. The mountains, the valleys, and villages they crossed on that catastrophic night before my birth. I felt my mother's pain and desperation. It was no longer a story I was trapped in; others were carrying it with me in the open now. In that sharing, I understood it better, I became clearer about my feelings and gained strength learning how it shapes my decisions. Playback Theater allowed for the story, the experience, the narrative to circle from the inside out

DOI: 10.4324/9781003302186-4

and then back from the outside in. Not surprisingly, PT became a central part of my artistic and professional life.

Coupled with my art therapy activism, it provides a perfect venue in Palestine to tell our stories of dispossession, displacement, and aspirations for dignity and freedom. Playback Theater creates a space for us to reflect, together, on what we know, to learn about and from our (grand)parents' stories and heal. We are all shaped by our parents, and ancestors' stories, whether we have heard them or not. Hearing them helps us understand how they shape us and decide how we want them to shape us. I want the world to know my people's stories the way I want the world to know my story. Telling our stories is, in a way, a mission. Although I have no power to free Palestine, at least, by telling my story I remind the world of the crimes committed against Palestinians and Palestine's refugees and how we have survived and continue trying to thrive and fight for our liberation. It's the story of a people who insist on restoring their lives on their lands with respect and dignity. Storytelling is one way to defend Palestine.

**Dr. Hussein-Shannan** (A Palestinian woman living in her homeland as a permanent resident)

Born in Colombia to Palestinian parents, I grew up hearing about peasant life in Kobar, their village, the far away olive groves where people spent nights during the season, the seven-day wedding celebrations, family feuds, love stories, and broken hearts. My parents also told stories about betrayals, relatives massacred in Deir Yasin, and heroic resistance in defense of Palestine. My father carried his scars in his heart and soul, but also on his body; I knew too well all the injuries he had sustained in 1947–48 defending Jerusalem and fighting in al-Qastal. The memories, pain, love, dreams, and aspirations infused in my parents' stories became central to how I understood and positioned myself in the world since as far as I can remember.

Once the family returned to Palestine, faces, places, family dynamics, and ways of living I had only heard of felt quite familiar. Questions I had never asked felt answered just like answers I thought I had turned into questions. Growing up in Jerusalem, I walked the streets and visited places my father fought for; I often could hear their voices, feel movements, and imagine their feelings as they fought for the Holy City. My passion for justice, dignity, and liberation is fueled by stories I have heard, stories I have told, and stories I have lived. Upon learning about PT from Khitam, I understood its power as a venue for accumulating generational knowledge through storytelling and learning about and from our young to better understand how they make sense of their world and their place in it. For Palestinians, a people who continue to resist colonization, violent displacement (internally and in the diaspora), dispossession, and geographic fragmentation, stories are central to the continuity of collective memory (remembrance, healing, imagination) and, ultimately, decolonization.

## Playback Theater (PT)

Founded by Jonathan Fox and his partner Jo Salas during the 1970s, Playback Theater is "an interactive, improvisational theatrical form used to illuminate life and incite dialogue" (Fox, 2008, para. 1). Co-founder Salas (1993) explains that the scope and purpose of PT is

> to reveal the form and meaning of any experience, even those which are ostensibly formless and ambiguous in the telling. [PT] dignifies stories with ritual and aesthetic awareness, and links them together so that they form a collective story about a community of people… [It] offers an arena in which the meaning of individual experience expands to become part of a shared sense of purposeful existence.
>
> *p. 22*

PT is a spontaneous, unscripted drama format grounded in real-life stories voluntarily shared by audience members, facilitated by a "conductor," re-enacted on stage by a corps of "performers" and "musicians." A conductor facilitates the Playback Theater group, which usually includes a corps of at least one musician and around five actors (Good, 1986). For a visual of the basic setting for a Playback Theater performance, see Playback Theater UK.[1]

Aiming to create conditions for open, warm, and respectful social interaction among the audience, the conductor directs the process through "rituals, theatrical aesthetics, dialogue, movement and music" (Motos & Fields, 2015, p. 4). After setting up the space and explaining how Playback Theater works, the conductor invites audience members to share a personal story that is significant for them (often, the group agrees on a theme). These can be memories, dreams, dilemmas, feelings, fantasies, etc. The conductor supports the storyteller through questions and reiteration to flash out core elements of the story, identify key events, name dilemmas or conundrums, etc., both to honor the narrator (and their story) and to deepen and expand the corps of actors' and the musician(s)' interpretation of the story. It is important that the conductor be familiar not only with PT goals and rituals but also with the context of the community and the participating audience to balance the three interactive elements of PT, namely, art, ritual, and social interaction (Fox & Dauber, 1999, p. 127). Adhering to a ritualized process (clear roles, definitive steps, predictable temporal, and spatial arrangement), shapes the artistic and aesthetic performance, encourages audience participation, and protects the space for stories to be shared, performed, and reflected upon. Salas (2005) explains that rituals "provide stability and familiarity within which unpredictability can be found" (p. 117). It is in this unpredictability that learning and healing can happen.

Rivers (2013) explains that "Playback Theater praxis is based on the assumption that stories are told for a purpose: to remember, to transmit a message or evoke certain responses in the audience" (p. 161). This necessitates the full presence and attentive listening of the corps of actors who are tasked with acting out their interpretation of the story in front of the narrator and audience, using their own words and movements, guided by the conductor, and accompanied by sound created by the musician(s). Performers often use objects and materials from a "cloth" or "prop tree" to bring to life characters, places, or abstract elements in the story. Although the performance requires no prior rehearsals, the corps of actors will have been trained in active listening, improvisational techniques, and other drama exercises. Music is an important part of the ritual "serving a dual purpose of 1) creating an atmospheric setting, and 2) giving the actors more time to reflect on their assigned roles" (Motos & Fields, 2015, p. 12).

After the performance, the conductor asks the storyteller about their feelings while watching the scene, whether the scene was close to the story that was narrated, and if there is anything they would add or share with the audience and the actors (Rivers, 2013). The narrator may accept it, choose to tweak the story to better capture the essence of their story, or decide to explore alternate possible choices. The dialogue that ensues pertains not only to the story and its narrators, but also the audience, the performers, and the musician(s). The participants can, through storytelling, reconsider their role in the events of the stories told and employ a multiplicity of languages to reflect on what is real, examine the impact of these experiences on them, and imagine their contribution to the future. Sharing and enacting real-life stories, they are deepening their thinking about themselves and about how others might experience common structures, and how these stories impact them and others. They can better understand their experiences and have the language and clarity of analysis to share with others as they garner support to imagine alternatives.

With the founding of The International Playback Theater Network in 1990, this versatile theatrical form has proliferated around the world with hundreds of Playback Theater companies now operating in over 60 countries (Ellinger & Ellinger, 2016). Given its flexibility, portability, and small number of props, coupled with its combination of storytelling, drama, and psychology, PT has proven attractive in different settings as a pedagogical practice in educational environments often with a focus on racial justice aiming to create a healing community (Sajnani & Wager, 2017). It has also been employed as a therapeutic art form in hospitals, prisons, youth centers, and even as community building in the corporate world (Salas, 2009). In educational institutions and cultural spaces, Playback Theater has been used in language training centers and classrooms to enhance second language acquisition and subject matter content (see Feldhendler, 2006 and 2007). In Palestine, PT has been used for various purposes (Rohrback, 2018) and as art therapy, which, as we argue in this chapter, becomes a pedagogical practice with strong potential for collective remembrance, healing, and envisioning.

## Palestine's Internally Displaced: Qalandia Refugee Camp

The Palestinian people, whether in their homeland or in neighboring countries, are routinely subjected to Israeli violence including invasions, bombings, murder, imprisonment, militarily imposed curfews, checkpoints, restriction of movement, unprotected from land theft, a captive economy and, since 1995, a sham of a

Palestinian political structure that manages and benefits from some administrative aspects of daily life under Israeli control. Palestinian youth are treated by the Israeli state as a "security threat" and are subject to killings, random beatings, arrests, prolonged detention, and sentenced under a "legal" system that, controlled and run by the military, imprisons minors without charges or even a trial under what the colonial powers call "administrative detention."[2] Losing a parent, a sibling, a friend, or a neighbor, or even the house often results in anger, pain, despair, and unhealed grief. Young people often participate in direct, quite often violent, confrontations at checkpoints with Israeli soldiers, and are at high risk of arrest, physical harm, and death. Living in a refugee camp only exacerbates these conditions.

The youth participants in the Playback Theater program in Palestine are all born in Qalandia refugee camp to parents (and grandparents) who became refugees after being forcibly evicted from their ancestral land in 1948. By the time the state of Israel was created in 1948 over 78% of the land of Palestine, Zionist paramilitaries had expelled 750,000 to 1 million Palestinians (then approximately 15% of the population) turning them into landless refugees in surrounding countries or internally displaced and dispossessed in historic Palestine. Home to over 11,000 Palestinians internally displaced in 1948, the Qalandia refugee camp is one of thirty-two refugee camps supported by the United Nations Relief and Works (UNRWA) in historic Palestine.[3] Denied their internationally recognized right to return to their ancestral land and homes, Palestinian refugees are trapped in small plots of land and live in high population density with inadequate infrastructure and poor socioeconomic conditions under a strictly imposed military rule that controls their movement in and out the camp, surrounded by physical barriers (barbed wire fencing, checkpoints, concrete wall, etc.). They are subject to frequent incursions and invasions by the Israeli military. Not surprisingly, refugee camps are home to fierce resistance to colonization and military rule.

Once a small prosperous village off the Ramallah-Jerusalem road, Qalandia was home to the Jerusalem airport, which later was heavily used by the British and the Jordanian occupying regimes (until 1948 and 1967, respectively). It has now been turned into an Israeli military base. The Qalandia military checkpoint, the largest one dividing Jerusalem from the West Bank, is placed at the entrance of the refugee camp. Tawil-Souri (2010) aptly captures how the colonization of Palestine has transformed the reality for Qalandia. "If in the past 'Jerusalem Airport was their [Palestinians'] gate to the world' today the Qalandia checkpoint is that gate" (p. 27). The Qalandia military checkpoint's proximity to people's houses and children's schools increases the oppressive intensity of colonial rule and military control as well as the frequency and intensity of acts of resistance, usually led by the youth.

These confrontations often lead to injury, arrest, and death in addition to mental and psychological harm. The ongoing deterioration of the situation for children and youth in Palestine is alarming and the need for interventions is dire. Not surprising, this context was vividly present in the stories shared during the study along with stories about school and family that echo worries, aspirations, and confusions of adolescents elsewhere.

## Playback Theater with Qalandia's Youth

Dr. Edelbi, a Palestinian art therapist, conducted a study to explore the role of Playback theater in youth development in the Qalandia Refugee Camp, Palestine. The study included 11 boys in ninth grade (14–15 years) who came from the same school, for 2.5 hours twice a week in an after school cultural center over a 2-month period. In 16 sessions, the study aimed to create a space for them to express themselves through drama activities and share their personal stories through Playback Theater. Dr. Edelbi's background in art therapy coupled with extensive experience as an art education trainer was important in creating a meaningful experience for all involved. In collaboration with a "conductor" Fida Ataya, a trainer with experience in Playback Theater, the art therapist designed the program, planned the sessions, and observed closely as the conductor led the sessions with the youth intervening only as necessary. The art therapist could thus focus on group dynamics, the youth growth individually and collectively, and, through regular debriefs with the conductor, assess the program as it unfolded.

Following informal check-ins, each session included group building, drama and movement activities as well as improvisational exercises and storytelling with content initiated by the participants. For example, one participant starts by saying or doing something. Group members voluntarily join, one by one, adding their own utterance or movement to develop a random scene based on a random idea. Not all participants have to interact with each other, and each participant could choose the other participants they want to work with for this activity. Throughout the two months, the youth learned techniques to improvise stories they hear from an audience, in this case, their friends and relatives, without rehearsals. They practiced, for instance, the "tableau" form whereby the actors perform the story they heard in a series of tableau images. Once the story is completely told, the conductor summarizes the first part of the story in a short sentence. The actors then create a still image based on the given sentence. Moving into the image, the actors can use their voices. The musician can also accompany them. The actors will then hold the image, while the conductor gives a second prompt relating to the next part of the story. The actors respond by moving into a second image. This process will be repeated 4 or 5 times, until the story has been played back through still tableaus. Providing the youth with a safe environment to express their own feelings including happiness, sadness, and pride, Playback Theater allowed for a collective space for the young participants to share concerns, aspirations, dreams, grief, and loss. The opportunity to learn and practice new skills together sharpened their ability to listen, focus, reflect, empathize, and build stronger and more positive relationships with each other.

Participants shared their feedback on how they experienced PT and what they learned in the process. For example, in their written feedback at the end of the program, Salam & Hammad reported that they "enjoyed the work a lot"[4] including storytelling, warm-up activities, and music. Hamza wrote that he enjoyed the experience "especially when we were acting and playing beautiful games" and Rateb reported that he enjoyed "acting and telling stories." Alqam's most enjoyable aspect was, he wrote, "when I was playing the musical instruments." The art therapist and the conductor observed participants' improved focus and heightened sensibilities as they heard (often for the first time) and improvised stories shared by their mothers and friends during the final performance. In addition to joy, they also wrote about learning. They reported that the program had a positive impact on their social interaction and helped them acquire new skills and were pleased with what they learned about themselves and those around them. Shahadah reported "I learned more than I could in front of the net." They also expressed that the performance at the end was healing as it created space for them to share their growth and new understanding of themselves and their context with friends and relatives. Asked about the positive impact of PT on them during the oral evaluation session, they responded:

> *Salam:* Yes, I feel I am less angry and reactive with other people and my acting became better.
>
> *Hammad:* Yes, I learned more how to deal with the group as a team, and how to collaborate with others on a specific project.
>
> *Hamzah:* I discovered new things about my acting and about playing musical instruments. It was my first time acting and playing music.
>
> *Naser:* Yes, I feel my whole personality has changed through this experience. For example, I hated to be photographed but now I actually like it. Through this project, me and the other participants became more respectful and kinder to each other.
>
> *Awwad:* I learned new things, things I never did before. At home, I became more active and even acted out stories at home with my siblings. This made my family happy about my work.

During the final performance, many of the youth were hearing their mothers' often devastating stories for the first time. For example, Mustafa, one of the participants, learned about his mother's terrifying experiences with Israeli soldiers during the first Intifada (Palestinian mass popular uprising against military occupation, 1987–1993) while on stage. Admitting that she had never spoken about that experience, Mustafa's mother shared during the debrief that "it felt good to see my story enacted on stage." Mothers who shared their stories in the final performance, many for the first time, and witnessed their sons acting them out on stage without rehearsal, also spoke about how powerful the experience was, in spite of the sadness the stories brought to surface. At their final evaluation, mothers shared their impressions of how participation in Playback Theater had a positive impact on their sons. They noticed how happy their sons were while getting ready for a session and after coming back home from a session, and saw their sons grow as they became more communicative, more mature, coming out of their shells and feeling more comfortable sharing their stories and listening to others.

Playback Theater may not have erased the anger, fear, pain, or grief that the adolescent refugees or their mothers carry, but it may have eased the burden, even if only temporarily. While their future and the potential impact of PT on the well-being and safety of the participating youth cannot be known, for the two months that they participated in PT workshops they were alive and filled with hope.

## Mental Health in Palestine

In the Palestinian land occupied since 1967 (i.e., West Bank including Jerusalem and Gaza), "entire generations of [Palestinian] children have grown up knowing nothing but violent war-like events and disruption" (Abdeen et al., 2008, p. 291). Long term exposure to war, curfews, closures, arrest, and torture result in traumatic events that are often repeated. A 2003 study in a refugee camp in Gaza found that 94% of participant children had been tear-gassed, 97% had witnessed a shooting, and 96% had seen funerals. As for mothers, 100% had witnessed shootings, 97.5% had been targeted by tear gas, and 95% had seen funerals (Qouta et al., 2003). Researchers notice a positive correlation between mothers who report high levels of PTSD and the occurrence of PTSD with their children, and vice versa (Allodi et al., 1985, p. 270).

While such research is indicative of the brutal impact of colonization and military rule on mental health in Palestine, it is important to question the validity of mental health assumptions and clinical measures and diagnosis tools such as PTSD in the context of ongoing colonization and the protracted state of terror inflicted on the Palestinian people. We concur with Hammoudeh (2020) that applied without proper attention to the complex interlocked forces shaping the reality in Palestine, mental health research positions the Palestinian people either as traumatized victims to sympathize with, or heroes, whose supposedly inherent resiliency explains our steadfastness in the face of draconian rule. "Both the victimization and the valorization miss the target" concludes Hammoudeh (2020, p. 78).

Focusing on PTSD in Palestine, Dr. Samah Jabr (2019), one of the few Palestinian psychiatrists practicing in Palestine, cautions us from the notion of "post" in the diagnosis of PTSD. "In Palestine," she writes, "traumatic threats are ongoing and enduring. There is no 'post-traumatic' safety." (Jabr, 2019, para.8). In an interview, Dr. Jabr alaborates that in Palestine, "there is no 'post' because the trauma is repetitive and ongoing and continuous." (Goldhill, 2019, para.3). PTSD, she explains, might be useful to describe "the experiences of an American soldier who goes to Iraq to bomb and go back to the safety of the United States. He's having nightmares and fears related to the battlefield and his fears are imaginary." (Goldhill, 2019, para.3). Palestinians, however, have no 'posttraumatic' safety to return to. While there might be similarity in some of the symptoms associated with PTSD, "for tortured Palestinian prisoners, such symptoms are reasonable reactions, insofar as the threat lives on; they may be re-arrested and tortured again at any time" (Jabr, 2019, para.8). For Palestinians, "the threat of having another bombardment is a very real one. It's not imaginary." Goldhill, 2019, para.3).

As such, interventions with young Palestinians need to account for the context in which such research and tools are developed and applied. What we need, according to Hammoudeh (2020), are critical mental health approaches so we can understand the complexity of people's experiences in relation to structural realities. She adds,

> Rather than numbing the pain of our individual wounds, what is needed is a mental health praxis rooted in social justice, one that seeks to strengthen communal solidarities and that identifies and addresses the structural (political and social) causes of collective ill-being at their root. Healing in a mental health praxis embedded within social justice and liberation becomes a call to action, an effort toward reconstructing a world that fosters our mental well-being.
>
> *pp. 80–81*

Playback Theater can potentially provide a space for youth to engage their pain and dreams together as they endeavor to make sense of the social and political forces shaping their lives. Articulating and explaining one's emotions, be it pain, joy, fears, or dreams, might be the beginning of a healing process that gently makes theorizing possible in spaces nurtured so that participants can connect their experiences with those of others, find commonalities, examine differences, question their context, interrogate how they are positioned and how they want to position themselves in and with the world. PT can become a communal act where participants weave histories, unique and common, creating both an environment of cooperation and exchange of experiences as well as creating a sense of communion among participants, in mind, body, and, no less important, imagination.

## Adolescents and Playback Theater

Discussing the participation of adolescents in Playback Theater, co-founder Jo Salas (2018, personal communication with the art therapist) emphasizes the imperative to welcome and accept any story the adolescents bring to the stage. She believes that adults should not urge adolescents to talk about a specific theme but to let them talk about what matters to them, not what matters to adults. In her experience using PT with adolescents, she notes that this approach allows adolescents to bring up what concerns them; to become open to discussion, and slowly feel comfortable in performing in the Playback Theater. When adolescents feel that they are heard and understood, she insists, they are freed up to experiment with happy and sad stories alike.

Through the Playback sessions at the Qalandia Refugee Camp, each participant had the opportunity to share stories of their choice and watched others act them out in front of them, simultaneously healing their wounds and learning a new language that incorporates the body. Language in this sense is understood beyond its utility in daily communication to language in its centrality to personal and communal identity that is always rooted in land for indigenous peoples like the Palestinians. Their stories revolved around the people and events that dominated their lives, which seemed to be rather common adolescent experiences about friends, family, and video games. For example, Zayed described a fight in his classroom. Hamzah talked about losing a friendship and not understanding why his friend's behavior had changed, and Awwad explained his love of the video game Fortnite. Alqam talked about the day he went to have lunch with his friends in Ramallah and the waiter in charge questioned whether they had paid the lunch bill before leaving the restaurant, and how angry he and his friends became when treated unfairly by that waiter. In settings like PT we can listen to ourselves, to each other, to our humanity, to our dreams, aspirations, our healing. In short, we reconnect with our agency as we express and share our stories with others and listen to theirs. During the final reflection, Dr. Edelbi asked participants whether and how Playback Theater offered them a platfrom to express themselves. Some of the responses were:

> *Salam:* Yes it did. Anyone who lives in the camp would like to share everything, and I managed to tell the group about a few things that happened to me.
> *Rateb:* Playback Theater offered me the ability to express myself in all different ways when acting, playing musical instruments, and doing the warm-up exercises.
> *Naser:* Yes, the project helped me to show my feelings and express my sadness.
> *Shahahdah:* Yes, and I felt good to see them acted out on stage. Also, when I acted out the stories of others I also expressed myself through them. I felt sad acting out their sad stories.

In the process of telling and performing, the young people not only acquired a new verbal language to talk about their experiences, their pain, their confusion, their pride, their (dis)illusions, their hopes, fears, aspirations, etc., but also practiced how their body can help them articulate and express their stories as well as others'. These verbal and body languages invite them to step into the worlds and experiences of others around them to deepen their understanding of their own as they share with others. In the "A Story Behind the Scarf" activity, the trainer put scarves on stage in front of the participants and invited each to choose a scarf. Salam chose a large white scarf and placed it on his body similar to how Muslims put a shroud on the dead body. Salam did not speak that day when participants shared what they did with the scarves and why, but in a following session, he explained that the white scarf represented his sadness over his martyred friend who had just been killed by the Israeli army.

As the youth became clearer about their positionality in the world, they acquired and practiced a language that helped them advance towards maturity. Their improved self-expression and deepened active listening strengthened their relationships with each other as young people and with an older generation. This new language made it possible for them to stand on stage and improvise sketches that tell stories verbally, physically, and artistically to each other and to an audience experiencing, even if only for a brief moment, the role of each of the characters, sometimes their own parents. They gradually built a safe enough space with guidance and support of the conductor and the art therapist, and relied on their body language to express feelings and thoughts that verbal language falls short of communicating. Naser, for example, reflected on the stories he shared, "It felt as if those stories were happening right now in the present. I was a little nervous when I acted out the stories of other participants." Similarly, Awwad shared that "it felt good seeing others acting out my stories, and watching the story unfold before me right now."

Back in their everyday lives, they reported feeling empowered with this new language they learned and practiced together in Playback sessions. One of the questions that was asked at the final evaluation by the researcher to the participants was "Did you learn/discover any new things about yourself through this experience or not?" The participants' responses highlighted how this PT experience affected them on several levels:

> *Salam:* Through the work, I discovered that I became less shy. I am less angry, and get angry less than I did before.
>
> *Shahadah:* I learned I can act. I did not know I would be able to do this.
>
> *Naser:* Yes, I discovered that I am a good person, and that I treat others with respect.
>
> *Awwad:* I learned that I could learn and apply new things that I had no idea about before. The experience changed and developed me as a person.
>
> *Khalil:* I learned about this theater method and how it is applied. I also discovered I could act, and became more courageous during the project.

Close observations allowed the art therapist to witness their gradual incorporation of facial and body movements to tell the stories, and no less important, feelings they typically suppress like anger, frustration, sadness, and rage. Watching them blossom during the sessions, and on stage during the final performance points to Playback Theater as one possible venue through which young people can acquire and practice multiple languages, colorful languages that ultimately help them connect with their inner power. These languages also help the group nurture their collective power through building trust as they support each other to believe in themselves and activate their own agency.

## Pedagogical Implications

The process of Playback Theater is complex yet not complicated. People involved in Playback Theater are creators of, not only witnesses to, stories – theirs and others'. As a pedagogical practice, Playback Theater thus allows for a participatory, interactive learning environment where the knowledge constructed emerges from and is grounded in stories voluntarily shared by the participants through ritual-istic, aesthetically artistic interpretations and enactment of their stories and the dialogue involved. Young people are encouraged to be storytellers, performers, and spectators practicing authentic communication in each of these roles as they listen attentively to stories that matter to them and narratives that are relevant to their here and now. This attentiveness is essential so they can take in the details and the spirit of the story and thus the corps of actors can, with musical support, perform it with "respect and aesthetic attention" (Salas, 2005, p. 46) and in ways that dem-onstrate "understanding towards the narrator" (Motos & Field, 2015, p. 13).

While the artistic element (acting out, music, props) enhances communication beyond spoken words, PT also has the potential to enhance verbal communication. Real-life conversations for real-life purposes with real-life human emotions help students to develop their "capability to relate to others and consequently become better communicators" (Alvarado, 2017, cited in Catherine & Devi, 2020, p. 2). Because Playback Theater does not involve rehearsing or practicing a script, young people have more freedom to communicate their interpretation of the story in their words, without worrying about formal language perfection or grammar. This impulsivity stands in stark contrast to how communication, when attended to in the classroom, tends to be taught through decontextualized language and scripts. Communication in PT, as Trivedi (2013) observes, is natural, spontaneous, and impulsive. This lowers the affective barriers and builds confidence in young people helping them develop new degrees of independence (Fabio, 2–15, cited in Catherine & Devi, p. 2).

Storytelling is here understood as healing, transformative, and decolonial. "Stories in Indigenous epistemologies are disruptive, sustaining, knowledge pro-ducing, and theory-in-action" (Sium & Ritskes, 2013, p. ii). Unlike liberal notions of "show & tell" and of depoliticized sharing, stories become verbal articulations of collective pain and aspirations that help us bridge theory and action. We concur with Sium and Ritskes (2013) that "the experiences of those who live out decol-onization are integral to the integrity of the movement, grounding it to the material realities of the people whose lives bear the scars of colonialism and the long histories of resistance and triumph" (p. iii). Grounded in an engaged peda-gogy that centers people in a learning environment where knowledge construc-tion includes the surfacing of collective pain, values and attitudes embedded in social relations, and acts of resistance, storytelling forms part of decolonization. "If stories are archives of collective pain, suffering and resistance, then to speak them is to heal; to believe in them is to reimagine the world" (Sium & Ritskes, 2013, p. iv). An engaged pedagogy acknowledges that learning can sometimes bring up feelings that we have difficulty processing alone. As bell hooks (1994) urges those committed to meaningful learning and teaching, "we have to learn how to appreciate difficulty, too, as a stage in intellectual development," which requires that we create spaces for young people to "feel that there is integrity to be found in grappling with difficult material" (p. 154). PT can create such spaces through its three elements: art, ritual, and social interaction. Collective engagement with our feelings and emotions is a central part of learning, healing, and envisioning, all of which require genuine connection with ideas. "If we are all emotionally shut down," hooks wonders, "how can there be any excitement about ideas?" (p. 155).

Young people in the classroom or any other setting participating in PT are part of history, part of communities whose stories and experiences are rarely allowed into teaching and learning spaces. Playback Theater creates space for participants to share and co-construct knowledge through stories, word choice, body posture, facial expressions, tone both for the narrator and the actors, and the dialogue between them facilitated by the conductor and for the audience in a different way. We are all shaped by our parents and ancestors' stories, whether we have heard them or not. Hearing them helps us understand how they shape us and decide how we want them to shape us. PT challenges the body/mind split inviting feelings, and perceptions to be enacted, aesthetically, through the body. The body here provides a representation of what is in participants' minds and hearts creating spaces for them to experience commonalities, differences, connections, and shared concerns with a strong potential to create "powerful moments when boundaries are crossed, differences confronted, discussion happens, and solidarity emerges" (hooks, 1994, p. 130).

A background in mental health and therapy, in addition to art education, undoubtedly enhances the conductor's role and enriches the experience. Deep knowledge of this theatrical form and the context, coupled with pedagogical clarity and skills in managing the tension between art, rituals, and storytelling, allows the conductor to create learning and healing spaces where experiences and interpretations are shared, reimagined, expanded, and possibly transformed. It is important that educators be trained in Playback Theater, its form, goals, and techniques, and that they have had opportunities to experience it, to live it, to experiment with it, as audience at least, though they will be much better equipped if they had shared a story and saw it enacted on stage. It is also imperative to honor students' full agency in sharing stories. Students should be explicitly encouraged to share only what they want to. If, for example, a student stops after starting to tell a story, they should be supported in that decision without having to explain their decision. In short, student participation should always be entirely voluntary in all ways. If a student shares a story that the educator feels unprepared and/or unequipped to handle, the educator might decide to seek guidance and support from qualified professionals. Since the role of the educator is to hold and protect the space for their stories, the focus should always be on the storyteller: their well-being, their feelings, their thoughts, and their needs at the moment. Understood as a pedagogical praxis that understands healing as part of critical thinking, PT can support learners in "creating a new language, rupturing disciplinary boundaries, decentering authority, and rewriting the institutional and discursive borderlands in which politics becomes a condition for reasserting the relationship between agency, power, and struggle" (Giroux & McLaren, 1994, p. ix).

Language here emerges in multiple forms and colors. Going beyond verbal, oral language to name experiences and feelings, PT creates the space for a colorful language that is experiential, artistic, verbal, written, performed, sculptured, theoretical, etc. Like indigenous peoples elsewhere, Palestinians are also well versed in the language of the land. We understand our relationship to the land as the foundation of our existence. Listening to this colorful language we remember, resist, and lean towards healing, nurturing our humanity and envisioning our liberation. For Palestinians, an indigenous people who continue to resist colonization, violent displacement (internally and in the diaspora), dispossession, and geographic fragmentation, stories are central to the continuity of collective memory: remembrance, healing, and imagination. Playback Theater allows us to listen to ourselves and to each other while we share and re-enact our stories, thus exploring commonalities, examining differences, forging connections, bonding, and healing together. Such colorful language emerges through dialogue, reflection, empathy, identification, and expression, all of which become communal through Playback Theater. PT can be a way for us to also care for our youth, protect them, prolong their lives, and to nurture them towards life and the living. This colorful language can communicate a message central to our future: we exist, we insist on life, we teach life, we create life, we heal, we recover, we rebuild. In the words of our beloved Palestinian poet, Mahmoud Darwish, "And we love life if we find a way to it."[5]

## Notes

1 https://playbacktheatreuk.wordpress.com/so-what-is-playback-theatre-and-how-does-it-work/
2 "Administrative detention is incarceration without trial or charge, alleging that a person plans to commit a future offense. It has no time limit, and the evidence on which it is based is not disclosed [...] Detainees cannot reasonably mount a defense against undisclosed allegations. Nevertheless, [Israeli] courts uphold the vast majority of orders." www.btselem.org/topic/administrative_detention
3 Almost 45% of the Palestinian people in Palestine are registered as refugees with UNRWA (not all who were displaced were registered as refugees). UNRWA recognizes a total of 58 Palestinian refugee camps in Jordan, Lebanon, Syria, and historic Palestine

where almost a third of Palestinian refugees (from both 1948 and 1967) reside. www. unrwa.org/palestine-refugees By mid-2013, almost half the Palestinian population worldwide was registered as refugees (approximately 5.3 million). www.pcbs.gov.ps/port als/_pcbs/PressRelease/Press_En_nakba65E.pdf Of every three refugees in the world, one is Palestinian (Badil.org).

4 Participants' names have been changed to protect their privacy.

5 www.slowdownshow.org/episode/2020/05/14/384-and-we-love-life

# References

Abdeen, Z., Qasrawi, R., Nabil, S., & Shaheen, M. (2008). Psychological reactions to Israeli occupation: Findings from the national study of school-based screening in Palestine. *International Journal of Behavioral Development, 32*(4), 290–297.

Allodi, F., Randall, G. R., Lutz, E., Quiroga, J., Zunzunegui, M. V., Kolff, C. A., & Doan, R. N. (1985). Physical and psychiatric effects of torture: Two medical studies. In E. Stover & E. O. Nightingale (Eds.), *The breaking of bodies and minds: Torture, psychiatric abuses and the health professions* (pp. 58–78). New York, NY: Freeman/Times Books/Holt.

Catherine, V. D., & Devi, V. A. (2020). Developing English language skills of the students through playback theatre techniques with special emphasis to speaking skills. *Journal of Critical Reviews, 7*(3), 1427–1442.

Edelbi, K. (2020). Using Playback Theater with Adolescents in Refugee Camps in Palestine to Tell Their Stories. Expressive Therapies Dissertations. 97. https://digitalcommons.les ley.edu/expressive_dissertations/97

Ellinger, A., & Ellinger, C. (2016). A Playback Theater toolkit: Through the lens of one company's experience. Boston, MA: Belmarlin Press.

Feldhendler, D. (2006). "La vie mise en scène, théâtre et récit," Le français dans le monde, Sondernummer Recherches et applications, 39, 155–168

Feldhendler, D. (2007). Playback Theatre: A method for intercultural dialogue. Scenario, 1(2), 46–55. Retrieved from http://publish.ucc.ie/scenario/2007/02/feldhendler/04/cn

Fox, H. (2008). Webpage supplement to chapter 1: Playback Theatre. Retrieved from www. interactiveimprov.com/playbackwb.html

Fox, J., & Dauber, H. (Eds.). (1999). Gathering Voices: Essays on Playback Theatre. New Paltz: Tusitala.

Giroux, H. A., & McLaren, P. (2014). Between borders: Pedagogy and the politics of cultural studies. New York: Routledge.

Goldhill, O. (2019). Palestine's head of mental health services says PTSD is a western concept. Quartz. Retrieved from https://qz.com/1521806/palestines-head-of-mental-hea lth-services-says-ptsd-is-a-western-concept

Good, M. (1986). The Playback Conductor, or How Many Arrows Will I Need. Retrieved from www.playbacktheatre.org/wp-content/uploads/2010/04/playbackconduct- good.pdf

Motos, T. & Fields, D. (2015). Playback theatre: embodying the CLIL methodology. In Drama and CLIL. Edition 1. Linguistics Insights: Studies in Language and Communication, LI194. Román, S. & Núñez, J. (eds). www.peterlang.com/view/9783035194098/cite.html

Playback Theater UK https://playbacktheatreuk.wordpress.com/so-what-is-playback-thea tre-and-how-does-it-work/

Qouta, S., Punamäkii, R., & Sarraj, E. (2003). Prevalence and determinants of PTSD among Palestinian children exposed to military violence. *European Child & Adolescent Psychiatry, 12*(6), 265–272. https://doi.org/10.1007/s00787-003-0328-0

Rivers, B. (2013). Playback Theatre as a response to the impact of political violence in occupied Palestine. *Applied Theatre Research,* 1(2), 157–176. https://doi.org/10.1386/atr.1.2.157_1

Sajnani, N. & Wager, A. (2017). Gaps, Complicities, and Connections: Stories from a Movement Towards Racial Justice in Higher Education. In Playback Theater Reflects. https://playbacktheatrereflects.net/2017/06/19/gaps-complicities-and-connections-stories-from-a-movement-towards-racial-justice-in-higher-education-by-nisha-sajnani-and-amanda-wager/#more-150

Salas, Jo. (1993). Improvising real life: Personal story in Playback Theatre. New Platz, NY: Tusitala Publishing

Salas, Jo. (2005). "Using Theater to Address Bullying," Educational Leadership 63/1, 78–82.

Salas, Jo. (2009). "Playback Theatre: A Frame for Healing" in David R. Johnson and Renée Emunah, eds., Current Approach in Drama Therapy (Second Edition), Springfield, Illinois: Charles C. Thomas Publisher Ltd., 2009), 445–459.

Salas. J, personal communication with Dr. Edelbi, the art therapist, May 18, 2018

Samah Jabr (2019). "What Palestinians Experience Goes beyond the PTSD Label," Middle East Eye, February 7, 2019, www.middleeasteye.net/opinion/what-palestinians-experience-goes-beyond-ptsd-label

Sium, A. & Ritskes, E. (2013). Speaking truth to power: Indigenous storytelling as an act of livingresistance. Decolonization: Indigeneity, Education & Society, 2(1), I–X.

Tawil-Souri, H. (2010). Qalandia checkpoint: The historical geography of a non-place. *Jerusalem Quarterly,* 42(Summer), 26–48. (https://oldwebsite.palestine-studies.org/sites/default/files/jq-articles/42_Tawil-Souri_Qalandia%20Checkpoint.pdf)

Weeam Hammoudeh, Samah Jabr, Maria Helbich & Cindy Sousa (2020). On Mental Health Amid Covid-19, Journal of Palestine Studies, 49(4), 77–90, DOI: 10.1525/jps.2020.49.4.77

# 2

# EDUCATION BEYOND WALLS

## Using the Arts to Awaken an Endangered Language

*Lorato Trok*

I would like to start this chapter with a quote from Kenyan novelist and playwright, Professor Ngũgĩ wa Thiong'o, who wrote

> The real aim of colonialism was to control the people's wealth. But its most important area of domination was the mental universe of the colonised, the control through culture, of how people perceived themselves and their relationship to the world. The domination of a people's language by the languages of the colonising nations was crucial to the domination of the mental universe of the colonised
>
> *(Thiong'o, 1986, p. 16)*

Here Ngũgĩ wa Thiong'o perfectly sums up the role that the brutality of colonialism and the repressive apartheid laws played in the demise of Indigenous cultural practices and languages.

Growing up in Kuruman, a small town in the Northern Cape Province of South Africa, my beloved mother, who had a sixth grade education and spoke very little English, was a master storyteller and without fail, she narrated oral Setswana stories, known as *ditlhamane,* to her six children every single night. Like many Black children of my generation growing up in townships and rural towns in the '80s and early '90s in apartheid South Africa, lack of resources and political instability meant that many families improvised a lot to entertain themselves. While my mother was a skilled narrator, my aunt was a gifted actress and she would act out her stories when it was her turn to tell a story. Our home became a melting pot of storytelling sessions and performance art, as more and more children in the neighbourhood learned of the entertainment that my mother had created for us. As the numbers grew, my mother asked each one of the children who came to

DOI: 10.4324/9781003302186-5

our house to prepare stories of their own and share them with everyone. All this was done in my mother tongue, Setswana, and I have been hooked on stories, languages, and the arts ever since. We may have lacked physical books and a local library, but these oral stories were good enough to make me understand the power of stories to a curious child.

Although at the time we were oblivious to the fact that what we were doing was literacy promotion, it laid the foundation for the beginning of my work in early literacy as an author, translator, editor, and activist in the promotion of multi-lingual literacies in South Africa and the African continent. I was thus automatically attracted to Katrina Esau's story in my work of activism in promoting African languages. I learned of her fascinating life story through a newspaper clipping and when I visited her at her home in Rosedale, a township on the outskirts of Upington, Northern Cape Province and saw her work firsthand, I knew she was an extraordinarily special individual.

In *Decolonising The Mind: The Politics of Language in African Literature* (1986), Ngũgĩ wa Thiong'o describes imperialism as a system that

> disrupts the entire fabric of the lives of its victims: in particular their culture, making them ashamed of their names, history, systems of belief, languages, lore, art, dance, song, sculpture, even the colour of their skin. It thwarts all its victims' forms and means of survival, and furthermore it employs racism.
>
> *(p. 51)*

This definition is true of apartheid South Africa, a country with a majority Black population, where the many years of minority rule dispossessed people of their culture, heritage, and languages, and employed racism to shame them for the colour of their skin. In post-apartheid South Africa, African languages are still struggling to find their rightful place in the arts, education, science, and medicine. Indigenous communities whose languages were in the minority were almost entirely wiped out by the then government language policies, one of which was to introduce Afrikaans as a language of learning and teaching (sahistory.org.za). Colonialism, imperialism, slavery, apartheid, Nazism, and all other autocratic governments that dispossessed, enslaved, and exterminated humans the world over robbed communities' physical ownership of their possessions like land and livestock, but also tore apart families, disregarded and disrespected their languages and cultural practices to the point of extermination.

The Khoisain, Indigenous peoples of South Africa and Botswana, used art as a means of communication. Their ancient rock paintings found in caves consisted of depictions of half-human hybrids, believed to be healers (Gall, 2003). This was not only artwork; it was their language of communication. While many of them were murdered in the course of colonization, surviving members of these hunter-gatherer communities were marginalized and linguistically assimilated. N|uu, one of the languages of the Khoisain, is considered one of the most endangered languages of Southern Africa. In fact, it was thought to be extinct for several decades. Then in the late 1990s, some 20 elderly speakers, scattered throughout the Northern Cape province of South Africa, revealed their competence in this language. Today, Katrina Esau, also known as Ouma Geelmeid, is the last fluent speaker of N|uu after the death of her two sisters, Hanna Kloper and Griet Seekoei, in 2020 and her brother, Simon Sauls, in early 2021. The N|uu language is believed to be one of the oldest languages in the world. Shah and Brenzinger (2017) explain that N|uu "one of the few surviving 'non–Bantu click languages' in Southern Africa, a term suggested by Westphal (1971)" (p. 109). All other Khoisan languages have vanished and their descendants speak Afrikaans, Nama, or other languages as their mother tongue.

South Africa is a multicultural, multiethnic, and multilingual society. The children that Katrina Esau teaches identify themselves as first language Afrikaans speakers, as do most people in their community. Her teachings use the art of oral literature to promote sociocultural awareness to this community that generations before them were deprived of. Katrina's unconventional teaching methods of an almost extinct language propelled linguists far and wide to create orthography for her language. That the orthography of a language can be designed from scratch through listening to the speaker is a testament to how artistic practices can be used to increase literacy and language abilities with multilingual learners. This is art as a way of listening.

## The Incredible Quest to Save a Dying Language

Katrina Esau was born in 1933 on Farm Klapien in Olifantshoek, Northern Cape (see Figure 2.1). They were a family of eight sisters and three brothers. Katrina's father was a Motswana and her mother a Khoisan. Even though Katrina's father was a Motswana, his children never learned Setswana. Their father spoke Afrikaans to them and their mother spoke N|uu with them, a language they considered their home language. They were farm workers and all their children were born and brought up on this farm. While they were growing up on the farm, the farmer

**FIGURE 2.1** A picture of Katrina Esau.

did not allow them to speak their native language, N | uu. Katrina recalls the farmer telling them that their language sounded horrible and ugly and should never be spoken around white children on the farm. The N | uu language was the only language that connected Katrina and her siblings to their culture. It was their home language. The farmer threatened to shoot them if they were caught speaking the language. Many Khoi people were scared of the farmer as they knew his threats were not hollow. They fearfully stopped speaking their N | uu language.

Katrina believes this contributed to the language's disappearance. It was already a minority language as the Khoi population was and to this day remains in the minority. Katrina says that even her identity was determined by the farmer. She recalls her mother telling her that when she was born she was yellow in colour, as are most Khoisan babies and children. When the farmer learned what the baby's name was, he was angry that she was given a proper name for "proper" children. Per the recollection of Katrina's memory the farmer told her mother, "Katrina for what? Don't you see how yellow this baby is? We'll call her Geelmeid!" "Geel" means yellow in Afrikaans and "meid" means maid. She was then called Geelmeid her whole childhood and the name stuck and is still used to this day.

Katrina's mother taught her children to speak Afrikaans to prepare them for jobs on the farm when they were old enough to work. None of the Khoisan children living on the farm were allowed to go to school. As children of farm workers, they were expected to work on farms like their parents. Katrina never went to school and she started working on Farm Koeipan, the same farm that employed her parents, at age 16. Katrina's family settled in Upington where her parents died in the 1970s.

Although she never went to school or learned to read and write, Katrina was educated in the cultural and environmental knowledge of her people. She and her siblings learned about medicinal plants, how to hunt, and how to make fire. They knew which plants were deadly and which were edible and healing. As is the history of the San people, they used creative ways for survival. For example, after a hard day in the field hunting springboks, one of the first things the hunters would do after a hard kill was to take out the springbok's stomach and press it hard until water came out. They would drink the water to quench their thirst. They used the Nha plant, a cabbage-like plant, and ripped the leaves off to expose the stem. They would then scratch two stones against each other next to the stem of the Nha plant. The stones' friction would cause a fire and catch the plant, which they would place under the firewood or dried grass. Katrina says when they moved out of the farm, they walked more than 100 kilometres (54 miles) and could have died of hunger and thirst if they did not have these survival skills. It is this cultural knowledge that fueled her determination to fight for the survival of her mother tongue since her culture has been eroded by modern ways of life.

## Growing a New Generation of Activists

Growing up in an Afrikaans-speaking community, it bothered Katrina that she had not passed her mother tongue, N | uu, to her four surviving children. For 15 years,

Katrina has been running a school from her home (a donated corrugated make-shift room) teaching the neighbourhood children her beloved N|uu language. She cannot read nor write but the language never left her soul, she told me during our conversation. She was assisted by the Centre for African Language Diversity (CALDi) at the University of Cape Town, which developed an orthography and teaching materials for N|uu (Shah & Brezinger, 2017).

To ensure the survival of her mother tongue, Katrina, with the help of linguists Drs. Sheena Shah and Matthias Brezinger, taught the language to her eldest grand-daughter Claudia Snyman (now 31) and David van Wyk, a council member for the Royal Khoisan Heritage Council. Claudia and David are the only two people in their generation who are able to speak, read, and write the language fluently. Claudia and David are teaching the children to formally read and write the lan-guage while Katrina teaches the cultural aspects of the language and ensures it's preserved orally.

Claudia Snyman was born in 1991 in Upington, Northern Cape. She is the third generation in the family tree and the heir to her grandmother's teaching and activism work in promoting the N|uu language. She has been at her grandmother's table of knowledge since she was a baby and took the mantle of teaching at the age of 16. Claudia has given all three of her children N|uu names and speaks to them in the language. From a very young age, they were exposed to speaking three languages at home, N|uu, Afrikaans and English. Claudia says it's important for her to expose them to the language and the cul-ture at a young age so that they carry the mantle over to the next generation to save the language from being extinct. Claudia and Katrina use the art of storytelling to create access for children and young people to learn a second language.

When developing the orthography, Shah and Brenzinger (2017) relied solely on Katrina's pronunciation and knowledge of N|uu. They adopted the writing conventions developed through research done over 15 years on the N|uu lan-guage by linguists Miller et. al (2007), through wordlists, recordings, and tran-scription of sentences. N|uu is characterized by one of the largest phoneme inventories in the world. In the N|uu practical orthography, 114 speech sounds are represented: 45 click phonemes, 30 non-click consonants, and 39 vowels. In Jones and Mooney (2017), Dr. Sheena Shah, a postdoctoral fellow and director of the CALDi Language Project, described the process in 2016 as, "Based on existing documentation, we worked closely with Ouma Geelmeid to identify the dis-tinctive sounds of this language. Ouma Geelmeid, assisted by her granddaughter Claudia, are using the alphabet charts and teaching materials developed in the CALDi project." (p. 111).

Ouma Geelmeid teaches the language in a fun and interactive way, and has developed many songs and games to teach the children the N|uu language. The children enjoy seeing themselves featured in the educational materials produced in the CALDi project. They sing the N|uu songs and play N|uu games even out-side class.

## My Language, My Heritage Project

The year 2019 was declared the year of Indigenous languages by UNESCO. It was befitting that we honoured the UNESCO mandate by honouring Katrina's quest to save her language by producing the first ever children's picture book in her language. My engagement with Ouma Geelmeid and Phenyo Modise of the Northern Cape Department of Sports, Arts and Culture, inspired Puku Children's Literature Foundation (www.puku.co.za) to secure support for the "My Language, My Heritage" project from the National Heritage Council and the Embassy of Switzerland in South Africa. The purpose of the project was to harness the power of Indigenous storytelling to produce books and digital content for children in the languages of the Northern Cape Province, especially the endangered languages. The project was informed by Puku's conviction that the oral storytelling traditions in Indigenous languages are not reflected in print and there is almost no content for children in the endangered languages.

A three-day writing workshop was designed to produce books in the languages of the Northern Cape Province: Setswana, Afrikaans, Nama, and N | uu. Participants were selected from a pool of authors from the Northern Cape towns of Kuruman, Namaqualand, Kimberley, and Upington. The original intention was to have a workshop in Upington specifically for the N | uu language and to spare old Katrina from traveling long distances, but that was not possible for various logistical and administrative reasons. We finally settled on a workshop in Johannesburg to which we invited Ouma Geelmeid, not really expecting that she would make it. There was great excitement when she attended accompanied by her daughter, Lena Du Plessis, granddaughter, Claudia Snyman, and great-granddaughter, N | aungkusi (see Figure. 2.2).

The four generations of the N/uu speaking people.

**FIGURE 2.2** Four generations of the Nluu-speaking people.

With an energy that belied her age, Ouma Geelmeid participated fully in the intense three-day workshop in which the mostly young authors and illustrators spent hours perfecting their stories in Nama, Setswana, and Afrikaans that had been submitted prior to the workshop. N|uu was the only language whose story was created at the workshop as Ouma Geelmeid and Claudia, who live in different cities, had to sit together and create a story. Ouma Geelmeid narrated the story in N|uu and Claudia wrote it down. They then worked with young Soweto illustrator Terence Maluleke to develop the first draft of the manuscript of the first ever children's picture book in N|uu.

Claudia wrote down the story narrated in N|uu by her grandmother, and then translated it into Afrikaans. A dedicated team of creatives came together to edit, translate, and proofread the story to see the project come to fruition. Puku's Afrikaans editor, Madelein Du Toit, did the first Afrikaans edit. The story was then passed on to Diana Ferris, who fleshed out some details in consultation with Ouma Geelmeid, and then translated it into English. Drs. Sheena Shah and Matthias Brenzinger checked the N|uu orthography for consistency. Production of the book was delayed when the original illustrations by artist Terence Maluleke were lost as a result of a computer crash. Artist Stanley Grootboom came to the rescue and produced a new set of illustrations "as a gift to Ouma Geelmeid."

Lack of funding in the arts is a global challenge and with 2020 having been such a challenging year, it took three years to produce Ouma Geelmeid's book, "Tortoise and Ostrich" (see Figure 2.3). With UNESCO's 2021 International Mother Language Day theme being "Fostering Multilingualism for inclusion in Education," to celebrate South Africa's multilingualism as well as the community that Katrina serves, Puku forged ahead with limited funding for this project to ensure publication of the book, as a trilingual picture book. The trilingual story (Afrikaans, N|uu, and English) was launched in May 2021 to coincide with Africa Day celebrations. For any language to survive, including and especially the N|uu language, it needs a vibrant children's literature.

After spending time with Ouma Katrina, it is easy to understand the accolades she has received over the years. She has a rare combination of assurance and humility. Her calm, serene presence gave a sense of gravitas to the proceedings and there was hardly a dry eye in the room when she related her life story.

Ouma Geelmeid is not short of recognition for her efforts but sadly it does not translate to financial rewards. In 2019 South African President, Cyril Ramaphosa paid homage to Ouma Geelmeid when he spent Heritage Day in Upington in the Northern Cape where he visited the Sandile Present Community library to listen to stories read by children in the Indigenous languages of the area. Referencing the United Nations Year of Indigenous Languages, the President emphasised the government's commitment to preserving all South Africa's Indigenous languages, especially the endangered N|uu, Nama, and Khwe languages. While all these accolades are an important recognition of the Nǀuu language revitalization efforts

!Qhoi n|a Tjhoi
Skilpad en Volstruis
Tortoise and Ostrich

FINISH

Story by Katrina Esau, as told to Claudia Snyman
Illustrations by Stanley Grootboom

**FIGURE 2.3** The outside cover of Katrina's book.

of Katrina and the community, much more governmental support would be required to save the language from extinction.

In 2021, as we celebrated International Mother Language Day under the cloud of the Covid-19 pandemic, we asked ourselves what progress has been made in efforts to ensure the survival of the ancient N|uu language. Following the death of two of the remaining N|uu speakers, it seems that the language is more endangered than ever. If resources were a problem before, they will be an even greater problem in the post-Covid era.

Ouma Geelmeid's situation should be part of a larger conversation on the Western academic paradigm where Indigenous knowledges are not always validated. Ouma Geelmeid is the world expert in the N|uu language and the culture of her people. No one knows more than her. As such, she should be given the status of Professor of the N|uu language and paid a professor's salary, which will make it easier to spend the rest of her days teaching N|uu. Her school should be supported with the books and learning materials needed to produce the next generation of N|uu speakers. If she was economically empowered through the recognition of her role as a repository of knowledge, an activist, a storyteller, and an organic intellectual, it would be an enormous boost to the efforts to save the N|uu language.

## In Conclusion

What is the solution? According to UNESCO's Atlas of the World's Languages in Danger, of the estimated 7,011 known living languages in the world today, nearly half are in danger of extinction and are likely to disappear in this century www. unesco.org/culture/en/endangeredlanguages/atlas.

This is what Katrina is trying to prevent through her school, transmission from one generation to the next. Language and culture are intertwined. By saving her language, by default Katrina is also saving her culture or parts therof. Despite the colonial and apartheid history, the N|uu language has a chance of survival. Although it was Ouma Katrina's undying spirit that preserved the language, its survival is dependent on the younger generation that she has given the baton to. It is refreshing to know that they have begun taking over by giving their children N|uu names and ditched the so called Christian names as dictated by white supremacy. They are taking pride in their cultural practices by celebrating their heritage through dance and song and their colourful attire.

## References

Gall, S. (2003). The Bushmen of the Kalahari. *Ecologist, 33*(7), 28–31.

Jones, M. C., & Mooney, D. (Eds.). (2017). *Creating orthographies for endangered languages*. Cambridge university press.

Miller, A. L., Brugman, J., Sands, B., Namaseb, L., Exter, M., & Collins, C. (2007). The sounds of Nluu: Place and airstream contrasts. *Working Papers of the Cornell Phonetics Laboratory, 16*, 101–160.

Shah, S. & Brenzinger, M. (2016). *Ouma Geelmeid ke kx'u //xa//xa N/uu*. University of Cape Town.

Shah, S. & Brenzinger, M. (2017). Writing for speaking: The N/uu orthography. In Mari Jones & Damien Mooney (eds.), *Creating Orthographies for Endangered Languages*. Cambridge: Cambridge University Press, 109–125.

Thiong'o, N. (1986). *Decolonising the Mind. The Politics of Language in African Literature*. East African Publishers.

www.news.uct.ac.za/article/-2019-01-07-uct-researcher-is-in-the-vanguard-of-preserv
    ing-threatened-languages
www.thepresidency.gov.za
www.specialcollections.uct.ac.za/news/giving-breath-dying-language.
www.unesco.org/culture/en/endangeredlanguages/atlas
YouTube: My Language, My Heritage by Puku

# 3

# ENACTING LANGUAGE RECLAMATION THROUGH PERFORMANCE AS EMBODIED PRAXIS

*Maria Cecilia Schwedhelm Ramirez*

"Tell me a story about language," I say to the class of student teachers at the University in Oaxaca, Mexico. Oaxaca is Mexico's linguistically most diverse state and the students reflect this demographic. They are also language learners and future language teachers, so I know there will be many stories. I would usually be in a classroom on campus, in a circle, facing the 25 students in the class, but the spring semester of 2020 started with a strike that delayed the start of the semester until March. Just as the University was about to open, the Mexican government announced the beginning of a lockdown as a response to COVID-19 that forced us (with much of the world) to re-invent our educational practices in a virtual environment.

The class I was facilitating, *Lengua, Poder y Arte*, aimed to collectively explore linguistic ideologies and language regimes through our own linguistic histories to (re)imagine and (re)create equitable multilingual policies and pedagogies through performance and the arts. The syllabus I had imagined and put together, the embodied activities, all had to be reinvented. But this sudden and complete shift in context also brought with it an unexpected lightness. Letting go of the predetermined, our constantly changing circumstances allowed me to embrace an ever-present praxis of exploration, creativity, and self-reflexivity.

Many of us have yet to meet in person. And while I long for daily interaction and face-to-face embodiment, I understand pedagogy not as a classroom-bound practice but as relational encounters that create opportunities for growth (Zembylas, 2017). Viewed this way, pedagogy is dynamic and adaptable, informed by practice, experience, and stories. So we come together with our stories through our screens, not knowing how this experience will develop.

Today, I am sitting in my bedroom in Oaxaca City, computer on my lap. About half of the students are able to connect to the synchronous Zoom class and I hold

DOI: 10.4324/9781003302186-6

my phone in front of my computer to transmit live on Facebook for everyone else. Outside, a voceador advertises warm tamales on the speakerphone. I wonder if they can hear him too.

> I continue addressing students, explaining what I mean by "language stories."
> — It can be a time when you felt different based on how you spoke or communicated, or when you noticed someone making a comment about someone's language use; it can be a moment when something was lost in translation; a story you inherited from parents or grandparents; a moment that stirred joy, anger or pain.
> After a moment of reflection, the stories start flowing.

In this chapter I explore the performances and discussions that emerged around one language story during a synchronous online class. Through the exploration and (re)telling of this specific story as an ethnodrama, I examine the possibilities of embodied, arts-based pedagogies for language reclamation, arguing that performance can be an important platform to foster critical ideological awareness and (re)create alternative spaces for Indigenous languages and cultures. The virtual landscape in which we were forced to work hindered some possibilities, but enabled different types of collaborations and modalities.

I begin the chapter by detailing the geographical and sociolinguistic background of the class and the experiences and theories that ground *Lengua, Poder y Arte*. In the second portion of this chapter, I introduce the story of José within an ethnodrama of a synchronous class session and discuss the implications of this work for language reclamation in multilingual settings.

## Background

Oaxaca is a southern state in Mexico where the Sierra Madre Oriental meets the Sierra Madre Occidental. This rugged landscape is home to some of the country's most diverse natural ecosystems, as well as the highest number of self-governed municipalities, communal land ownership, and people with distinct languages and cultures (Martinez Luna, 2010). There are around 16 different languages, though this number is contested because some of these languages have multiple, sometimes mutually unintelligible variants, and according to census data, 31.2% of the population identifies as a speaker of an Indigenous language (INEGI, 2020).

Perhaps because of this cultural, linguistic, and natural diversity, Oaxaca is also characterized by a long history of political resistance against a neoliberal economic model and assimilationist policies—from capitalist mega-projects in Indigenous communities (e.g., García, 2021) to standardized assessments for teachers (Bautista, 2020)—that have seized land and natural resources, and aimed to unify and Spanishize a nation-state in the name of "progress." These policies have profoundly affected Indigenous communities, resulting in societal changes that have disrupted cultural and linguistic intergenerational transmission (de León, 2017). While many communities continue to transmit their language to the younger generations, there is a growing shift to Spanish as the hegemonic language.

As a response, many scholars, activists, and teachers have engaged in local processes and efforts to create spaces of resistance in everyday life, as well as in schools where many local, alternative educational models and pedagogies are being developed from the ground up, following Indigenous forms of knowledge (Schwedhelm, 2019). It is against this backdrop of hegemonic policies and local resistance that the class took place.

The University of Oaxaca is a public institution located in the City of Oaxaca that attracts students from multiple communities throughout the state. Within the Language Teaching and Learning Department, students are required to take English language classes and choose a "third" language. While most students take Indo-European languages like French, Italian, or Portuguese, spaces for Indigenous languages have been growing gradually over the years, with the recent offering of Isthmus Zapotec and Mixe language classes. Both language courses are taught by former students of the University who were invited to teach their languages. Zapotec is the most widely spoken language in the state, with more than 420,000 speakers (INEGI, 2020). It is generally divided geographically into four macro variants: Sierra Norte, Sierra Sur, Central Valleys and the Isthmus, and over 60 variants, many of them mutually unintelligible (INALI, 2020). The sociolinguistic context varies greatly by district and community. While the Central Valley varieties within and nearby the urban areas are being more rapidly displaced (Brügmann & Acevedo, 2013), Isthmus Zapotec or Diidxazá has the largest numbers of speakers and enjoys a long tradition of activism due to economic, political, and academic support that has resulted in the development of a growing body of literature and other art-based initiatives (DeKorne, 2021).

Mixe or Ayuuk is spoken by 118,000 people (INEGI, 2020) in a small mountainous area in the northeast of Oaxaca that borders and intertwines with Zapotec languages in some communities. It is characterized as one of the most vibrant languages of the state due to a geopolitical delimitation and collective identification that has generated multiple strategies of resistance through the daily practice of comunalidad, an ideology, theory, and way of living (Díaz, 2007) briefly described as "the principle and practices of communal life and the source of indigenous identity and resistance" (Meyer, 2010, pp. 30–31).

The growing recognition of the linguistic and cultural diversity within the University, and the role and responsibility of the Language Department to make spaces for Indigenous languages has also fostered the development of new events like multilingual song competitions, projects, and workshops through partnerships with other institutions (e.g., a workshop on linguistic auto-documentation) and a new translation and interpretation master's degree program for Indigenous languages.

Some students are speakers or learners of an Indigenous language; thus, they are already bilingual or multilingual when they enter the program. Many more have parents, grandparents, or close friends who are speakers or have been exposed to the linguistic diversity of the state in their communities and in Oaxaca City, where it is common to hear multiple languages in markets and other public places.

## Conceptual Groundings

It is through storytelling that we make connections between the personal and the political, the local and the global, for the intimate and the global are continuously invoked and constituted through storytelling (Nagar, 2019). My story, growing up trilingual—in German, English, and Spanish—in Mexico City, yet unaware of the living presence of multiple languages indigenous to Mexico, reflects a global history of erasure of linguistic, cultural, and epistemological diversity. It was only when I was far from home that I first questioned and became struck with the erasure of Indigenous languages and ways of knowing. I had been studying Mandarin Chinese in China, discovering new ways of seeing and being in the world through a language completely unrelated to my own when I realized I didn't have to travel that far.

A long history of colonialism and centuries of oppression and discrimination have displaced and invisibilized Indigenous peoples, languages, and cultures. My ignorance and my story were both a consequence and driving force of these policies of erasure. There were only rumors that my great grandfather, a book-seller in the Mexican market of La Lagunilla, spoke Hñañu, a language indigenous to Central Mexico. My grandfather never shared that story. His mother was a woman of Spanish descent and he was raised in the city, his father's language and stories lost within one generation. In many ways, this research is grounded in my journey to make sense of this generational loss and (re)weave the many loose threads of my own story.

### Towards an Embodied Praxis for Language Reclamation

Many different terms and metaphors have been used to refer to the work to reverse language shift. "Language revitalization" is the most widely used among scholars, who've also referred to it as a new field (McIvor, 2021). Alternatively, the term "language reclamation" has been put forth and described by Leonard (2012) as encompassing common language revitalization strategies, including language documentation, description, and language learning, but with a wider focus on the embodied and dynamic nature of language and its inextricable and reciprocal links to human and non-human interaction. Like Zapotec poet Irma Pineda, Zoque poet Mikea Sánchez, and Tsotsil poet Enriqueta Lunez (Canal 22, 2019) remind us, there is no language without people, *no hay lengua sin pueblo*. Language reclamation is therefore never only about the language. It is a decolonization effort, a reclamation of knowledge(s), and a way of being in the world, connected to autonomy, self-determination, land rights, and a sense of identity for communities and individuals (Hinton, 2001; Smith, 2012).

The idea for *Lengua, Poder y Arte* developed slowly through experiences living, doing, and trying different strategies that I threaded into a syllabus aimed at questioning hegemonic power structures and reimagining equitable worlds. A syllabus that conceives of language as inseparable from its speakers, deeply entangled with questions of race, gender, social class, land, and politics of knowledge production. I aimed to connect these questions to action and transformation, using all the senses to feel and do what we cannot express with words alone and found performance as a clear vehicle to achieve these goals.

## Weaving the Trenza

As a field, language revitalization (and reclamation) is inherently interdisciplinary (Córdova Hernández, 2019; McIvor, 2021), drawing from any body of work that will help advance the aims of countering language shift. Such interdisciplinarity or theoretical promiscuity (Simpson & Smith, 2014) is also common among scholars and educators engaged in critical theories and pedagogies.

Chican@ scholars like Francisca Gonzalez (1998) and Dolores Delgado Bernal and Enrique Alemán (2017) employ the trenza, a metaphor of a braid, an Indigenous hairstyle with important cultural meanings, as an analytical tool. For Delgado Bernal and Aleman, the trenza refers to their critical feminista praxis that braids together Critical Race Theories and Anzaldúan Chicana feminist theories with Chican@ Latin@ and Indigenous knowledges and pedagogies. The project described here embraces its own trenza grounded on feminist theories (e.g., Anzaldúa, 1987; 2002; Nagar, 2014; 2019), critical pedagogies (e.g., Boal, 2000; Freire, 2005; hooks, 2014), and Indigenous theories and praxis (e.g., Simpson, 2017; Martínez Luna, 2010).

Scholars engaged within these approaches and pedagogies have challenged the modern division between theory and practice (e.g., Freire, 2005; hooks, 2014; Mignolo & Walsh, 2018; Simpson & Smith, 2014; Smith, 2012). Paulo Freire, for example, embraced the concept of praxis, conceptualized as "reflection and action upon the world in order to transform it" (2005, p. 51). Similarly, the Latin American decolonial school of thought understands praxis as a continuous flow of movement of "thought–reflection–action," stressing that the possibilities for transformation or "re-existence" cannot just be thought or imagined, they have to be lived and continuously practiced (Mignolo & Walsh, 2018, p. 7).

But whereas these conceptions of praxis focus on (re)mending a theory-practice divide, feminist and Indigenous scholars have foregrounded the embodied nature of knowledge-making, emphasizing the inseparability between mind, body, and spirit (Anzaldúa, 2002; hooks, 2014; Simpson, 2017). Native scholar Leanne Simpson, for example, draws from Nishnaabeg creation stories to assert that theory is storytelling, woven with kinetics, spiritual presence, and emotion. It is contextual and relational, intimate, and personal (p. 151).

Embracing theory as praxis, as emerging from action, relationships, stories, and everyday life experiences not only enables transformation, but disrupts hegemonic ideas of what counts as knowledge, creating spaces for ancestral stories and other forms of knowledge that have not been considered valid within schools and academia. *Lengua, Poder y Arte* was conceived with the aim of disrupting this infrastructure of inequality (King, 2017) by foregrounding our individual and collective stories and knowledges as theory and enacting change through praxis.

## Performance as Embodied Praxis

As Grosz (1994) noted, "it is in and through our bodies that we experience the world and develop consciousness" (p.106). The arts, like language and as language, are inherently embodied and afford multiple possibilities for reflecting, theorizing, and engaging in different ways of knowing and being in the world, opening up spaces for alternative epistemologies. Movement and performance in particular have a special power to contest divisions between theory and practice through the emphasis on "doing" as meaning-making and activism (Madison, 2014, p.15).

*Lengua, Poder y Arte* turns to performance and specifically to Augusto Boal's Forum Theater (2000) as a strategy of collective analysis and action. Within Forum Theater, the community comes together, creating an improvisational forum that explores shared experiences, ideas, and concerns. Spectators are encouraged to become active participants, referred to as "spect-actors." Every participant has the power to interrupt and intervene performances, "forcing the other actors to improvise and realign themselves in relation to the changing action" (Babbage, 2004, p.45).

Augusto Boal (2013) notes that performance has a quality of abstraction in that it enables people to see themselves from the outside. The performing body becomes a site of analysis that allows us to view markings of class, gender, race, sexuality, language, etc., meanings ascribed to our bodies and the characters we are embodying, both a subject and an object of analysis. These bodies merge and remain distinct, allowing people to see themselves and others, to see themselves in others and others in themselves.

This chapter looks at how performance operates as a mode of embodied analysis and critique; specifically, how a critical embodied pedagogy can foster language reclamation by empowering students to question hegemonic ideologies that work to marginalize and displace Indigenous languages and knowledge systems.

## Ethnodrama as Method

In relation to research, performance can be 1) an object of study, 2) "a pragmatics of inquiry, an optic and operation of research," and 3) a tactic of intervention (Conquergood, 2002, p. 152). *Lengua, Poder y Arte* and the subsequent research project encompass all three. Above all, performance was conceived as a space of struggle or tactics of intervention to create spaces for Indigenous languages and knowledges. As an object of study, I analyze the performances of students' language stories, yet even before this round of analysis, the performance served as a site of analysis or "pragmatics of inquiry." Thus, the intervention *was* performance as a pragmatics of inquiry, theory, and practice merged into one.

I also employ performance as a pragmatics of inquiry by writing the narrative of the virtual in-class performance and subsequent discussion as an ethnodrama, an arts-based-research approach. Unlike ethnotheater, ethnodrama is not meant to be a performance event, but more specifically a genre of writing that can serve both as representation of data and analysis (Saldaña, 2005). Ethnodrama recognizes knowledge as socially constructed, drawing attention to the representational nature of data, or what Mignolo calls enunciation, as there is not one world that someone (me) has the authority to represent, but "a world that is constantly invented in the enunciation" (in Getzambide-Fernandez, 2014, p. 198). Ethnodrama draws attention to the many choices that researchers and writers have to make when writing down data to enunciate findings, central to and present in any analysis. For example, while quotes are largely verbatim, I translated them from Spanish and I edited them for clarity, cutting repetitions and hesitations. Space constraints also meant that I had to make choices on what quotes to include and how they would fit together, creating a narrative and telling a specific story.

Another choice involved referring to myself in the third person. I imagined the script as an independent document that can be shared and possibly performed. This decision also opened different possibilities for analysis, making myself, along with the other cast members/participants, a subject/object of study. It allows, for example, for an analysis of positionalities, in this case, interactions between facilitator and students and how hierarchies are upheld and disrupted (Malhotra & Hotton, 2018). Except for Beatrix, a pseudonym, the names and descriptions of participants in the ethnodrama correspond to the participants in the class.

Ethnodrama as a method is consistent with a framework of embodiment by foregrounding the experience of the scripted event and the experience of the reader. My hope is that it will evoke feelings in the reader, just like the event itself evoked feelings in the participants. The purpose of this chapter and ethnodrama, as was the purpose of the performances of the language stories, remains the same, to learn from stories and inspire actions.

In the next section, I present an ethnodrama of a virtual class meeting where students performed and discussed the story of José. Next, I add my reflections as analysis to illuminate the possibilities of performance as an embodied praxis for language reclamation.

## The Story of José

### Prelude

It is a May afternoon in 2020 and the class is about to start on Zoom. During the previous week students shared their language stories and then got together in groups to write a script based on or inspired by their stories. The original syllabus envisioned the class doing improvised performances based on the language stories. Yet, lack of access to a computer and the Internet, bad connectivity, or other issues means that not everybody can connect to the synchronous sessions. Co-writing scripts allows those students who cannot connect synchronously to participate in the process in an asynchronous way. Today is the first day of performances. None of us knows how performance will work on Zoom, this being a new experience for all.

## List of Participants

### ABRAHAM

Student and co-author of José's story. Plays 10-year old José. He was born in a Zapotec village and moved to the city when he was young. It was then that he stopped speaking Zapotec. He can understand his language but finds it difficult to speak it.

### RUTH

Student and co-author of José's story. Performs as the narrator in the story. Her mother comes from Veracruz, a state neighboring Oaxaca and is a Spanish speaker. Her father comes from a Zapotec village near Oaxaca City where she still lives. She learned Zapotec from her father and in the community.

### KARLA

Student and co-author of José's story. Plays José's mother. She comes from a village by the coast of Oaxaca where Spanish is now the predominant language. She's very attached to her village and finds it difficult to be away in Oaxaca City.

### BEATRIX

Student and co-author of José's story. Plays José's father. She comes from Oaxaca City.

### CESAR

Student. He traces his roots to Oaxaca City where he lives with his mother and grandmother. He is a learner of Mixtec and is collaborating on a revitalization project in a Mixtec village alongside a fellow student from that village.

### AREMI

Student. She grew up in Oaxaca City. Her father comes from a Zapotec village and speaks the language with family and friends. Her mother is a Spanish speaker and the lingua franca at home is Spanish.

## JOSELINT

Student. She grew up in Oaxaca City. Her father is a Spanish speaker and her mother is a Huave speaker from a coastal town. Huave or Ikoots is an independent linguistic group spoken by around 14,000 people on the coast of the Gulf of Tehuantepec, primarily in the towns of San Mateo del Mar and San Dionisio del Mar (Brügmann & Acevedo, 2013). She can understand the language, though she and her mother communicate in Spanish.

## EMMA

Student. She comes from a Zapotec village near Oaxaca City where Spanish is now the predominant language. One of the last few speakers was her late grand-mother. She is studying Isthmus Zapotec at the University and wants to start a revitalization project in her home village.

## VICTORIA

Student. She grew up in Oaxaca City. Her mothers' family comes from the Isthmus, where Zapotec is still widely spoken, but neither her mother nor grand-mother are speakers.

## MARIA

Facilitator. She grew up in Mexico City. She has German and Mexican roots. Spanish is her home language, but she has been living and studying in the United States for the past 15 years.

## Background

*There are 15 names on rectangles on a screen, some with faces flickering in and out of the virtual room. Three rectangles are black, a melody coming from behind one of them. Nine or ten cameras are on, showing faces against brick or painted walls. Some faces are barely visible, others look deep into the camera, some move about the room, attending simultaneously to the screen and to other people in the house. María holds her phone in front of her, transmitting live on Facebook for students who are not able to join.*

*The session starts with a quick check-in. Students share about their days and developments related to COVID in their hometowns. They express a desire to return to in-person classes and note the importance of doing collaborative work and building relationships through the class in a time of uncertainty and isolation. María leads students through stretching exercises to make bodies present and aware. One person models one exercise and the others follow.*

### Act 1: Activating the Body

*EMMA:* [*Stands up. Only half of her body is visible through the screen. She leans to the right and then to the left. Others stand up and follow, letting out deep exhalations.*]

*MARIA:* Thank you, Emma.

*ABRAHAM:* I can go next, but my camera isn't working.

*MARIA:* That's OK. You can narrate what you're doing.

*ABRAHAM:* OK. So put your arm behind your head and with your other hand pull your elbow to the other side. [*He pauses. Others follow his directions.*] Now do the same with the other arm. [*Four students are standing, others are sitting down. All the elbows are up, bodies swinging left and right.*]

*MARIA:* Thanks Abraham. Now let's get started. Who is performing today? Abraham, you're with Ruth, Karla…

*ABRAHAM:* Yes, and Beatrix.

*MARIA:* Perfect. Then you're complete.

### Act 2: José's Story

*ABRAHAM:* Listos?

*NARRATOR/RUTH:* OK. [*Clears her throat and looks down, reading from a text*]

Zaku chi' lo ra:tib-tu. Buenas tardes a todos. This is the story of José, a boy who has developed the interest and skill to learn the Zapotec language spoken in his community. The boy arrives home after school. He starts saying some Zapotec words that he has heard in school.

*JOSÉ/ABRAHAM:* Na:ra va b-dzinya ma'.

*MOTHER/KARLA:* What did you say?

*JOSÉ/ABRAHAM:* I'm here mom.

*MOTHER/KARLA:* Since when do you speak Zapotec?

*JOSÉ/ABRAHAM:* Everybody speaks it at school, it's a lot of fun. It sounds very nice, but I don't understand them.

*MOTHER/KARLA:* And would you like to know what they say?

*JOSÉ/ABRAHAM:* Yes. That way I could have friends. Nobody played with me today.

*MOTHER/KARLA:* It's great that you want to learn. I am happy that you like it and that you start speaking.

*NARRATOR/RUTH:* The mother turns to the father, who has just arrived home.

*MOTHER/KARLA:* [*to the father*] Have you heard your son speak Zapotec?

*FATHER/BEATRIX:* No [*surprised*].

*MOTHER/KARLA:* [*to José*] Son, tell me something in Zapotec. What did you learn today?

*JOSÉ/ABRAHAM:* Today one boy said "xhupa," which means "father."

*FATHER/BEATRIX:* Little by little you will learn and get used to it.

*NARRATOR/RUTH:* The next part takes place in school. José is with a classmate who is teaching him Zapotec.

*JOSÉ/ABRAHAM:* [*to his classmate*] Hello, will you teach me new words today?

*CLASSMATE/RUTH:* Of course, we will go little by little, first with the basics. First we have to introduce ourselves. If I say "tu:lalu'?" I am asking what your name is, then you respond "na:ra lá José."

*JOSÉ/ABRAHAM:* Na:ra lá José.

*CLASSMATE/RUTH:* Good, now you will say, I am 10 years old. "Báal iss nú:u?" means how old are you. To answer you say "na:nú tsi'is."

*JOSÉ/ABRAHAM:* Na:nú tsi'is.

*CLASSMATE/RUTH:* Very good. You learn fast.

[*There's a short silence, then Ruth looks up from the text, signaling the end of the performance.*]

*RUTH:* That would be all.

*ABRAHAM:* That is the first part because the boy learns but then he starts forgetting. He moves to the city and he doesn't want to speak anymore.

*MARIA:* Oh! So there's one part missing?

*ABRAHAM:* A little [*chuckles*]. The boy let's say grows up and moves to the city and stops speaking Zapotec. That's how the story ends.

*MARIA:* Oh! OK. So for those of us who were observing. What did we see?

[*silence*]

Let's start descriptively. There was a boy in a scene at home. The boy speaks in Zapotec to his mother, and it seems like the parents don't speak the language, right?

*RUTH:* In this story, the father speaks Zapotec, but not the mother. It was a little bit like in my story, I think. We're putting them together. Doing a fusion of our stories.

*MARIA:* That's a great idea.

*JOSELINT:* I think so too. It is very nice that he is a boy and he wants to learn. He talks to his mother in Zapotec even though she doesn't understand. Then… I think there is a loss from the father because he hasn't taught the child, but he is learning from somewhere else. I think that happens often. Many parents don't teach their children anymore. Languages are lost because parents don't teach their children and in this case the boy became interested somewhere else and the father says, if he's interested, well, I'll teach him.

*MARIA:* That's a good question. It seems like the parents are glad he is learning, but like you said, Joselint, why hasn't the father taught him? And what about the mother, is she from another community? Did her parents not transmit her the language? What else is there to this story?

*AREMI:* My case is similar to this story because my father speaks Zapotec very well and he can write it, but not my mom. Then, when he talks to his family and friends my mother doesn't understand. My father said he didn't do it, talk to us in Zapotec, because my mother doesn't know how to speak it. He needs another person who can teach us the language.

*MARIA:* That's an interesting theme because often we talk about language displacement because of linguistic oppression, the relationship between the dominant language and the minoritized Indigenous languages, but seldom do we mention cases like in your family, where Spanish is the lingua franca. So this could be a theme in this story. Why doesn't the boy speak Zapotec? Why did his father not teach it to him? Why does the mother not speak? What do they feel when the boy is learning the language in school? What did you feel, Beatrix, as the father, and Karla, as the mother?

*BEATRIX:* He is surprised that he is learning by his own initiative even if he hasn't taught him.

*KARLA:* It's a different experience. In this case it's a positive influence. The mom could take the joy and learn the language. In this case, Zapotec is the language of the community, so it would be to adapt to a new place.

*MARIA:* So there's joy and surprise. Abraham, how do you feel as the boy?

*ABRAHAM:* I would feel excited about being able to learn a new language. Because it is easier to learn it as a boy. You don't have so much pressure and you enjoy it more. I would be very excited.

*MARIA:* I propose then to do it again, but exploring the feelings of your characters. You can add and improvise. Imagine how you feel, where you come from. Imagine the father. His son is learning his language in school. How would he feel?

*CESAR:* I have a suggestion. We can use the same context, but instead of everything being positive, explore a negative scenario where the mother or father start reprimanding the son for speaking Zapotec. I don't know if it is the mother, because she doesn't understand and is afraid they might talk about her, or the father, because he is afraid people will think less of him. I don't know. Because now it's a very positive story and there's a great acceptance. It would be interesting to see the contrast. What happens when a boy is interested in learning an Indigenous language? I would suggest that.

*[students nod, showing interest]*

*MARIA:* OK, then let's, why not, do this as an exercise. [*To the co-authors of José's story*] Remember these are exercises, not judgements towards your work. You can develop your story in any way that you decide. This can help us explore different scenarios, feelings and ideologies. So, César, why don't you take the role of the father. You can all improvise.

Ready?

*ABRAHAM:* Yes.

*[the group takes up the performance with the mother addressing the father]*

*MOTHER/KARLA:* Have you heard your son speak Zapotec?

*FATHER/CESAR:* What? Why? Zapotec? No, no, no, no, there is no reason to! He is speaking Zapotec? [*agitated, he raises his voice*] What are people going to think? They are going to think… that we're poor or something, it is forbidden that you speak that.

*JOSÉ/ABRAHAM:* [*Looking down*] But I like it, dad.

*FATHER/CESAR:* [*Speaking fast and loud, gazing at the camera*] Well, I don't care, or have you seen that we speak that at home? No, no, because we have taught you other things. And you're not going to argue. We send you to school to learn other things, not that.

*JOSÉ/ABRAHAM:* But I have to talk in school to make friends.

*FATHER/CESAR:* You can make friends in other ways, with children who teach you other things, better things. Why that? Besides, teachers can discipline you for speaking like that. They can point at you, they can bully you. And besides, what if… you can't even pronounce it correctly.

[*José nods, his voice defeated, his eyes looking down*]

*JOSÉ/ABRAHAM:* OK dad, if you want it so, I will stop learning.

[*The group responds with silence. Overwhelmed, like José, trying to recollect what happened. After a moment, Joselint speaks.*]

*JOSELINT:* I think that reaction is more common. There are some places where belonging to a community where a native language is spoken means belonging to a region that can be poor, so many people still hold that view… it could be a more realistic example of what we're still living.

*EMMA:* [*nods*] I think she's right. I feel it's a more common reaction. At least before, that is why many languages have been lost, for that idea that speaking an Indigenous language makes you a lower socioeconomic status and worth less for society. And that's what parents were guided by.

*MARIA:* Why did he get so angry?

*JOSELINT:* Maybe in a way it can be something to try to defend the boy, to avoid him being treated badly.

*VICTORIA:* I think he also suffered, and he reflects that on his son. He doesn't want that for his son. He was scared, perhaps.

*CESAR/FATHER:* Yes, I was scared and angry, because I believed José was learning other things in school. The goal was not to go to school to learn a language. As a dad you worry that your son has to learn what he has to learn, like Spanish or math. I also imagined that I was discriminated against and bullied for speaking Zapotec, and not only in school but beyond. I was othered, pointed at: "he's speaking his language" or "speaking funny" or "messing with the words," or worse, "it sounds Indian, Chinese." All of that I am reflecting on this character. These are things that I have heard.

*MARIA:* There are so many themes surfacing in this story: the historical load of coloniality that the father carries in his body, language as intersecting with socioeconomic status, the inter-linguistic marriages with Spanish as a lingua franca, puristic ideologies that deem a language not "well spoken" not worthy of speaking at all, and as an epilogue, not yet performed, migration to the cities and subsequent linguistic assimilation. We can choose to explore any of them and how they interlock. Through performance, questioning, improvising, dialoguing. But for now time is running out.

*STUDENTS:* What is next?

*ABRAHAM:* Do we change the script?

*MARIA:* It is up to you. What do you want these stories and performances to do? Keep playing with them. Let's not leave them static. We might be able to perform them again; this is something dynamic. Even if and when we record them, the work will be dynamic and in progress as long as it keeps growing, provoking reflection and action.

## Performance as an Embodied Praxis for Language Reclamation

Performance operates as a mode of embodied analysis and critique through questioning, empathetic reflections (Nagar, 2019), and engaging contradictions, and can become a site of struggle and action towards language reclamation. José's story was one among several told, scripted, performed, improvised, re-scripted, re-improvised, and recorded. There was a story of a girl from a Zapotec community bullied and pushed out of an urban school, a story of linguistic estrangement and discrimination within migration from Oaxaca to the United States. There was a story of another girl, discovering, when visiting her grandmother and listening to her speaking in Huave, how language is not just a translatable code, but reflects different ways of being in the world. And there was a story of native languages, embodied and living, narrating their losses, presence, and dreams. Some stories, like José's, explored challenges, weighed so large they can seem insurmountable. Others, like the story of the girl visiting her grandmother or the languages sharing their joys, foregrounded hope.

Issues such as structural and curricular barriers and constraints may affect a performance and arts-based pedagogy (e.g., Louis, 2005). In the case of *Lengua, Poder y Arte*, I was given complete trust and flexibility in terms of course design and evaluation, determined through participation (broadly defined) and self-assessment. Instead, the most salient issue was the need to adapt an embodied praxis to a virtual context. The reality of remote learning completely re-shaped the process of analysis, engagement, and critique. No two journeys are ever alike, and it is impossible to know where this journey would have taken us had we been able to meet and work together in person. But while our bodies were located physically apart, performance still requires us to think in and through our bodies, preserving the embodied processes of knowledge construction even when communicating across screens, being only able to see our faces, or just a black square where our faces would have been. We bring our backgrounds, our voices and silences, faces, gestures, or absences to the spaces within and beyond the screens, like Abraham, his body moving and narrating itself behind the absence of a camera. We ascribe meanings. Virtual interaction is still embodied, still performative.

Performance is also intensely relational. We make meaning in interaction and in community with one another in a form of co-authorship where we take risks in sharing, receiving, and engaging with each other's stories (Nagar, 2019). Sitting in my bedroom looking at the screen I am in two spaces at the same time. Never fully in one place. Yet, there is a yearning to do this work, relational and healing, to recognize each other, each other's bodies and stories.

Like Ruth mentioned, the collaborative work was indispensable and created a bond of companionship and co-existence, essential in the situation we are facing.

Through sharing and co-writing scripts, students were able to consider and learn with and from one anothers' stories, creating a dialogic culture in an evolving co-authorship, "creating and learning by sharing authority with one another" (Nagar, 2019, p. 212). Ruths's story is one of growing up in a Zapotec community, in a home where her father is a speaker and her mother, coming from the neighboring state of Veracruz, is not. She recalls the joy and pride of showing off her new words to her grandparents in Veracruz. Abraham too grew up in a Zapotec community, but left with his parents to live in the city, where he has gradually forgotten the language. Seeing himself struggle to communicate, he recalls with nostalgia the ease and joy of speaking and learning as a child. Pieces of these stories became the story of José. Others too were able to find pieces that translated into their own experiences; Aremi, whose father also speaks Zapotec but whose mother does not; Emma and Joselint, who recognized the linguistic ideologies held by César's portrayal of the father; César, who embodied the words that he too had many times heard.

Through its quality of abstraction where the body is both subject and object of analysis, performance invites reflection and questioning. It also encourages empathy, as it invites people to think and feel from the perspective of different characters. Karla narrates the process of creating the video for the story of José, using dolls, drawings, or socks as puppets: "We had the dialogue but we didn't use it because we wanted to improvise… Putting yourself in the role allowed you to see a different perspective… it tells a story that is sad, but emotional. It was like living the moment and creating a new feeling" (Karla, September 12th, 2020).

Especially powerful is the ability of performance to elicit emotion and what Nagar (2019) calls empathetic reflection as we strive to see and feel from the perspectives of an Other, "even in situations where we're critical of those others' arguments" (p. 212). In the class narrated here, I asked students to consider how the characters might have felt, and actors to feel and answer from the perspective of the characters themselves. Within the improvised version, the father became the antagonist, the figure embodying every deficit language ideology, molded into arguments for why his son should not learn Zapotec. Looking deeper, we locate the contexts and structures from which the position of the father is emerging. Perhaps he is fearful, students suggest. He doesn't want his son to experience the discrimination that has marginalized him. Within this fear, he has internalized hegemonic discourses about the purpose of schooling "we send you to school to learn other things," and paradoxically, puristic ideologies about language "you can't even pronounce it correctly," suggesting that Zapotec with a Spanish accent or Spanish influence, sometimes referred to as "Zapochueco" or "crooked Zapotec" (DeKorne, 2017), can be more harmful than not speaking at all.

Empathetic reflections (Nagar, 2019) call for empathizing with those deemed as the antagonist, trying to understand the specific contexts from which the character of the father emerges. Inayatullah (2013) refers to this as "generosity to the antagonist." Recognizing every person/character from the context that produces them/us helps us recognize the ways that we too are implicated in reproducing and changing the structures that perpetuate violence, and use that as a catalyst for change. Through empathetic reflection, we understand these arguments within the sociohistorical context of coloniality. Colonizers repressed the epistemologies of the colonized, their knowledge production, symbolic universe, and forms of expression, engendering an epistemic hegemony that is manifest today through a rhetoric of modernity that maintains a logic of coloniality. Mignolo and Walsh (2018) make note of the complicities that bring us to participate in what they call the modernity/coloniality matrix of power by negating, distorting, and denying "knowledges, subjectivities, world senses, and life visions" outside hegemonic epistemologies and ontologies (p.4). As Leigh Patel (2016) notes, in order to engage in decolonization (and language reclamation as decolonization), one has to first "attend to the ways that we come into relation with coloniality" (p. 8).

Embodying complex characters, feeling the need to protect our own as the father does, fosters empathy, illuminating the ways that we as the father come into relation with coloniality, how we come to internalize and reproduce the social discourses that assign value to certain language varieties, while negating our own language, cultural practices and epistemologies. We are able to step out and recognize the ideologies inscribed on our bodies.

The embodied doing of performance and speaking for the characters enables us, students and teachers, to engage contradictions. Emma and Joselint ascribed ideologies that associate Indigenous languages with poverty to existing in "some places" and "in the past," yet they both recognized the reactions informed by these ideologies as "more common" than those supportive of learning Zapotec. By characterizing them as geographically and temporarily remote, they distance themselves from these ideologies. They understand the father's arguments as located and stemming from global pressures and violences, but at the same time recognize these same arguments as contributing to the same global violences, thus seeking distance. In performance, the meanings we ascribe to the actions of the characters, or the performing body, might not be ascribed to us as individuals. Thus, it provides a space of rehearsal where we identify and de-identify.

We bring our ideological bodies, entangled with our multiplicities, for we do not embody a single ideology, but an ideological assemblage (Kroskrity, 2018), feelings we gather from our families, communities, and from our journeys in schooling and academic settings. These ideologies, both indigenous and imposed, "may complement, contest, or otherwise dynamically interact with each other to modify language ideologies and linguistic practices" (p. 134). As teachers and students engage in performance, as we see ourselves from the outside, our ideological assemblages illuminated through the performing bodies, our identities are destabilized, critiqued, and reimagined (Louis, 2005, p. 344).

Students display embodied identities, recognizing themselves as the antagonists in the father, scared and angry, fighting for his son to have a good life, and perhaps simultaneously as the marginalized, robbed of the languages and knowledges of ancestors, navigating a world of structural inequalities and injustices. Performance entails vulnerability and risk. We risk discomfort as we co-author a pedagogy where we are the subjects to be disentangled and observed closely, analyzed within the contexts and conditions that engender us. Performance illuminates both limitations and possibilities.

After all the groups had performed their stories and we had watched all the videos that resulted from this project, I asked the group about the purpose of this work, from sharing their stories to co-authoring scripts, performing, and making their videos. We talked about the emotions, the sadness and the anger, we felt in some of the stories. So, how do we analyze these emotions so the work doesn't end in hopelessness? Can it drive us to start actions to change the conditions we've seen in these stories, in our communities?

"Maybe it's hartazgo," Victoria said, "getting to that point where action is inevitable." Hartazgo is that no longer bearable feeling of satiety, of not being able to bear sadness, anger, or pain any longer, feelings about to burst into action that moves towards remediating the social inequities around us. Performance scholar Elyse Pineau noted that her research and teaching "need to be motivated by a gnawing disturbance at the inequities that plague our society" (In Louis, 2005, p. 436). Making ourselves vulnerable, learning with and from each other's stories through performance can fuel the hartazgo to motivate action.

Language reclamation is, like performance, intensely relational, recognizing the complex social contexts in which languages exist (Leonard, 2021). It is also affective, and as Hermes, Bang and Marin (2012) have noted, deeply personal. Generating hartazgo to fuel reclamation work is not a benign process. It requires seeing yourself in these stories, as protagonist and antagonist, engaging contradictions. It requires recognizing violent histories and how they operate at local and personal levels to gain an embodied awareness of structural inequalities and injustices. But alongside hartazgo, there is also joy, the joy of collaboration, of relationality, its significance never more salient than in times of social isolation, the joy of creating something together and the hope of where it might lead.

## Conclusion

So where does this work lead? What are the possibilities of embodied, arts-based pedagogies for language reclamation? Performance provides a space to wrestle with questions of identity and justice, to question ideologies that we hold and the language regimes within which we live. But beyond recognizing the causes and conditions within which language exists and is displaced, performance can be a site of struggle and rehearsal that fuels hartazgo and joy towards a reclamation of identity, culture, and language.

Nancy Hornberger (2002) posits that "multilingual language policies are essentially about opening up ideological and implementational space in the environment for as many languages as possible […] to evolve and flourish rather than dwindle and disappear" (p. 30). Many bodies came together during *Lengua, Poder y Arte*, each of us with our own linguistic histories. In a diverse setting where our ancestors' languages are many, the goal of the performances was to create ideological spaces for Indigenous languages, which in turn might open more spaces for Indigenous languages. These spaces could be ideological, by raising critical language awareness in our families and our communities. They could be implementational, by creating policies and pedagogies that encourage students' Indigenous languages and epistemologies within classrooms and schools, and actual spaces, by engaging in the teaching, learning, and promoting of our ancestral languages.

Each one of us might take this journey into different directions. Abraham wrote down his story growing up in a Zapotec community. Joselint recorded a story in Huave from her mother, which she then translated into Spanish, using it as a language learning opportunity. Emma made a video of her community, where her grandmother was one of the last speakers of Zapotec and where she is planning to start a revitalization project. César recorded the history of his community. Ruth shared about the Zapotec bilingual school she attended in her community and Victoria made a video of the class, inciting others to action. The possibilities are dynamic. As Louis (2005) noted, they lie in the process of doing.

Few spaces exist within institutional education settings where young people can critically question, feel, and analyze the meanings ascribed to languages and bodies. At the same time, much of the work in language revitalization and reclamation is concerned with a single language or language community, often presumed homogeneous. There are, however, many communities, especially within institutional settings like the University of Oaxaca, where multiple people come together with their/our diverse linguistic histories and multiple languages, visible or invisibilized. There is thus a great need to expand the work of language reclamation to spaces deemed non-Indigenous, like this University, and among both Indigenous and non-Indigenous identifying youth. For we also know that identity is changing and dynamic and all of us have a role in language reclamation, that is, engaging in the decolonial actions that resist language and epistemological displacement and erasure. Moreover, embodied, arts-based pedagogies, including performance, invite different ways of knowing into often rigid education settings. Learning through stories and the body, through the senses in a pedagogy that is dynamic, guided through relational encounters also invites alternative epistemologies. We learn from the knowledges that have been handed down from our families and communities.

There is much that we can learn from one another and one another's stories and languages. Performance provides a platform for a collective labor of language reclamation where empathetic reflection, hartazgo, and joy can generate ideological, implementational, and actual spaces for Indigenous languages.

## Acknowledgments

I would like to thank everyone at the University of Oaxaca who supported this project, and most importantly, to all participants in *Lengua, Poder y Arte*, for sharing your stories. This research was supported by the Leadership in Equity, Inclusion and Diversity (LEAD) Fellowship of the University of Minnesota.

## References

Anzaldúa, G. (1987). *Borderlands: la frontera* (Vol. 3). San Francisco: Aunt Lute.

Anzaldúa, G. E. (2002). Now let us shift… the path of conocimiento… inner work, public acts. In G. Anzaldúa & A.L. Keating (Eds.), *This bridge we call home*, pp. 554–592. New York: Routledge.

Babbage, F. (2004). *Augusto Boal*. New York, NY: Routledge.

Bautista, E. (2020). La asamblea popular de pueblos de Oaxaca, crisis de denominación y resistencia. *Bajo el volcán 1*(12), 115–134.

Boal, A. (2000). *Theater of the Oppressed*. London: Pluto Press.

Boal, A. (2013). *The rainbow of desire: The Boal method of theatre and therapy*. Routledge.

Brügmann, M.T. & Acevedo, M.L. (2013). *La dinámica sociolingüística en Oaxaca: Los procesos de mantenimiento o desplazamiento de las lenguas indígenas del estado (Tomo 1)*. México: CIESAS (Publicaciones de la Casa Chata)

Canal 22. (2019, November 6). La raíz doble: No hay lengua sin pueblo [Video]. YouTube. www.youtube.com/watch?v=mYlZiUUATzM

Conquergood, D. (2002). Performance studies: Interventions and radical research. *TDR: The Drama Review, 46*, 145–156.

Córdova Hernández, L. (2019). *Metáforas ecológicas, ideologías y políticas lingüísticas en la revitalización de lenguas indígenas*. Oaxaca, México: UABJO.

De Korne, H. (2017). The multilingual realities of language reclamation: Working with language contact, diversity, and change in endangered language education. *Language Documentation and Description, 14*, 111–135.

De Korne, H. (2021). *Language Activism: Imaginaries and Strategies of Minority Language Equality*. Boston/Berlin: De Gruyter.

De Léon, L. (2017). Indigenous language policy and education in Mexico. In T.L. McCarty & S. May (Eds.), *Language Policy and Political Issues in Education*, pp. 415–433. Cham: Springer International Publishing.

Delgado Bernal, D., & Alemán, E., Jr. (2017). *Transforming Educational Pathways for Chicana/o Students: A Critical Race Feminista Praxis*. New York, NY: Teachers College Press.

Díaz, F. (2007). Escrito: comunalidad, energía viva del pensamiento mixe = Ayuujktsënää'yën - ayuujkwënmää'ny - ayuujk mëk'äjtën, Ciudad de México: Universidad Nacional Autónoma de México.

Freire, P. (2005). *Pedagogy of the oppressed*. New York: Bloomsbury.

García, A. R. V. (2021). Despojo y resistencia en el Istmo de Tehuantepec, Oaxaca, en la era del "capitalismo ecológico.". *Punto Cunorte, 12* (Enero-Junio), 38–68.

Gaztambide-Fernández, R. (2014). Decolonial options and artistic/aestheSic entanglements: An interview with Walter Mignolo. *Decolonization: Indigeneity, Education & Society, 3*(1), 196–212.

Gonzalez, F. E. (1998). Formations of Mexicana ness: Trenzas de identidades multiples Growing up Mexicana: Braids of multiple identities. *International Journal of Qualitative Studies in Education, 11*(1), 81–102.

Grosz, E. (1994). *Volatile Bodies: Toward a corporeal feminism*. Bloomington. IN: Indiana University Press.

Hermes, M., Bang, M., & Marin, A. (2012). Designing Indigenous language revitalization. *Harvard Educational Review, 82*(3), 381–402.

Hinton, L. (2001). Language revitalization: An overview. *The green book of language revitalization in practice*, pp.3–18. Leiden & Boston: Brill.

hooks, b. (2014). *Teaching to transgress*. New York & London: Routledge.

Hornberger, N. H. (2002). Multilingual language policies and the continua of biliteracy: 11 An ecological approach. *Language Policy, 1*, 27–51.

INALI. (2020). Catálogo de las lenguas indígenas nacionales: Variantes lingü.sticas de México con sus autodenominaciones y referencias geoestadísticas. https://www.inali.gob.mx/clin-inali/html/v_zapoteco.html#62

Inayatullah, N. (2013). Pulling threads: Intimate systematicity in the politics of exile. *Security Dialogue, 44*(4), 331–345.

INEGI (2020), Censo de Población y Vivienda, México. Retrieved from http://cuentame.inegi.org.mx/monografias/informacion/oax/poblacion/default.aspx?tema=me&e=20

King, J. E. (2017). 2015 AERA presidential address morally engaged research/ers dismantling epistemological nihilation in the age of impunity. *Educational Researcher, 46*(5), 211–222.

Kroskrity, Paul V. (2018). On recognizing persistence in the Indigenous language ideologies of multilingualism in two Native American communities. *Language and Communication 62*, 133–44.

Leonard, W. (2012). Framing language reclamation programmes for everybody's empowerment. *Gender and Language, 6*(2), 339–367.

Leonard, W. (2021). Language reclamation through relational language work. Keynote lecture at the International Conference on Language Documentation and Conservation (ICLDC), March 7, 2021. https://www.youtube.com/watch?v=2Oqye0gvCdA.

Louis, R. (2005). Performing English, performing bodies: A case for critical performative language pedagogy. *Text and Performance Quarterly, 25*(4), 334–353.

Madison, D.S. (2014) Narrative poetics and performative interventions. In N. Denzin, Y. Lincoln & L.T.Smith, *Handbook of Critical and Indigenous Methodologies*, pp.391–406. Thousand Oaks: SAGE.

Malhotra, N., & Hotton, V. (2018). Contemplating positionalities: An ethnodrama. *The Journal of General Education, 67*(1–2), 152–171.

Martínez Luna, J. (2010). The Fourth Principle. In L. Meyer and B. Maldonado (eds.) *New world of Indigenous resistance: Noam Chomsky and Voices from North, South, and Central America*, pp. 85–100. San Francisco: City Lights.

McIvor, O. (2021). Race Racial Justice and Indigenous Language Revitalization [Video]. AAAL Webinar series: https://www.aaal.org/race-racial-justice-and-indigenous-language-revitalization

Meyer, L. (2010). Introduction: Hemispheric conversation among equals. In L. Meyer and B. Maldonado (eds.) *New world of Indigenous resistance: Noam Chomsky and Voices from North, South, and Central America*, pp. 7–37. San Francisco: City Lights.

Mignolo, W. D., & Walsh, C. E. (2018). *On decoloniality: Concepts, analytics, praxis*. Durham: Duke University Press.

Nagar, R. (2014). *Muddying the waters: Coauthoring feminisms across scholarship and activism*. Urbana: University of Illinois Press.

Nagar, R. (2019). *Hungry translations: Relearning the world through radical vulnerability*. Chicago: University of Illinois Press.

Patel, L. (2016). *Decolonizing educational research: From ownership to answerability*. New York: Routledge.

Saldaña, J. (Ed.). (2005). *Ethnodrama: An anthology of reality theatre*. Walnut Creek: Rowman Altamira.

Schwedhelm, M.C. (2019) Reclaiming languages, decolonizing knowledge(s): Articulating Indigenous knowledge(s) in and for language reclamation, *Center for Urban and Regional Affairs* (CURA), University of Minnesota. https://conservancy.umn.edu/handle/11299/208319

Simpson, A. & Smith, A. (2014). *Theorizing native studies*. Durham: Duke University Press.

Simpson, L. B. (2017). *As we have always done: Indigenous freedom through radical resistance*. Minneapolis: U of Minnesota Press.

Smith, L. T. (2012). *Decolonizing methodologies: Research and indigenous peoples*. London: Zedbooks Ltd.

Zembylas, M. (2017). The contribution of non-representational theories in education: Some affective, ethical and political implications. *Studies in Philosophy and Education, 36*, 393–407.

# 4

# THE *KULEANA* OF *ULANA LAUHALA*

## Reflecting on Our Weaving

*Cherie Okada-Carlson and Marit Dewhurst*

Sitting at a long folding table, a group of *lauhala* weavers count their *moe* and *kū* (weft and warp, respectively) as their *pāpale* (hats) take shape (see glossary at end for translations). Like Hawaiian ancestors who wove necessities such as sleeping mats, ceremonial mats, canoe sails, and baskets, these contemporary artists use the dried leaves, or *lau,* of the *hala* (pandanus) tree to weave hats, purses, bracelets, and jewelry in addition to the more traditional baskets and mats. It is a form of art that has been passed through generations and has evolved into a lively form of creativity and cultural production in many communities in Hawai'i. Many of today's weavers, in addition to gifting and selling their *lauhala* artworks in galleries, festivals, and online spaces, also participate in community teaching workshops (for images that depict the process, see Figure 4.1). In these workshops, *haumana* (students) of diverse backgrounds and experiences work under the apprentice-ship of *kumu* (teachers) in both formal workshop settings and informal weaving sessions on weekends or evenings—perhaps gathered at a kitchen table or under a back porch awning. Watching these groups of weavers—some focused quietly and intently on their plaiting, others "talking story" or telling tear-jerking jokes—one can't help but wonder if the craft of turning a bundle of *lau* into a beautiful hat is the only thing being learned.

As educators, we have often asked ourselves about the nature of our participa-tion in *lauhala* weaving and our interest in education. What does it mean for us to learn in contexts where the very ways and modes of teaching and learning are different than those we typically experience in schools? How do these experiences communicate not only how to create a work of art, but also about a cultural way of being and of relating to each other? In engaging in a form of art-making deeply rooted in a specific cultural *way of making* we have also learned a specific *way of being*—one that prioritizes the interdependent connections and mutual

DOI: 10.4324/9781003302186-7

**FIGURE 4.1** The process of *ulana lauhala*, from harvesting to weaving.

responsibilities between teachers and learners. Throughout this, we are aware of the particular role of language—our forms of communication—that are steeped in lessons in themselves.

In this chapter, we reflect on our experiences in *ulana lauhala* to better understand how language—in this case, both Hawaiian language and weaving-specific terminology—can open portals of understanding that enable us to learn more about our lineages of history, our relationships with community, and ways of being within a culture. Through our own experiences both as *kumu* and *haumana* we have seen how weaving can unlock pedagogical points of entry that are rarely accessible in other learning settings. Our reflections help us consider how the art of weaving *lauhala* can be a space for historical, relational, and cultural learning.

## Who We Are: Educators, *Haumana*, *Kumu*, Weavers, Friends

In 2005, Aunty Harriet Soong made sure to introduce us at Cherie's third and Marit's first *Ka Ulu Lauhala O Kona* conference. Knowing Aunty Harriet, she probably already knew we would become friends despite the many miles that separated us and our very different backgrounds. With shared interests in learning and teaching, we began chatting in between our weaving classes and in late-night weaving sessions. Cherie Okada-Carlson began weaving *pāpale* in 2003 with the late Aunty Gladys Grace, then she learned from Margaret Lovett, Pohaku

Kahoʻohanohano, Marcia Omura, Lynda Saffery, and the late Ed Kaneko through *Ka Ulu Lauhala O Kona*. Prior to that she learned *ulana* from Shirley Kauhaihao and the late Aunty Harriet Soong. Cherie has worked in rural public schools in Kona, Hawaiʻi since 1996, off and on as a high school teacher then as a Student Services Coordinator. She has recently become a *kumu ulana*. Marit learned *ulana lauhala* from the late Aunty Harriet Soong, Aunty Shirley Kauhaihao, the late Aunty Elizabeth Lee, the late Uncle Ed Kaneko, and Aunty Margaret Lovett, Aunty Lola Spencer, and Cherie Okada-Carlson with encouragement and support for several other *kumu* and *haumana* from the *Ka Ulu Lauhala O Kona* community. She lives in New York City (where it's often too cool and dry to *ulana*) where she works with pre-service arts educators to prepare them for culturally relevant teaching.

Although our childhood experiences had been quite different—Cherie growing up in Kona on Hawaiʻi island and Marit on the U.S. continent in Michigan—we connected over the *lau* and over our mutual respect for the process of weaving, the knowledge of our *kumu*, and the sense of community we experienced in weaving. These initial experiences launched conversations about how weaving connected to our lives in public school contexts, leading us to begin writing and reflecting more together over the years. Together, we blend our perspectives to reflect on particular vignettes from our own weaving experiences where spoken and unspoken language provided powerful learning opportunities. Weaving together our words, we offer a meditation on how moments of weaving specific language—both the voiced and the unspoken—have served as key pedagogical doors into worlds of deeper understanding about ourselves and our relationships with a wider weaving community.

## Chapter Structure: Talking-Story

While we have both written about our experiences in weaving from an academic perspective (Dewhurst, et. al, 2013; Dewhurst & Okada-Carlson, 2012), when we began this chapter, each of us social distanced across multiple time zones, we started it much as we started our initial weaving friendship—through stories and remembered moments. The memories of gathering with other weavers to *talk story* and learn weaving patterns and traditions reminded us of the powerful relationships and learning opportunities we've been missing over these pandemic years. In talking about the kinds of learning and teaching that emerge from weaving together, we've realized that much of it is embedded in both the shared stories and silences. To honor that, we've tried to capture some of the ways in which our reflections about weaving unfold in overlapping reflections. We've identified several recurring questions that have shaped our thinking about weaving as a pedagogical space. As we meditate on these questions, we share both our individual perspectives and our collective ideas.

### Before We Begin, Let's Share How We Came to Weaving. What Drew Us to This Form of Art-making and How Does It Relate to Who We Are?

*Cherie:* I was born in Honolulu, my family moved to Kona when I was a baby. Although part Native Hawaiian, I was not raised traditionally Hawaiian. Growing up in Hawai'i, rural Kona, was relatively multi-cultural: various ethnicities, cultures, religions, and mixed-race friends and family. In my world, Hawai'i is more like an amalgamated stew than a salad. I went into education as a career because I enjoyed learning, working with young adults, and wanted to stay in Kona without having to work in the tourism industry. *Ulana lauhala* started as a hobby that became a much needed supplemental source of income when recession caused teacher furloughs and pay reductions. Teaching *ulana lauhala* is a "*kuleana* thing," a way to pay it forward for all the generosity in knowledge that *kumu* and other weavers have shared with me.

*Marit:* I came to weaving almost reluctantly. In the mid-2000s, my folklorist parents—white folks with Western European heritage—were interviewing weavers in Kona at the annual gathering of *Ka Ulu Lauhala O Kona* weavers for a collaborative exhibition on Native American basket weaving traditions from the United States. Eager for a reprieve from East Coast winter weather, I tagged along for what I thought would be a beach-side break from my doctoral research in education. However, before I even unrolled a beach towel, Aunty Harriet had convinced me to pick up some lau to weave a bracelet with the group. I sat there listening to *kumu* tell stories, laugh, reminisce, and share weaving tips as we plaited strips of *lauhala* together and I was hooked. The sense of connection and community felt so different from the conventional kind of learning I was experiencing as a student in a competitive higher education setting. There was collaboration, joy, and respect. There was an understanding of the materials, honor for the people who prepared the materials, care for the teachers and students, and a sense of celebration in the act of making. It was the kind of educational experience I was writing about in my own research, the kind of learning and teaching I was trying to facilitate in my own education.

### Get Close to Any Gathering of Weavers and You'll Overhear a Mix of English and Hawaiian Terms as Weavers Trade Patterns, Stories, Jokes, and Tips. How Much Does the Hawaiian Language Shape Our Experiences with Weaving?

*Cherie:* I connect with my Hawaiian culture not only through the action of *ulana lauhala*, but using Hawaiian terminology whenever I can. When teaching *ulana*, if I get a blank look from my *haumana*, I will use the English word, but then by using the Hawaiian term over and over in context, they learn the meaning of the word. While it is a "broken" Hawaiian-English sentence, there is useful vocabulary and a verbal shorthand. Instead of saying, "start the center, weave four rows using the double weave twill pattern, and then tie that flat portion to your hat block," I could say "make your *piko*, *ulana* four *maka 'o'eno*, then tie the *pā* on your *ipu*." I imagine *'Ōlelo Hawai'i* and English instructors may cringe at the mix of words, but I think it's important to keep Hawaiian words alive and relevant when doing Hawaiian things like *ulana lauhala*. I've also learned from a *kupuna*, who grew up with native Hawaiian speakers in the home, that certain terms such as *"hi'a"* have different meanings depending on context. *"Hi'a"* can mean "to make a fire," but in *ulana* it is the pulling/threading tool that pulls strips of *lauhala* through the weaving to splice or overlay.

*Marit:* I still have the notes from classes I took with Aunty Elizabeth Lee who encouraged me to write down the Hawaiian terms as she used them to teach me how to start the *piko* for my first mat. For a cultural outsider, learning these terms felt like I was being trusted with a set of keys to unlock the process of weaving; without them I'd be lost. As in learning any language, they also allowed me to suddenly understand more of the stories and jokes being told around me as other weavers laughed and talked story with each other. When I tried using them myself to ask a *kumu* for help they felt clunky at first, almost like they didn't belong in my mouth. But the more I wove, the more I listened and learned, the more comfortable I became describing to my *kumu* how I had again dropped a *kū* and needed to *hemo* (undo and start over). The confidence I gained with these terms aligned with the increasing sense of understanding I had for weaving; I realized I could not deepen my knowledge of weaving without speaking some Hawaiian words—the language could not be parsed out from the actions of weaving.

*Cherie:* There is no "majority" enthnic group in Hawai'i. Although English and Hawaiian are official languages of the State, pidgin (actually a creole) English developed as a common language so that the various plantation workers could communicate. The grammar structure was Hawaiian but the words were a mix of Hawaiian, English, Chinese, Filipino, Japanese, Portuguese, and Spanish. English was a second language to pretty much 95% of the population. To promote English as a first language in the Kingdom (and then Territory) of Hawai'i, all other languages were forbidden in schools including Hawaiian. Children were punished for not speaking English at school and discouraged at home. The *kupuna* native speakers were passing away. The Hawaiian language almost died out had it not been for active preservation and the development of Hawaiian language immersion programs.

Weaving and using Hawaiian terminology makes the vocabulary relevant and easier to learn. The quiet focus required to learn *ulana* allows me to hear my internal dialog. My mind could only focus on one thing at a time. When I first started to weave, it took a few years before I could hold a conversation while weaving.

### We've Both Felt The Importance of Listening and Observing in Our Weaving Practice. As Much Is Communicated Within the Silences of Weaving As Within The Talking. How Have We Experienced This As Both Learners and Teachers?

*Cherie and Marit:* Much like the traditional saying, *'ōlelo no'eau*, "*Nānā ka maka, ho'olohe ka pepeiao, pa'a ka waha*" (look with your eye, listen with your ear, close your mouth) (Pukui, 1983, p. 248), oftentimes in weaving there is a need to listen and observe in order to learn. Unlike our Western schooling experiences where we were both often encouraged to participate by asking questions, vocalizing what we learned, and to demonstrate engagement by talking, our experiences in weaving have often been focused on close looking and listening.

*Marit:* This focused listening felt very unusual to me when I first started weaving. Like Cherie, I had to (and still have to) concentrate fully on what my hands and fingers are doing. While my hands are working though, I could listen. I was accustomed to learning spaces where the teacher would briefly demonstrate a task and then guide me through it, basing her assessment of my performance on the questions I asked, the quickness of my repetition of the task, and my vocal participation. To show engagement, I was encouraged to double-check my progress, to ask for constant feedback, to pose questions that demonstrated that I was processing the information. This new kind of listening felt immersive; my whole body had to take in the process of weaving without constantly peppering my *kumu* with comments and questions. This different kind of listening demanded of me a new kind of patience and slowness. As a cultural outsider, I certainly didn't know all the language, the nuanced commentary, or the double-meaning embedded in some of the jokes. Were I to just jump into a conversation, I would certainly flounder. And yet, sitting in a circle of weavers as they talked story and I focused on my fingers, I listened. Unlike in other art classes I had taken, I was almost forced to be attentive to the conversations circling around me by more advanced weavers. As an immersive experience the listening was almost a class in itself.

*Cherie: Ulana* is meditative. As I sit quietly concentrating on the tension, the pattern, the texture (is it time to spritz it with water?), and trying to remember to sit up straight and take deep breaths, I have to quiet all other thoughts and focus on consistency. In the quiet, I hear the voices of my *kumu* echoing in my head. Instructions. Admonitions. Funny anecdotes. Of the voices, Aunty Harriet is probably heard most often. She was not a bio-logical relative, she was my friend's aunt. Aunty Harriet taught us *lei* making,

Hawaiian quilting, basket weaving using banana *poka* (passionfruit) vines, *lauhala* weaving, and unknowingly mentored me in life. Aunty Harriet gave me cues on being a better *haumana ulana*. Through her influence I strove to be a good *haumana*: be quiet, to absorb as much as I could from my *kumu*, don't ask too many questions or complain, and give them *makana kūka'a lauhala* (rolls of cleaned and softened *lauhala* as a gift) in appreciation. As a result, my basic *ulana* skills were able to develop to my art medium. My art is a way for me to silence the outside noise and listen to my inner self. Through *ulana* I can hear the voices of my *kumu*, those still living and those who have gone before. When I look at past projects, usually *pāpale*, that I had woven with each *kumu*, I remember the time with them in a tactile way. *Ulana* allows me to practice my culture, and in the process of creating, meditate on the things my *kumu* have taught me about *lauhala* and life.

## We've Both Learned to Connect Our Own Weaving to the Community of Weavers with Whom We've Learned. What Role Does Language Play in Connecting Us to Lineages of Other Weavers? How Do Certain Terms Open Up and Make Clear Those Connections?

*Marit and Cherie:* In each of our weaving kits at home, we both have a common tool: the "Peter Park Pulling Tool." Even just typing the name of the tool conjures up the mischievous smile of Uncle Peter and illustrates how the naming of this tool connects *kumu* and *haumana* alike in a specific lineage of weavers.

*Cherie:* I first knew it as the "Uncle Peter tool" as the late Uncle Peter Park, a master weaver, used to make and give them out to us as little *makana* (gifts). Aunty Harriet corrected me and said "it's a *hi'a*!" So from then on, it was a *hi'a*. When I thought "*hi'a*," the image of that tool came to mind. I did not know the "official" English word for "*hi'a*" until a Hawaiian language instructor informed me that a *hi'a* was a "shuttle." As in a tool used for weaving fabric. In learning the art of weaving *lauhala* I am hearing Hawaiian words in a literal and culturally relevant way.

*Marit:* For someone who is not from Hawai'i and only visits occasionally to weave, the naming of my "Uncle Peter Park tool" helps me feel connected to weavers who have shared knowledge with me for brief moments in time. It has also contributed to my feeling that I am a part of a community of weavers—albeit one that is physically distant and culturally different than any of my other communities. In being able to name the tools, I can share in a common sense of relationship to other weavers. Suddenly, I'm connected to people when I can shift from calling a tool by its dictionary name to calling it by the name used in this specific community (I think it's unlikely that I'd find a group of *lauhala* weavers in New York City who would use the term "Uncle Peter Park tool." Although if they did, I bet we would feel instantly connected.) Unlike learning, an artform in a format devoid of context—in a class, via a kit, book, or series of YouTube videos for example—the community-specific naming of tools, patterns, or stories has made my learning of weaving more personal. Calling up Uncle Peter Park's name as I reach for a weaving tool while miles away has kept me connected, even in small ways, to the weavers who taught and nurtured my learning in Hawai'i.

*Cherie:* As I feel connected to my *kumu* before me, many of which have now passed on, I think it is important for new weavers to know where their knowledge is coming from. As I describe steps when I'm teaching I am careful to "cite" who taught me the various steps or skills. I feel it is my *kuleana* (responsibility) to pass on what was generously given to me.

*Marit:* This "citation" process reminds me of when I finished my very first *pāpale*. I started mentioning who I might give it to and Aunty Lola told me that I should not give away my first *pāpale* since it contains all of my knowledge. We laughed as we discussed where I should sign and date my *pāpale*. And, if memory serves me, I recall us half-joking that we should note Aunty Lola's name on my *pāpale* as well since she had been my primary *kumu* for this hat. This connection though is something I think about often and comes up in conversation with other weavers who ask who I learned from. Unlike in conventional art classrooms or online tutorials, the naming of my *kumu* connects me to a particular community of weavers in a specific time and place. In this way, the practice of *ulana lauhala* helps me expand my own understanding of who I am in relation to this group of weavers who live primarily on an island thousands of miles from the urban island I live on in New York City. Weaving reminds me that we are interconnected across those many miles and cultural differences.

## The Concept of Community is a Powerful One in Weaving; We Often Speak of Weaving Together as Core to the Practice. How Does This Emphasis on Community in Weaving Also Teach Us Values That Shape Our Experiences as Learners and Teachers?

*Cherie:* The experience of weaving in a group of friends or in a class with your *kumu* and other *haumana* is a bonding experience. Aunty Gladys, with her *haumana*, started *Ulana me ka Lokomaika'i* (Weave with the Goodness Within) weaving club on O'ahu. She often reminded us to focus on good thoughts and intentions because that energy goes from your head and heart through your hands. Those emotions will show in one's work. Changes in tension, both psychological/emotional and literal physical tension in the pulling of the *mau'u* (strands), will be obvious in the woven item: rows may be crooked, *mau'u* (strands) may break from being pulled too hard, patterns may be uneven. It is difficult to weave unless one is in a calm state of mind

or actively calms oneself. Weavers are generally very encouraging and supportive of one another. Interpersonal relationships are valued. We live on an
island, what we do affects each other, we cannot hurt others without hurting
ourselves. It seems difficult to teach *ulana* without teaching relative values.

*Marit:* I came to weaving as a stressed out graduate student worn down by
the focus on individualism, competition, and perfectionism in my doctoral
program. When I was welcomed into weaving with warmth, compassion,
and care, I suddenly realized I was experiencing an entirely different way of
being as a learner and artist. In learning *ulana lauhala*, I was encouraged to be
patient, to respect the collective and cultural knowledge, and to see myself as
connected to both the weavers around me, those who came before, and those
who will come after. It was unlike anything I had experienced previously and
the more I learned to listen to the values that were embedded in how I was
taught weaving, the more I came to see myself as a weaver, not just someone
who takes a weaving class. Even now, years and miles away from the last time
I sat near Cherie to *ulana* together, I can call upon the values I learned in
weaving to recenter my own teaching in the arts. In doing so, I remind myself
to bring a greater focus on patience, listening, cultural lineages, and above all,
on nurturing the relationships amongst communities of artists.

### How Have Our Experiences Shifted as We've Become both Haumana and Kumu? How Has It Changed our Relationship to Weaving and to Education?

*Cherie:* As a *haumana ulana*, I just focused on learning to weave and being
respectful to and appreciative of the *kupuna*, *kumu*, and fellow *haumana*. I went
to the weaving conferences to absorb as much as I could from everyone - other
*kumu*, *haumana*, vendors - so I could go home and try it. As a *kumu*, I still need
to focus on interpersoal relationships, but I also need to teach *ulana*. I thought
I could teach the way I learned, but found that adult *haumana* have more filters
and unspoken expectations. Experienced *kumu ulana*, Emily Claspell, told me
before my first time as a *kumu*, "there are people who want to weave and there
are people who want to be weavers. Knowing the difference will make things
easier." I learned quickly that people who "want to weave" are at the conference to make their project. They want to be able to say "I made this ____."
That's it. People who "want to be weavers" are the ones who pay attention to
the interpersonal relationships, the nuances, and names of the master weavers
cited as sources. They are taking the knowledge with them to continue weaving
on their own. As an introvert, speaking/teaching/interacting takes a lot of
energy from me. Some *haumana* just want to know what to do to hurry up
and finish. Other *haumana* take their time to know the why and how and who.
Understanding a *haumana's* motivation helps ascertain how much information

to give them to avoid information overload, it saves my energy, and all of us from unnecessary frustration. I need to listen less to their verbiage and more to their art. I have only taught "basic *pāpale*" at two conferences so far. I think I may be transitioning from "what do I teach them?" to "how do they want to learn?"

Marit: Although I spend my working hours training pre-service art teachers, I only recently started sharing more about my weaving with my students. Since I teach about cultural appropriation and culturally responsive and sustaining pedagogies, I was too scared to do disservice to my own *kumu* and the cultural traditions that shape *ulana*. Having learned how people are invited to be *kumu* and not self-appointed, I have feared harming the very community that so generously welcomed me as a *haumana* if I were to claim to be a teacher myself. Add to this that I'm a *haole*, or white person not from Hawai'i in Hawaiian terms, it has all felt quite fraught. However, in reflecting on what I have learned in *ulana* I realized that it is also a story worth sharing.

While I am not a *kumu* in the sense of *ulana lauhala*, I have come to share my experiences as a *haumana* with my own students as I introduce to them the knowledge I have learned in community with other weavers. In these moments, I strive to share not only some of the technical aspects of weaving as I introduce the process of making a simple woven fish toy, but to also convey some of the cultural lessons I have learned, such as the importance of caring for materials, using appropriate terminology, and naming one's connection to a lineage of *kumu*. These conversations take place in a classroom in New York City, where I have no access to *lauhala*. However, I seek to engage my students in conversations about how many culturally-specific art forms can provide opportunities to learn more about ourselves, our relationships with our students, and new ways of knowing and being. As I share my reflections on trying to teach about forms of art outside of my own cultural context, I hope to model for my students ways in which they can teach about cultural art forms with respect for the socio-economic and cultural contexts from which those arts emerge.

Cherie: Hawaiian culture has been appropriated for as long as I can remember. *Hula* and *aloha shirts* are known and misappropriated globally. Hawaiian culture has been commodified to the extent that our economy relies on tourism at the expense of our native ecosystem and quality of life. Marit differentiates that she is teaching <u>about</u> the act of *ulana* in a culturally sensitive tactile way, not claiming to teach ulana as a *kumu ulana*. She is exposing her students to *ulana* in New York, the opposite side of the country from Hawai'i, with such respect and cultural sensitivity. I believe this is a good thing. Just as our *keiki* (children) need to know there's a whole world out there beyond our island in the middle of the Pacific Ocean, teaching others that Hawai'i is more than just "hula girls and grass skirts" is a much needed conversation.

### Since We Both Have Experiences in Public School Settings, We Spend a Lot of Time Reflecting on the Lessons We've Learned in Ulana Lauhala. How Have Our Experiences Weaving Altered Our Teaching and Learning in Other Contexts?

*Cherie:* In the eighteen plus years I've been learning, weaving, and teaching *ulana lauhala*, I've seen shifts in public education from using personality surveys and learning styles, to emphasizing high stakes testing, and now to restorative justice, trauma-informed teaching, and Social and Emotional Learning. The latest of which puts focus on relationships and context and being with and of each other. It is very much like my entire time learning *ulana* within the context of respectful interpersonal relationships. I learned with my friend from a *kupuna* master weaver: we felt responsible to learn well and behave respectfully because we were representing not only ourselves and our *kumu*, but the people who recommended us as *haumana* to our *kumu*. Students, especially those labeled "challenging" by our educational systems, need to feel a connection to engage in school. Interpersonal relationships are vital to make them feel connected. Having a relationship with their teacher allows them to feel invested in themselves and their learning community. My greatest challenge is adapting to teaching adults. While I felt competent in my Department of Education positions, I do not think I am a good *kumu ulana*...yet.

*Marit:* My experiences *ulana lauhala* and reflecting on the experience have shifted how I think about teaching and learning in profound ways. While I had researched and taught about different modes of teaching, it was only in *ulana* that I *experienced* the ways in which both a cultural and linguistic context can deeply shape not just what one learns but how and why. *Ulana lauhala* has taught me to be aware of the ways in which knowledge is shared, respected, and cared for. Unlike my experiences in conventional public schools where vocal participation, questioning, urgency, and individual ownership of knowledge prevail as dominant modes of being, *ulana lauhala* has shown me a different way to engage in education. From my weaving, I have experienced the importance of culturally specific language in learning, how naming and honoring our teachers can connect us to lineages of knowledge, and the quiet power of observation and listening. In my own teaching, I now try to bring in these elements into my classroom.

## Closing Thoughts

*Cherie: Kuleana* has many meanings: privilege, concern, responsibility, etc. My *kuleana* in *ulana lauhala* is not only the privilege to be part of a community of *kupuna*, master, legacy, and aspiring weavers, but a concern for the *mālama* (care) of *nā puhala* (the pandanus trees), and the responsibility to perpetuate the knowledge that was given to me.

*Marit:* In collaborating on this chapter, I have learned the term *kuleana*. It is not a word of my own home language, and yet, in knowing Cherie and in learning weaving, I have come to understand its meaning. As an educator, I hope to bring *kuleana* to my teaching and learning. The term offers guidance for me to deepen my practice as both an educator and weaver.

★ ★ ★ ★

While Aunty Harriet might have known that we would become quick friends when she pulled us towards each other several years ago over bundles of *lau*, we wonder if she also knew that we would come to regularly reflect on and write about our experiences *ulana lauhala*. Perhaps she had a sense that our shared interest in education would connect us, even if it has been our shared experiences in weaving that have cemented our friendship. In some ways, it is the language of weaving that connects us across time zones and climate zones. The languages of *ulana lauhala*—the silences necessary to listen and observe, the naming of tools and techniques to link us to other weavers, the modes of teaching that instill values, and the sense of community as we "talk story"—these are the languages that we carry with us. These languages, if brought into conventional school settings, could radically transform how young people learn and how their teachers teach. We know that the pandemic has torn through our schools in yet to be understood ways. We encourage educators to imagine what might happen if they were to tend to the languages we've learned in *ulana lauaha*. What might shift? What spaces might open up in the pauses? What new relationships might emerge? How might we weave together our communities with values steeped in the lessons we have learned in *ulana*?

As weavers, artists, *haumana*, *kumu,* students, and teachers, it is our *kuleana* to observe, listen, reflect, and share the knowledge that our *kumu* have so generously shared with us as we seek to support our own students. Through the languages of *ulana lauhala* we have grown as learners and educators. With each overlapping *moe* and *kū*, our knowledge and understanding deepen. The weaving and our ongoing reflections about it continue to open up new possibilities for understanding who we are and how we can become more connected, caring, and compassionate educators.

## Glossary

aloha - nvt., nvs. aloha, love, affection, compassion, mercy, sympathy, pity, kindness, sentiment, grace, charity; greeting, salutation, regards

aloha shirt - also referred to as a "Hawaiian shirt," is a style of dress shirt originating in Hawai'i. They are collared, buttoned, and usually short-sleeved and made from printed fabric. They are often worn untucked, but can also be worn tucked into the waist of trousers.

hala - n. pandanus tectorius

haole - nvs. white person, caucasian; any foreigner; foreign, introduced, of foreign origin, as plants, pigs, chickens

haumana - n. student, pupil

haumana ulana - n. student of weaving

hemo - v. to loosen, undo, unfasten, take off

hi'a - nvt. the act of making a fire; shuttle or needle for making nets; pulling tool for overlay or splicing lauhala strips

hula - nvt. the hula, a hula dancer; to dance the hula

ipu - hat block

keiki - nvi. child

kū - n. the vertical element in weaving, warp; vs. to stand, upright

Ka Ulu Lauhala O Kona - founded by the late Aunty Elizabeth Maluihi Lee, with the mission, to "perpetuate, preserve and ensure the growth of traditional art of Lauhala Weaving"

koana - n. width of pandanus strips used in plaiting

kūka'a - nvt. rolled pack, as of pandanus leaves ready for plaiting

kuleana - nvt. responsibility, privilege, concern, business.

kumu - n. teacher, tutor

kumu ulana - n. teacher of weaving

kupuna - n. grandparent, ancestor, relative or close friend of the grandparent's generation, grandaunt, granduncle.

lau - n. leaf

lauhala - n. pandanus leaf

lei - n. garland, wreath; necklace of flowers, leaves, shells, ivory, feathers, or paper, given as a symbol of affection; worn around the head or about the neck

mā.lama - nvt. to take care of, tend, attend, care for, preserve, protect, beware, save, maintain

makana - n. gift

maka 'o'eno - n. twill plaiting, as in hats, mats

mau'u - n. general name for grasses, sedges, rushes, herbs; kava strainer; strand of pandanus plaiting, as in hat making.

moe - n. the horizontal element in weaving, weft; vi. to sleep, lie down

nā pūhala - the pandanus trees

'ōlelo - nvt. language, speech, word, quotation, statement, utterance, term, tidings; to speak, say, state, talk, mention, quote, converse, tell

'ōlelo Hawai'i - nv. Hawai'ian language, speaking Hawai'ian

'ōlelo no'eau - n. proverb, wise saying, traditional saying

pā - n. Flat top of a hat

pāpale - n. hat

pāpale lauhala Hawai'i - n. Hawai'ian lauhala hat

piko - n. center, beginning

poka vines – n. Passiflora mollissima; passion flower vines

pūhala – n. pandanus tree

talking story – colloquialism in Hawai'i meaning "to chat informally"

ulana – vt. to plait, weave, knit, braid

ulana lauhala – vs. weaving pandanus leaves

Ulana Me Ka Loko Maika'i – one of the most respected weaving clubs on Oahu founded by Master Weavers, the late Aunty Gladys Grace and the late Uncle Frank Masagatani.

## Bibliography

Dewhurst, M. and Okada-Carlson, C. (2012) Becoming *Haumana. Cultural Arts Resources for Teachers and Students,* Volume 12. New York, NY: City Lore.

Dewhurst, M., Keawe, L. O., Okada-Carlson, C., MacDowell, M., & Wong, A. K. (2013) *Ka ulana 'ana i ka piko/* In weaving you begin at the center: Perspectives from a culturally specific approach to art education. *Harvard Educational Review. 83*(1). 136–146.

Pukui, M. K. (1983) '*Ōlelo No'eau: Hawaiian Proverbs and Poetical Sayings.* Honolulu, HI: Bishop Museum Press.

Pukui, M. K. and Elbert, S.H. (1986) *Hawaiian Dictionary: Hawaiian-English, English-Hawaiian. Revised and Enlarged Edition.* Honolulu, HI: University of Hawai'i Press.

# 5

## ZAPOTEC YOUTH VISUALIZING THEIR LANGUAGE

### Using Cellphilm and Visual Methods to Support Language Revitalization

*Joshua Schwab Cartas*

*I was scrolling Facebook when suddenly I got a notification of a memory from 12 years ago! It is a picture taken by a friend from Ranchu Gubiña, Pedro, of a wicker basket lined with a white linen cloth and three guetabiza-blackbean tamales. The image commemorates the time our media collective—Binni Cubi (new people)— created a documentary film with an Elder Modesta Vicente, but it also marks a significant moment when the Elder Modesta taught our collective how to find balance between our ancestral traditions, language, and the influences of the globalized world and its byproducts, such as technology. It was a moment of intergenerational bonding and learning!*

*Following this incredible encounter, our media collective had hoped to do a series of food-related documentaries celebrating our rich gastronomic traditions and the Elders who keep them alive. As I look at the picture I recall the hardships we endured due to the lack of technology (we had to borrow a camcorder) and ponder whether or not we would have made more documentaries had we had cell phones. Due to this lack of accessible technology our collective never realized our goal of creating a series of food related documentatries. I remember Pedro's words after taking the picture of the tamales. I recall we both unwrapped the **bacuela** (corn husk, one of the words taught by Na Modesta) to reveal the delicious black bean tamales, known locally as **guetabiza,** as we both sat silently savoring the tamale, Pedro broke the silence, "I never knew how much work and how much history is behind making this dish." Pedro was reminiscing on the fact that we had to wake up at 3am to help Na Modesta cook the corn to make the tamale masa. "I can't believe that Na Modesta only charges 15 pesos for 3 tamales." Pedro spoke candidly about how he took this dish for granted, not realizing the amount of work, history, and even personal connection behind this humble dish. He mentioned that speaking to his parents of his experience of making guetabiza with Modesta Vicente he learned that his mother's grandmother used to make the dish and would bond with his folks over their shared experience of a Zapotec tradition in the form of food. Through this experience we learned that food has the power to create memories as well as transmit*

DOI: 10.4324/9781003302186-8

*culture and language. As we ate our guetabiza we both marveled at being another link in a
long line of cultural inheritors of our Binnzá (Zapotec) culture.*

It has been a few years since I completed my PhD project entitled, *Learning
to Live Our Language: Zapotec Elders and Youth Fostering Intergenerational Dialogue
through Cellphilms,* which applied cellphilming, a participatory visual research
method, that was grounded in a Zapotec experiential pedagogy (Schwab-Cartas,
2016; 2018). This chapter revisits the project to further explore questions that
have arisen from that work: Why cellphilm? And more specifically, why a visual
method to revitalize a language? What role does the visual play in language reclamation and intergenerational transmission? How can cellphilm play a role in
language restoration? And finally, I examine how youths' visual expression through
mobile media continues to expand how Indigenous language can be expressed or
communicated and the role digital technology plays in Indigenous knowledge and
culture transmission.

This chapter is based on my experience and observations as a bi-racial Binnzá
(Zapotec), a diidxazá (Zapotec) language learner, community activist, father
teaching his binnzá daughter our language, and researcher working in our community of Union Hidalgo for the past 18 years. Although this chapter is an example of
a local and personal account of an Indigenous Zapotec methodology, the insights
I learned through this encounter are not soley my own, rather they speak to a
shared communal learning based on inter-relationships with Elders, the land and
ancestral practices all which are rooted in thousands of years of communal knowledge. Therefore, this cellphilm approach, knowledge gained and considerations, is
the result of years of working collectively on various initiatives in our community
that grew from insights gained through ongoing relationships, discussions, and
being immersed in a community for extended periods of time. Where collectivity is underscored above, individuality continues to permeate our teachings and
actions. That is why what is shared in this chapter is not just my insight, but rather
they are *our* insight.

## Language Revitalization

Language revitalization has many appellations, such as language awakening (Linn,
Naranjo, Nicholas, Slaughter, Yamamoto & Zepeda, 2002), reversing language shift
(Fishman, 1991), and language resurgence (McCarty, Nicholas, & Wigglesworth,
2019), to name a few examples. Each of these terms has a specific history, political motivation, and justification. While throughout this chapter, I will use the
term language revitalization because it is more commonly known of all the aforementioned terms, my understanding of this practice aligns with Amanda Holmes'
(2018) concept of language restoration explained below.

Language revitalization is typically thought of as being concerned with halting,
reversing the decline or shift of an endangered language, and or even attempting
to "save" one. Costa (2015) notes that "'endangerment' and 'revitalization' are

generally understood in quantitative terms: while the former is the disappearance of languages, the latter consists in fostering the expansion of domains of use of numbers of speakers" (Costa, 2015, p. 2). Kanienkehaka scholar Amanda Holmes (2018) cogently notes that classic approaches to language revitalization are typically embedded in a Western linear epistemology that is tied to a discourse of extinction and salvation where humans assume a scientific interventionist approach to language revitalization. In this approach "*we* do the revitalizing *to* the language" (Holmes, p. 88), not the other way around. In this dynamic Holmes notes, language is objectified, conceived as something that is separate from us, something we as humans do to it, speak with it, treated as an abstract system or code rather than a "conduit and catalyst for social relationships"(Perley, 2012, p. 134). However, learning diidxazá and participating in numerous language restoration initiatives is so much more than just about learning how to speak the language. Languages are connected to stories, practices, histories, and ancestral knowledge and are much more than something that is spoken. Critical Indigenous language restoration and renewal, as Holmes (2018) notes, is about:

> deepening a conversation with sense-making, with places where the People have lived, walked, storied, and walked on. It means listening for and attending to the relationships and ways of relating that the language holds onto and that its speakers use to invigorate memory, create meaning, and locate identity.
>
> *p. 91*

Holmes' words, grounded and guided by an Indigenous framework, capture the embodied, holistic, and emotional nature of what learning and working to restore our ancestral language of diidxazá has meant for me personally and while working in our community on the cellphilm project.

## Methodology

### What is a Cellphilm?

Cellphilming is a participatory visual method that "straddles the realms of research practice, documentation, and creative expression to encourage new and potentially transformative skills and representational forms" (Mandrona, 2016, p. 183). As a method it responds to the influx of new digital technology, particularly mobile devices, such as cellphones, tablets, and iPods, all which have ushered in new modes of communication and interaction. This digital technology and new media engendered what Henry Jenkins (2006) refers to as participatory culture, where everyday citizens participate in this participatory ecology, not as passive consumers, but rather as prosumers or active participants creating and distributing their own DIY content on an array of social issues, such as gender, race, or the environment.

Cellphilm utilizes everyday digital, on hand, local technologies (i.e., mobile phones/devices) that tap into the citizen's preexisting everyday digital media skills, reducing the overdependence of technology typically brought in by an outside researcher (Schwab-Cartas & Mitchell, 2014). Furthermore, researchers cannot assume the role of "expert" when it comes to knowledge of video or editing software either, particularly in an age when the average citizen creates, edits, and shares visual content with their mobile devices on a daily basis. In many ways, cellphilm is about fostering a more horizontal and equitable way to do research with individuals or communities, moving away from traditional research practices of "rescuing" or "giving voice" to marginalized communities or individuals. It is about promoting research that works with, alongside, and for community, rooted in principles of co-learning and shared knowledge practices, as opposed to research projects that are on or about community for the sole purpose of academic knowledge production. Mandrona (2016) asserts that as a methodology it requires researchers to take up a critical perspective that pays close attention to one's privilege and positionality, potentially leading to hierarchical power dynamics between researchers and participants. Part of this critical perspective is asking yourself as a researcher a series of critical questions, such as, what is your role if participants are proficient digital media users? Ally? Co-facilitator? Co- participant? Learner? Witness? How will it benefit the community? How are you accountable to your, or *the*, community? What do you as a researcher gain from this process? Am I listening closely enough? How do I learn from the community? Also, this participatory methodology moves away from the assumption that marginalized individuals or communities need an intermediary to tell their stories to one where communities and individuals tell their *own* stories for themselves. Instead, the goal of cellphilming as Mandrona (2016) argues is to highlight different experiences and perspectives from those of the mainstream. For example, with the proliferation of cell phones or mobile devices in our community, videos become personal journals or blogs that highlight a more individual community member experience. Problematizing the idea of the community as a monolithic or homogenous group, it plays with the individual and communal at the same time; one does not negate the other.

*Cellphilming steps:*

Here I offer eight steps that were used in our cellphilm workshop. Note that these steps can be modified for the specific community context or topics that you are working with. For example, in the context of my community and language restoration we chose to use Zapotec prompts. These steps are not prescriptive and can be changed to fit the community/context/topic.

1.  Developing a prompt,
2.  Introduction and discussion of visual ethics,
3.  Brainstorming: participants brainstorm and discuss a prompt,
4.  Storyboarding,

5. Filming,
6. Screening,
7. Reflection, discussion and future action,
8. Archiving, storage, and future viewership.[1]

## Diidxaza/Zapotec: A Brief Overview

*Diidxazá (dee-jah-saa)* or Isthmus Zapotec in English is the language spoken in my grandfather's community of Ranchu Gubina, located in the southern Mexican state of Oaxaca. The late Binnizá intellectual Victor De la Cruz once said the "'Zapotec language' is not one language with numerous dialects, as is often believed; it is multiple languages, as different among themselves as are the Romance languages" (as quoted in Frischmann, 2005, p. 20). There are 58 varieties of Zapotec listed by Ethnologue and 49 of them have fewer than 10,000 speakers. This includes our own community of Ranchu Gubiña, also known as Union Hidalgo.

According to the Mexican National Institute of Statistics and Geography 2015 census, our community of 15,347 inhabitants has 7500 speakers, an alarming number considering that according to the Elders less than 40 years ago our entire community spoke our language. Now, a generation later, only 56% of our community speaks our language, with the majority of speakers being over the age of 60.

## Grounding Cellphilm in the Teachings of an Elder: An Indigenous Approach to Cellphilming

The cellphilm project applied a Zapotec pedagogical approach that was taught to us by the late Elder, Modesta Vicente (see Schwab-Cartas, 2016; 2018). It emphasizes language learning and knowledge acquisition as both embodied and multimodal through direct engagement with "linguistic, visual, auditory, gestural and spatial" multiple literacy methods (Kalantzis & Cope, 2005) that are key elements to learning and communication (Schwab–Cartas, 2012). Through direct engagement with her blackbean tamale making process, Na Modesta taught us Zapotec by reciting and getting us to repeat and recall the name of all the ingredients, cooking utensils, and processes, thus fully immersing us in an ancestral practice. Na Modesta understood that putting a practice like making *blackbean tamales* at the center of language learning instead of isolating our language learning to a classroom setting or focusing on grammar provided us with an accessible entry point into our language for speakers at any level of language proficiency, while grounding her teachings and our language in a Zapotec epistemology. Na Modesta also saw that technology, which at the time was a camcorder (See: Schwab-Cartas, 2012), was the catalyst to making her practice both appealing and relevant to us as young people, which is why cellphilm was chosen as the methodology above other participatory visual methods.

Cellphones in our community, due to their global affordability, have entered the diidxazá lexicon and are referred to as *bichugale*. *B*innzá youth in Ranchu Gubiña, like many Indigenous youth around the world, are growing up as digital natives in a complex pluricultural, multimedia, multilingual world; a world that is saturated with networked devices, such as smartphones, images of global culture, and other visual practices (Jewitt, 2008). Cellphones were used in this project because of their relatability and importance to youth everyday experience in our community. Youth use mobile devices to communicate and to express themselves, their identity, and a vision of the type of world they want to see.

A cellphilm approach is not intended to initiate the adoption and use of new technologies, but rather to *refocus* current use patterns and preexisting media creating skills in a way that encourages Zapotec language and cultural learning amongst youth. This was done through a series of intergenerational workshops focused on language and traditional practice as a means to bridge the generational gap of understanding between Elders and youth—a gap that is currently the most significant barrier to language and cultural transfer for new generations of Indigenous people. Cellphone technology created a more reciprocal exchange between Elders and youth. Both parties are knowledge holders that play critical roles in language revitalization; Elders as language and cultural experts and youth as technology and digital media specialists. The emphasis on intergenerational bonding with Elders also ensured that cell phones or mobile devices are understood as tools that can act as catalysts to action and even documentation for future generations. Language restoration and learning always lies in engaged and committed interaction with Elders and one's community surroundings. In the end participants felt that through this process they had a stronger and more connected relationship with their language, culture, and Elders.

## Visualizing our Zapotec Language: Zapotec Visual Culture and Speaking Through Cellphilms

I gravitated towards using cellphilm as a visual methodology because of the technological relevance to our youth, and also because I understood it to be a more equitable and culturally adaptable approach. I was also interested in cellphilming because visuality is so central to the method and to understand how the practice of looking, filming whilst also doing, can support the learning of our language and or cultural practice.

My Elders, and Indigenous friends and colleagues, concur that we learn best through watching and observing, since we are visual learners (see Figure 5.1). Comanche and Kiowa scholar Cornel Pewewardy (2002) asserts:

> Visual learners learn best when they are able to see the material they are expected to master. They tend to learn best when the teacher provides a myriad of visual learning opportunities such as graphs, films, demonstrations,

FIGURE 5.1 Three participants discussing their shot.

and pictures. American Indian/Alaska Native students are taught by observing parents or Elders (Red Horse, 1980). When skills are taught, parents or Elders generally teach through demonstration. Children watch, and then imitate the skills. For example, the father, mother, or elder might teach the child a skill by modeling. Children are expected to watch, listen and then do. Therefore, many American Indian/Alaska Native students appear to perform best in classrooms with an emphasis on visualization.

*p. 29*

Pewewardy's description of Indigenous visual learning mirrors our interaction and experiences with our Elders in these workshops, and perfectly describes our inspirational encounter and teaching learned from Na Modesta, who gifted us this approach. Zapotec pedagogy as taught to us by Na Modesta's "values a person's ability to learn independently by observing, listening, participating with a minimum of intervention and instruction" (Battiste, 2002, p. 11). The visual is emphasized as an integral element of teaching and learning to pass on knowledge used in ours and other Indigenous communities. While learning about language revitalization approaches that utilize visual technology, the *visual* is not emphasized beyond the role of documentation and possible reflection. Through engaging with these workshops, I experienced how critical the role of the visual was in learning our language and culture. Indigenous knowledges and ways of learning are embodied; the visual, oral, and tactile all play a critical role in Indigenous modes of learning and teaching, which speaks to the interconnectedness and the interrelationships of all life.

A key component to igniting a critical language consciousness (Lee, 2014) amongst youth was through our juntas (talking circles) coupled with the use of visual elements to engender deep conversation on an array of topics (Bennett et al., 2019). Juntas allowed us to create a space to honor the ancestral traditions while also "imagining" new futures (Duarte & Belarde-Lewis, 2015), different possibilities that allow us to begin and complete our journeys of decolonization one day. Duarte and Belarde-Lewis (2015) best describe imagining for us as "envisioning and discovering the beauty of our knowledge" (p. 687) and continue with:

> Envisioning is a strategy that Indigenous peoples have employed effectively to bind people together politically ask[ing] that people imagine a future, that they rise above present-day situations which are generally depressing, dream a new dream and set a new vision." Discovering the beauty of our knowledge refers to the processes in which Indigenous peoples focus on "making our knowledge systems work for the benefit of their communities".
>
> *p. 687*

It was important to try to ensure that our juntas created a non-judgmental and compassionate space as a means to help stimulate the process of decolonization amongst the young participants. This required myself and my co-participant Jose Arenas Lopez, founder of the binni cubi and longtime collaborator, to be vulnerable and candid about our language capacities, struggles, and experiences of how language loss has affected us both in similar and yet different ways. It was also about creating space free of suppositions, focused on deep listening, to better comprehend youths' needs when it comes to learning our language instead of assuming that we knew what they needed or that they simply were not interested in learning our language, an assumption made by their parents and Elders.

Another key element to simulating decolonization and igniting critical language consciousness is grounding our juntas, discussions, and activities in a Zapotec Indigenous pedagogical praxis known as comunalidad. Comunalidad describes a way of living that has been around for thousands of years. Mexican activist and public intellectual Gustavo Esteva (2012) describes it as "both a collection of practices formed as creative adaptations of old traditions to resist old and new colonialisms, and a mental space, a horizon of intelligibility: how you see and experience the world as We" (Esteva, 2012, n.p.). The foundation and vitality of comunalidad, according to Alvarado (2013), has three inseparable elements: (1) ideology (a way of thinking rooted in the old ways); (2) a structure that supports this world view (the community or a collective or both); and (3) a way of organizing that supports collectivity over individualism (communal work). Comunalidad proposes an Indigenous identity, as Zapotec scholar Sanchez-Lopez

(2017) notes, not based on physical, biological, or linguistic traits, but rather on the work one does for their community. Thus, emphasizing interdependence and "kincentric" (Salmón, 2000) relations that have been key to our survival and resilience as Zapotec people. These ideas were underscored throughout the entire workshop, explaining to participants that through this collaborative work of creating cellphilms with Elders, we are creating and restoring intergenerational relationships, transferring knowledge, and becoming *we,* so as to emphasize our comunalidad.

**Using visuals to support language revitalization:** To help unpack and connect with the topic(s) related to language loss and revitalization as mentioned above we used many visuals, like documentaries (such works by Ikoots female documentarist Teofila Palafox Herranz), photographs, and food, to function as visual and physical prompts to engender conversation on an array of subjects and or emotions pertaining to our language. Topics discussed included ancestral traditions, history, loss, trauma, pride, fluency shaming (how Elders or fluent speakers make learners feel ashamed for not being able to speak fluently), expanding concepts of fluency, and cultural identity. We also introduced and talked about visual ethics and storyboarding by combining both activities. Visual ethics is a critical aspect of creating a cellphilm because it is about ensuring images/visuals are used in the safest way possible to do the most good and least harm, while always taking participants and/or the community's rights and concerns into consideration. However, as integral as this topic is, many of the participants found the topic a bit abstract and hard to comprehend, which is why we used the heuristic method in a real-life context. We discussed the basics of visual ethics, such considerations of consent and ownership of the process and visual outputs, what was permissible and not permissible, the importance of protecting people's identity, and also what to do when working with children and how to get them to participate without having them actually be on screen. Parental consent was sought when uploading films to social media platforms.[2]

The heuristic method we used to help our young participants experience and comprehend these aforementioned activities/topics in a lived context was to shadow an Elder before making their cellphilm. Shadowing an Elder had a fourfold purpose: first and foremost to build a relationship and establish trust with an Elder, second to get the youth to understand and immerse themselves in the practice that they were choosing to base their cellphilm on, to help understand the significance of the ancestral practice, and to begin to think of their storyline in terms of a visual narrative. By fostering the process of thinking visually about their cellphilm by asking what it would look like, what time and where it would be filmed, and what key elements or words of the practice were to be used by the Elder moves away from an abstract idea to a more concrete one that understands how and what to film. Through shadowing an Elder the storyboard process becomes more dynamic and embodied by the viewer, and intersects with concerns about visual ethics because the cellphilmer learns from the Elder or co-participant in the film what is sharable and what is not shareable and why. Perhaps it is sacred knowledge, or perhaps it is personal knowledge that the Elder only wants to share with a select few people. Also, through this process you can ask and collectively decide who is the audience for the cellphilm, how it should be shared, and other potential caveats, such as the Elder having the last word on whether it is shared or can be taken down from a website or social media website in the future. The process of visual ethics becomes grounded in the concerns and goals of the community alongside Elders and other community members. This lived process allows youth to understand storyboarding and visual ethics in a grounded and practical way that reflects Elders knowledge and community concerns.

During these juntas we learned that our youth were in fact very interested in learning their language, but they did not know how to navigate the mixed messages they were receiving. That is, on the one hand, Elders and parents lament that they are not speaking the language, yet they are not being taught diidxazá, while also being discouraged to learn it, speak it, and actively being told to learn a global language such as English. This required unpacking and discussion. In these juntas we learned that talking, listening, and sharing are a critical part of reclaiming and reconnecting to our ancestral language and that it requires a great deal of emotional labour on the part of the person reclaiming their Indigenous language. It takes time to process, to reclaim, to reconnect to your Indigenous language. Indigenous languages, like diidxazá, are not like learning a global language, such as English or Spanish. Global languages have over centuries become standardized and delocalized in order to serve as national and global trade languages, whereas Indigenous languages continue to encode local ontology rooted in practices and understandings related to everything from food gathering and processing to cosmovisions, from understandings of weather phenomena to animals, to landscape and ethics in a particular place. Learning our language is more than just learning how to speak our ancestral tongue; it is also about reconnecting and restoring our relationship to our culture, each other, the land; and our Elders teachings. Also, using and creating images allowed participants to describe those ineffable feelings they felt for the rapid decline of their language, language loss, its history, and their emotional journey. For example, how does one verbalize what they feel for their ancestral language in English or Spanish, a language colonizers imposed on us, which represents a history of violence, oppression, and trauma? How do you put into words the profound sadness, hopelessness, and anger one feels that our ancestral language continues to decline because colonizers and government(s) wanted to get rid of any aspect of who we are as Indigenous peoples? Or how do you put into words the joy and pride one feels teaching their child words in our ancestral language, feeling and seeing intergenerational knowledge transfer and continuity in action, knowing you are part of the long line of ancestors who brought forth these traditions?

The adage of "an image is worth a thousand words" comes to mind because images, whether they are cellphilms, drawings, or photographs, are a powerful means to encapsulate a multiplicity of emotions, histories, and stories. With this in mind it is important for facilitators to recognize that images can be difficult for participants to view and/or create at times, so as much as an image can be empowering it can also be triggering of past traumas for some participants. This is why it is critical to ground discussions around the creation and viewership of images in your own Indigenous culture, so as to be able to use culturally relevant and specific teachings to unpack and discuss these elements before, during, and after using or creating images or videos to ensure the well-being of your participants. However, having, using, or creating images or videos, grounded in your own Indigenous culture, instead of having to revert to using the colonizer language to express your deepest emotions, is also a powerful act of resistance, reclamation, and self love.

## Speaking Diidxaza with and Through Cellphilms[3]

In this section I express an understanding of our Indigenous language that came from working in our community with digitally literate youth that goes beyond strict notions of "fluency" and the oral/textual dichotomy that as Indigenous peoples we have been placed in. Cellphilms and other mobile expressions play a dual role; the first as positive Indigenous representation and second as a form of communicating diidxazá as non-fluent speakers.

Art critic John Berger (1972), said:

> Seeing comes before words. The child looks and recognizes before it can speak. But there is also another sense in which seeing comes before words. It is seeing which establishes our place in the surrounding world; we explain that world with words, but words can never undo the fact that we are surrounded by it.
>
> *p. 7*

Ba'du ca'—the young people—in our community grow up immersed in a binnzá world, where they continue to *see* an uncle or relative using an oxen cart to go to the corn fields, where they *hear* the the sound of their mother or an aunt's needle as it pierces the fabric, while they thread in brightly coloured silk threads of fuchsia, aqua marine, lavender to create an incredible *bidaani'* (huipil) (see Figure 5.2), or smell the familiar *smell* of burning wood ovens of a grandmother or Elder making *gueta biguii*.

Our young people grow up seeing these familiar scenes, hearing these familiar sounds and smells. While they may not be actively being taught diidxazá in their homes or at school, they are actively immersed in a Zapotec environment. Young people in the community, like so many youths around the globe in the 21st century, are also immersed in a hypervisual globalized world that is "saturated with images, visual technologies and visual practices" (Jewitt, 2008, p. 6). At the center

**FIGURE 5.2** Woman in Huipil.

of this visually enhanced world are mobile devices—cellphones and tablets—which for most people have become a quotidian medium through which they express themselves, receive and send information, and even experience their world. These technologies have also affected language practices in the 21st century and as a result modes of communication have become "multimodal—oral and written—and linguistic modes of meaning are intricately bound up with other visual, audio and spatial semiotic systems" (García, 2009, p. 376). In many ways, cellphones are extensions of people themselves; media created through them are new ways of transmitting culture and language. In this hypervisual world, youth speak through the visual, using emoji and memes, sharing their digital stories with friends and family on Instagram, TikTok, Facebook, and Youtube about millennial old practices, such as harvesting corn, *regadas de frutas(the giving away of fruits and other stuffs on saint's holidays), mediu xiga(a tradtional dance done at weddings).*

Indigenous youth around the globe are tired of not seeing themselves or topics of actual concern to them represented in the mainstream. They are taking up digital media to both decolonize and Indigenize the digital mediascape. Many youth in our community, like other Indigenous youth around the world, are using their mobile devices to actively and creatively speak back to the ongoing and lasting effects of colonialism through everyday mobile productions. And through these Do-It -Yourself (DIY) media productions shared on various social media platforms, Indigenous youth are sharing their critical and diverse perspectives on topics such as gender-based violence, access to clean water, environmental and climate justice, and cultural and language continuity (Mitchell, 2017). Illustrating that Indigenous Zapotec people are not a monolith and don't speak or act as a homogenous entity, through their DIY videos they express the diversity of opinions that exist within all communities. Their visual narratives therefore function much like a "contemporary talking stick that creates space for diverse experiences, perspectives and stories to be shared both within and between communities at great distances" (Tabobondung, 2010, p. 130). But perhaps most importantly these videos are about finding ways to connect with other Indigenous peoples as well as our own traditions, languages, and ancestral ways of being in the world.

Binnizá youth in our community continue to be immersed in a Zapotec visual culture and expressions from a young age, which according to Hopi filmmaker Victor Masayesva (2005):

> shapes one's instinct to pounce on the record button at the epiphanic moment. Deciding when to record is shaped by these early experiences. The defining moment is the pounce, which is executed not by the first or second hand, but by the third hand - the flourish of the Indigenous aesthetic
>
> *p. 168*

This Indigenous, or rather Zapotec, aesthetic was clearly evident in the cellphims produced in our community. Not having grown up in the community, unlike the young participants, I would not not catch the subtle seemingly insignificant visual elements to my untrained eye, such as culturally meaningful hand gestures, or facial expressions, or elements of nature to noticing well known community members in the background, are culturally more significant to those who are born and raised in their culture. These youths, unlike myself, understand binnzá visual grammar and language that they read and speak fluently with great ease. I argue that they utilize images and their knowledge of binnzá visual culture much in the same way speakers use words to express their culture and or communicate with one another. These videos are representations of how youth represent their culture, as well as their way of speaking diidxazá. In other words, through their adept knowledge of both digital media and binnzá visual culture, youth are able to successfully communicate intergenerationally. I argue that this is one of the few ways many of our young people know and or feel that they can *speak* or express themselves in diidxazá for the moment. It is their way to speak to their peers in diidxazá and to the community at large without fear of ridicule or shame by "fluent" speakers. The visual functions as an important bridge or transitional medium in the process and journey of restoring and renewing their relationship with their language (see Figure 5.3), not to mention that using this visual technology is a way to also extend the language domain of the Zapotec language.

**FIGURE 5.3**  Cellphilming Leonel.


Rather than losing their language and culture, youth in our community are innovating their language practices as a result of being more connected to mainstream global culture than their parents.

In contrast to the vision of fluency held by older Zapotec speakers who perceive a direct link between linguistic competence and cultural identity, the younger generation expresses cultural identity as inherent in a process associated with a broader definition of language as a cultural practice (See: Nicholas, 2011, Pennycook, 2010). Their videos reflect their search for ways to stay connected to their communities, culture, and language as they articulate their lives to the world outside of their communities. Ofelia García (2009) correctly points out that youth's ease with digital and mobile technology is shaping language practices so they are more flexible and fluid, thus challenging and expanding traditional notions of what it means to be able to communicate in your traditional language.

Despite living in a radically different world from their parents and even more so from their Elders, youth are continuing to do what our Elders and *Binnigula'sa,* our ancestors, did before them. That is, to be resilient and innovative so as to bring our binnzá language and culture forward for the next generations. My Uncle Narno Arias Cartas told me that the gula in the word *Binnigula'sa* can refer to a "form of strength that is rooted, like a sapling, in [our peoples] relationship to the land and to the members of our community who are living, have lived or are still to come" (Horner, 2013, p. 208). And like our binnigula'sa who were able to be flexible, to bend, when necessary, but also to be resistant is why we maintain our binnzá way of life. Using a cellphilm approach to language revitalization recognizes and engages with these complex multilingual and multimedia environments—speaking to the ethos of the participant's experiences of having to navigate the complicated learning environments. Also, to be able to negotiate these complex language settings requires embracing a biculturalism that Na Modesta approach taught us. Through Na Modesta's teachings we learned our Zapotec culture is not necessarily in opposition to Western technologies, such as camcorders and cellphones or ways of knowing, but she reminded us to not forget the strength, sacrifices, and beauty of our ancestral Zapotec traditions and technologies. Therefore, this cellphilm approach guided by lessons learned from Na Modesta included Elders, practicing ancestral traditions, to foster intergenerational bonding and learning, but also to ensure that our way of seeing and understanding the world would continue to guide the way digital technology is used in the future.

## Notes

1  This link will provide the reader with a more in-depth discussion and resources on and about creating a cellphilm. https://internationalcellphilmfestival.com/2013/10/24/cellphilm-tips/
2  For further guidelines on Visual Ethics please refer to this resource:

> Wiles, R., Prosser, J., Bagnoli, A., Clark, A., Davies, K., Holland, S., & Renold, E. (2008). Visual ethics: Ethical issues in visual research.

3  This is an example of a cellphilm created by one of the workshop participants, Giovanny de Jesus Rodreguiez Cazorla, which shows an array of different Zapotec cultural practices from his community of Chicapa de Castro, Oaxaca.
   www.youtube.com/watch?v=LOnc6vwW-S4&t=66s&ab_channel=TheGR-records Producciones.

## References

Alfred, T. (2005). *Wasase: Indigenous pathways of action and freedom*. University of Toronto Press.
Alvarado, B. M. (2013). Comunalidad y responsabilidad autogestiva. *Cuaderno del Sur, Revista de Ciencias Sociales, 34*, 21–27.
Battiste, M. (2002). *Indigenous knowledge and pedagogy in First Nations education: A literature review with recommendations* (pp. 1–69). National Working Group on Education.
Bennett, B., Maar, M., Manitowabi, D., Moeke-Pickering, T., Trudeau-Peltier, D., & Trudeau, S. (2019). The Gaataa'aabing visual research method: a culturally safe Anishinaabek transformation of Photovoice. *International Journal of Qualitative Methods, 18*, 1609406919851635.
Berger, J. (1972). *Ways of seeing: Based on the BBC television series with John Berger*. British Broadcasting Corporation.
Cope, B., & Kalantzis, M. (2005). Introduction: Multiliteracies: The beginnings of an idea. In *Multiliteracies* (pp. 3–8). Routledge.

Costa, J. (2015). Is language revitalization really about saving languages? Some insights from 150 years of language revival in Occitania. In *Proceedings from the Annual Meeting of the Chicago Linguistic Society* (Vol. 51).

Duarte, M. E., & Belarde-Lewis, M. (2015). Imagining: Creating spaces for indigenous ontologies. *Cataloging & Classification Quarterly, 53*(5–6), 677–702. https://doi.org/10.1080/01639374.2015.1018396

Esteva, G. (2012). Hope from the margins. In D. Bollier & S. Helfrich (Eds.), *The wealth of the commons: A world beyond market and state.* Levellers Press. Retrieved from www.wealthofthecommons.org/essay/hope-margins

Fishman, J. A. (1991). *Reversing language shift: Theoretical and empirical foundations of assistance to threatened languages.* Multilingual Matters.

Frischmann, D. H., & Montemayor, C. (2005). Words of the true peoples: Anthology of contemporary Mexican Indigenous-language writers. University of Texas Press.

García, O. (2009). En/countering indigenous bilingualism. Journal of Language, Identity, and Education, 8(5), 376–380. https://doi.org/10.1080/15348450903305155

Holmes, A. L. (2018). *Geographies of home, memory, and heart: Mohawk Elder praxis, land, language, and knowledge woven in place* (Unpublished Doctoral dissertation) The University of Arizona, Tucson. Retrieved from https://repository.arizona.edu/handle/10150/628178

Horner, G. A. (2013). *Caminando y miando: A reflection on academic practice* (Unpublished Doctoral dissertation). University of British Columbia, Vancouver. Retrieved from https://open.library.ubc.ca/cIRcle/collections/ubctheses/24/items/1.0073677

Jenkins, H. (2006). Confronting the challenges of participatory culture: Media education for the 21st century. An occasional paper on digital media and learning. *John D. and Catherine T. MacArthur Foundation.*

Jewitt, C. (2008). The visual in learning and creativity: a review of the literature. A report for creative partnership.

Lee, T. S. (2014). If I could speak Navajo, I'd definitely speak it 24/7: Diné youth, language consciousness, activism and reclamation of Diné identity. *Diné perspectives: Revitalizing and reclaiming Navajo thought (Critical Issues in Indigenous Studies)*, 158–169.

Linn, M. S., Naranjo, T., Nicholas, S., Slaughter, I., Yamamoto, A., & Zepeda, O. (2002). Awakening the Languages. Challenges of Enduring Language Programs: Field Reports from 15 Programs from Arizona, New Mexico and Oklahoma.

Mandrona, A. R. (2016). Visual culture, aesthetics, and the ethics of cellphilming. In MacEntee, Burkholder and Schwab-Cartas (Eds). *What's a Cellphilm? Integrating Mobile Phone Technology into Participatory Visual Research and Activism* (pp. 183–198). Brill Sense.

Masayesva, V., (2005) indigenous experimentalism. In Claxton, D., Loft, S., & Townsend, M. (Eds). Transference, Traditions, Technology: Native New Media Exploring Visual and Digital Culture. *Banff: Walter Phillips Gallery / Art Gallery of Hamilton / Indigenous media Arts group.*

McCarty, T. L., Nicholas, S. E., & Wigglesworth, G. (2019). A world of indigenous languages: Resurgence, reclamation, revitalization and resilience. A world of Indigenous languages: Politics, pedagogies and prospects for language reclamation, 1–26.

Mitchell, C. (2017). "The Girl Should Just Clean Up the Mess" On Studying Audiences in Understanding the Meaningful Engagement of Young People in Policy-Making. International Journal of Qualitative Methods, *16*(1), 1609406917703501.

Nicholas, S. E. (2011). How are you Hopi if you can't speak it?": An ethnographic study of language as cultural practice among contemporary Hopi youth. *Ethnography and language policy*, 53–75.

Pennycook, A. (2010). *Language as a local practice*. Routledge.

Perley, B. C. (2012, July). Zombie linguistics: Experts, endangered languages and the curse of undead voices. In *Anthropological forum* (Vol. 22, No. 2, pp. 133–149). Routledge.

Pewewardy, C. (2002). Learning styles of American Indian/Alaska Native students: A review of the literature and implications for practice. *Journal of American Indian Education*, 22–56.

Salmón, E. (2000). Kincentric ecology: indigenous perceptions of the human–nature relationship. Ecological Applications, 10(5), 1327–1332.

Sánchez-López, L. (2017). Learning from the paisanos: Coming to consciousness in Zapotec LA. Latino Studies, 15(2), 242–246.

Schwab-Cartas, J. (2012). Learning from communities: Personal reflections from inside. In E-J. Milne, C. Mitchell, & N. De Lange (Eds.), *Handbook of participatory video* (pp. 383–396). AltaMira Press.

Schwab-Cartas, J. (2018). Keeping Up with the Sun: Revitalizing Isthmus Zapotec and Ancestral Practices through Cellphilms. Canadian Modern Language Review, 74(3), 363–387.

Schwab-Cartas, J., & Mitchell, C. (2014). A tale of two sites: Cellphones, participatory video and indigeneity in community-based research. *McGill Journal of Education/Revue des sciences de l'éducation de McGill, 49*(3), 603–620.

Tabobondung, R. (2010). Indigenous perspectives on globalization: Self-determination through autonomous media creation. In Blaser, M., De Costa, R., McGregor, D., & Coleman, W. D. (Eds.). (2011). *Indigenous peoples and autonomy: Insights for a global age.* (pp.130–147). UBC Press.

# 6

# DIGITAL LANGUAGE KINSCAPES

## Twitter-based Pedagogical Possibilities for Indigenous Youth Language Learning in Canada

*Ashley Caranto Morford, Samantha McCormick, and Jeffrey Ansloos*

### Positioning Ourselves

We come to this work from a diversity of backgrounds, experiences, and positions. We open by recognizing the lived experiences and knowledge we bring with us to this work, to make clear our responsibilities to communities when doing this work, and to recognize any limitations to our own experiences and practices as we do this work.

Ashley Caranto Morford (she/her) is a diasporic Filipina (Visayan and Luzonian) and British settler scholar who is writing this piece as an uninvited occupant in Lenape territory (colonially called Philadelphia, Pennsylvania, USA). Ashley's community and scholarly work is at the intersections of Indigenous studies, Filipinx/a/o studies, anti-colonial methodologies, BIPOC (Black, Indigenous, and people of color) solidarities, and digital humanities. Ashley recognizes with humbleness the limitations of her perspective and experience as she approaches this work. She is currently a monolingual English speaker, having grown up disconnected from the ancestral languages of her Filipino relations, specifically Tagalog, Cebuano, and Pangasinan. Recently, she has been beginning the journey of reconnecting with various words and concepts from these languages, and hopes to one day more earnestly commit to and undergo the journey of learning one or all of these languages.

Samantha McCormick (she/her, them/they) is an Anishinaabe and English/French scholar who is writing this piece currently in Tkaronto (Toronto, Ontario, Canada). Samantha is from Northern Ontario and calls Baawaating (Sault Ste Marie, Ontario, Canada) region home. Samantha's father is Anishinaabe and a member of Sagamok First Nation, while Samantha's mother is of French/English settler ancestry. Being the grandchild of a residential school survivor who was

DOI: 10.4324/9781003302186-9

forbidden to speak her native language, Samantha values the opportunity to honor her ancestors through speaking Anishinaabemowin, even if it is only a few words. Samantha identifies as an Indigenous language learner. Samantha writes as a queer and Indigenous woman and her work is within Indigenous feminisms, language, and clinical psychology.

Jeffrey Ansloos is Nehiyaw (Cree) and English and is a member of Fisher River Cree Nation (Ochekwi-Sipi; Treaty 5). He was born and raised in the heart of Treaty 1 territory in Winnipeg, Manitoba. He is writing this piece while currently residing in Tkaranto (Toronto, Ontario, Canada). Ansloos writes as a multilingual language learner. Having grown up in a predominantly English context, he continues to learn French, Spanish, and Cree. His work considers anticolonial and critical approaches to Indigenous health and education.

We wish to extend deepest thanks to Dallas Hunt, Jay Odjick, and Bryson Syliboy, whose insights we have drawn on in the writing of this chapter. They generously offered their time, knowledge, and perspectives regarding language learning and resurgence processes through participating in interviews for this research project. We are humbled, honored, and thankful to have connected with and learned from their wisdom and work.

## Content Note

Please note that this piece engages, sometimes in graphic detail, with the violence enacted on Indigenous youth at Canada's residential schools.

## Introduction

It is a cold November day in Tkaronto/Toronto, but inside a small office on the 7th floor of the Ontario Institute for Studies in Education, the air is warm with stories of joy. Through Zoom, Algonquin language revivalist Jay Odjick talks with Ashley about his experiences sharing Algonquin on Twitter and the story of how his Twitter-based Algonquin Word of the Day saw "17,000 impressions a day" (Jay Odjick, personal communication, November 4, 2019). A month later, Cree language revivalist Dallas Hunt connects via Zoom and fills the office space with more stories of joy, sharing how his Twitter-based Cree Word of the Day inspired community members to write messages to him completely in the language (Dallas Hunt, personal communication, December 3, 2019). In April 2020, in the midst of the Covid-19 pandemic, Mi'kmaw language revivalist Bryson Syliboy and Ashley share in a moment of joy through Zoom, as Syliboy tells stories about how seeing tweets written in his language "brings a smile to my face because it's such a beautiful language" (Bryson Syliboy, personal communication, April 17, 2020). These stories illustrate how rich and expansive the resurgence, ongoing life, and vitality of Indigenous languages in (colonially called) Canada are, including within online social media platforms.

The Twitter environment features an ever-growing series of Indigenous language networks. For instance, there are tribal-specific Words of the Day on Twitter—including Nêhiyawêwin, Mi'kmaw, and Anishinaabemowin, just to name a few—which are led by Indigenous Twitter users. Twitter hashtag networks like #SpeakGwichinToMe and #CreeWordOfTheDay teach and celebrate Indigenous languages in culturally grounded ways specific to each distinct language and Indigenous nation. Through these movements, Indigenous Twitter users are transforming the social media platform into an important Indigenous cultural, community, and learning environment. In so doing, they are creating dynamic and nourishing digital spaces for Indigenous people to engage with and practice speaking their ancestral languages.

Indigenous scholars and community organizers are doing important, necessary language learning work within institutional spaces throughout Canada as well, from the Bachelor of Nsyilxcən Language Fluency program at the University of British Columbia Okanagan to the University of Victoria's Certificate in Indigenous Language Revitalization. Beyond learning how to express and understand an Indigenous language, these programs also emphasize how Indigenous histories and worldviews are embedded within Indigenous languages. Importantly, Indigenous language learning work also engages with connections to Indigenous lands, cultures, communities, and the pragmatics of day-to-day life (Hermes & King, 2013).

We are interested in the pedagogical possibilities, opportunities, and methods of online spaces for Indigenous youth language learning in the Canadian classroom. Our objective is to understand the pedagogical implications of how Indigenous community members and educators engage with Indigenous language learning on Twitter. This objective is aligned with and seeks to support the Calls to Action of the Truth and Reconciliation Commission (TRC) of Canada's Final Report, which include the key foci of asserting the importance of Indigenous language rights and expanding funding for Indigenous language initiatives (recommendations 13–17; TRC, 2015). Through a holistic qualitative analysis, we consider four pedagogical implications and tensions that emerge for Indigenous language learning on Twitter. First, we draw on the idea of language kinscapes, a term we learned from Cherokee scholar Daniel Heath Justice (2018) and which we understand as the culturally grounded, intimate, yet transnational networks of Indigenous community members collectively navigating language learning within Twitter. These networks are enabled, in large part, through the hashtag and keyword. Second, we examine the concept of relational pedagogy—a process of framing language as being in close relations with land and place, human and more-than-human, and intergenerational knowledge—within these networks. Relational pedagogy requires various relational protocols to be approached, taught, and learned in ethical ways. Third, we discuss the idea of place-based bridging, speaking to how language learning networks on Twitter offer accessibility to cultural and land-based language learning for Indigenous youth physically distanced from Indigenous community. We then consider the issues and possibilities of accessibility that arise within these spaces. Finally, we reflect on the implications of social media community networks, and the language learning that occurs within them, for classroom learning.

Overall, this chapter will discuss how Indigenous people on Twitter are actively carving out networks for Indigenous language learning, revitalization, and advocacy. This work builds on and can help to shape the rich efforts of Indigenous language teachers and scholars to consolidate Indigenous languages as meaningful and important. These frameworks exist as healing and decolonial spaces where Indigenous languages are valued and energized. The ways in which Indigenous people are creating online spaces and networks for language learning are rich with opportunities to build decolonial worlds and futures. Twitter provides many opportunities for Indigenous community members to story language learning, and this chapter's investigation of Twitter highlights a unique medium by which Indigenous people creatively reclaim their ancestral languages.

## Indigenous Languages, Colonialism, and the Canadian Education System

Colonialism has had direct impacts on Indigenous languages as they are spoken and understood in Canada. Since contact, colonialism has relentlessly campaigned to eradicate, efface, and eliminate Indigenous languages. The colonial agenda seeks to separate language from Indigenous peoples due to the intricate connections between language, culture, land, and identity (Iseke, 2013). This violent severing of language is one way that the process of language shift—that is, the shift of the use of one language to another—has manifested (Fishman, 1991, 2001). Once language is severed, this enables an easier transition to becoming colonized.

The Canadian residential school system (1876–1996) is a horrific and primary way that language has been shaped and a language shift has occurred within this territory. The residential school system was a product of the British North America Act (1867) and the Indian Act (1876), designed to assimilate Indigenous peoples into Canadian society (Haque & Patrick, 2015). Since their inception, Indian residential schools worked to "kill the Indian in the child" (Starblanket, 2017, p. 171), and extinguishing Indigenous languages and cultures from the students is an essential stage of this genocide. Indigenous children were instructed in English or French. When a student spoke their native language, they were punished. Accounts of residential school survivors describe beatings, discipline, and even torture as consequences for speaking their native languages. Celia Haig-Brown describes her father's experiences as a survivor of Alberni Indian Residential School; he "was physically tortured by his teachers for speaking Tseshaht: they pushed sewing needles through his tongue, a routine punishment for language offenders" (1988, p. 11). The impact of Indian Residential Schools not only ruptured intergenerational language transmission, but instilled traumas in connection to speaking the language, the impacts of which last to this day (Fontaine, 2017).

Canadian educational systems continue to marginalize Indigenous languages through situating English and French as official languages. Notably, the Royal Commission on Bilingualism and Biculturalism (1963–1970) was a policy document that mandated English and French as the "official" languages of Canada (Haque & Patrick, 2015), ignoring the irony that Indigenous languages were originally spoken and continue to be spoken widely throughout this territory. Serving a political motive to solidify a Liberal minority government gaining popularity with French-speaking Canadians, this document effectively "othered" non-English and non-French languages and cultures. The most noticeable impact has been on Indigenous peoples, further enacting colonial disenfranchisement from Indigenous languages, lands, and cultures. Effectively, this policy situates English and French as the essential means of communicating in educational and healthcare institutions, government and policy, and commerce. Thus, to obtain a livelihood and grow up in Canadian systems, Indigenous peoples are forced to adopt these "officially recognized languages" (Haque & Patrick, 2015). By perpetuating a focus on teaching and learning in English and French, and failing to include Indigenous languages in instruction and practice, educational institutions participate in continuing to enact colonial violence.

Language scholars and revivalists have emphasized that, for a language to thrive in long-lasting ways, it must have a community of speakers who can converse in, embody, live, breathe, and dream the language in the day-to-day and through the generations. Indigenous language learning spaces and the pedagogical approaches these spaces utilize can play an integral role in reversing language shift. Developed by Fishman, the process of reversing language shift entails emphasizing variables that promote the vitality of the minority language, reclaiming the language that was lost during the shifting process (Dion, 2009). Regarding pedagogical practices that enable languages to thrive both in and beyond classroom spaces, Hermes and King (2013) stress that "[f]or language revitalization efforts to be successful, they need not just to instruct the language in formal or school domains, but to promote its use and transmission across generations in informal contexts such as the home and family" (p. 127). Language pedagogy that is focused primarily on grammar and vocabulary risks de-emphasizing routine daily usage of the language. Hermes and King (2013) observe that "[d]ecades of research have indicated that school-based efforts—while effective in teaching some vocabulary and grammatical structures alone—tend not to promote use and transmission of the language outside of school" (p. 127). Similarly, Squamish language revivalist Khelsilem observes that, in mainstream classroom settings, "[y]ou might become knowledgeable in aspects of the language, but it won't make you into a conversation speaker that can talk to fluent speakers, or describe events, people, and locations" (quoted by McCue, 2016, CBC). Their insights emphasize that it is not sufficient to teach and learn Indigenous languages without a relational context where conversations and connections with others are actualized. To support the vitality of Indigenous languages, then, it is integral for educators to teach in a way that encourages and promotes daily and intimate use of and conversation within the language.

This intimate use includes centering the interconnections between language, culture, and land. Hermes and King (2013) write that "[w]hile [mainstream] school efforts can provide much needed support and status for Indigenous languages (Hornberger & King, 1996), they also tend to transform that language, both in form and in function, into an academic, frozen, and culturally disconnected register" (p. 127). Teaching Indigenous languages disconnected from their cultures, lands, and worldviews poses an immense hindrance to the true thriving of these languages. As Kroskrity (2018) writes, "any thriving language cannot only 'speak the past,' it must also 'push the envelope' of the language and develop new forms, and contexts of use that fit it to the ever-changing communicative needs of speakers in the present" (Kroskrity, 2018, p. 2). These scholars' words suggest the importance of placing Indigenous language learning in the modern and future-building day-to-day, and within the living relationality between language, culture, land, and worldview.

There are many Indigenous language scholars and activists fighting for changes and implementation of evidence-based language and cultural pedagogy within Canadian education. For example, Mi'kmaw scholar Marie Battiste (2017) popularized the notion of "decolonizing education" by exemplifying the importance of Indigenous language learning and cultures in the classroom. Battiste does tremendous work in battling systemic barriers to education for Indigenous students. Belinda Daniels-Fiss' (2008) work centers on her discovery of what it means to be Nêhiyaw through language learning, and particularly through her participation in a language immersion camp designed as a project for her master's thesis. There are also Indigenous-led language programs within Canadian universities, including (but by no means limited to) the Bachelor of Nsyilxcən Language Fluency program at the University of British Columbia Okanagan, a program that Okanagan scholar Jeanette Armstrong worked to establish; the Boodweh Centre for Indigenous Knowledges and Languages at Trent University, which works closely with Elders and local Indigenous communities; the University of Victoria's Certificate in Indigenous Language Revitalization, which formed through a partnership between the university and the En'owkin Centre, a community-based educational and arts collective run by the Okanagan Indian Educational Resources Society; and the Ciimaan/Kahuwe'yá/Qajaq language program currently led by Jenny Blackbird (Nehiyaw/Finnish) at the Centre for Indigenous Studies at the University of Toronto. These examples demonstrate the potential that universities hold for developing Indigenous pedagogies and supporting Indigenous community-driven and student-driven interest in Indigenous language learning.

Indigenous educators, community members, and language revivalists embody ongoing leadership in developing language programs in classroom settings— programs grounded in community, livingness, relationality, and futurity. As one example, Indigenous communities and teachers have furthered language learning efforts by drawing on digital technology to support kinscape-oriented language pedagogies and practices (Galla, 2016; Hermes & King, 2013). For instance, Indigenous language revivalists have developed the Ojibwemodaa Indigenous language learning software, which has been created especially for children and for families. What is particularly special about Ojibwemodaa and its utilization of digital technology is that the software was created by the community for the community. The software's purpose is to teach learners how to speak Anishinaabemowin in everyday kinscapes, such as conversing with family at home. That is, Ojibwemodaa strives to teach the language in a way that promotes everyday community-based conversational use through immersive simulated components. Since the software is easily accessible at home, it encourages intergenerational family learning that can occur both in and beyond the classroom space (Hermes & King, pp. 127–8).

The digital pedagogy that Indigenous language revivalists and educators are engaged in has helped to address some of the key issues that can occur in language pedagogy, and to expand and transform the possibilities of what classroom language learning can look like. We have observed exciting pedagogical possibilities in Indigenous language learning networks on Twitter. Through community-made hashtag networks like #NativeTwitter, Indigenous people utilize Twitter to connect with other Indigenous peoples. #NativeTwitter is a space where Indigenous people come together to collectively discuss the issues they face, share resources that are relevant to Indigenous life, support the artwork that they create, organize around land-based initiatives, and promote cultural knowledge such as language resurgence. #NativeTwitter provides another opportunity for Indigenous language educators and learners to access their languages in community-immersed ways.

## Methodology

The reflections shared in this chapter are derived from an analysis of the *#DecolonizingDigital* archive at the University of Toronto created by Ansloos (Principal Investigator) and Caranto Morford (Co-investigator), and supported by a team of graduate student researchers, including McCormick.[1] We draw on a collection of this archive entitled *Language Learning and Resurgence*, which focuses on Indigenous language revitalization in the Canadian context. In total, this collection included 3812 social media samples (text-based and multi-media tweets). These tweets were sourced through 1900 Twitter user accounts, and drew on searches of 35 hashtag networks and 57 keywords. The network and keyword search included in this collection are based on the 60 federally recognized Indigenous languages within Canada. In this chapter, we cite specific examples from interviews with participants, and describe text or image-based materials. No direct use of images or social media materials occurs in this chapter in efforts to maintain the anonymity and privacy of individual Twitter users.

## #NativeTwitter as a Pedagogical Community Space for Language Learning

The language learning networks of #NativeTwitter center Indigenous epistem-ologies, thereby enabling Indigenous language students to learn their languages and cultures in relationship with one another. These networks privilege how to name and express cultural worldviews in the language. These networks also form Indigenous language learning communities, which are made possible through digital infrastructures that bring Indigenous language learners together in a shared space with shared goals, despite connecting from diverse geographical locations, nations, and affiliations. We reflect on three overall themes that speak to the cul-tural and land-based teaching approaches occurring within #NativeTwitter: lan-guage kinscapes, relational pedagogy, and place-based bridging. As well, we reflect on a key tension within this collection: issues of access.

### *Language Kinscapes*

A key theme that emerged is the ongoing importance of language learning that is occurring through culturally based language networks — what we call kinscapes (Justice, 2018) in the context of digital networks. Here we understand kinscapes as the culturally grounded yet transnational networks of Indigenous communities navigating digital spaces for the purpose of language resurgence (Justice, 2018). These Twitter-based kinscapes, enabled through the hashtag and keyword, help language learners to learn in kinship connection and relationality with their cultural communities. The *#DecolonizingDigital* archive features, for instance, Indigenous people fostering active and culturally grounded lan-guage learning kinscapes on Twitter through encouraging Indigenous language learners to use particular hashtags to practice their language and build com-munity. By community-building, we mean people building relationships across both digital networks and in analogue spaces. These hashtags are numerous and include #SpeakMikmaq, #CreeWordoftheDay, #SpeakOjibweToMe, and #SpeakGwichinToMe. Other tweets in the archive exemplify how Indigenous people build and expand their kinscape communities with these hashtags to shout out, encourage, build a following, and support the work of fellow Indigenous lan-guage revivalists (#DecolonizingDigital Archive).

Learning alongside other members of the community is a crucial aspect of meaningful language pedagogy. Dallas Hunt has emphasized, for example, how integral it is to be able to have conversations in the language that you are learning. Speaking of Indigenous language kinscapes on Twitter, he says,

> [T]here is the ability for exchange and conversation and all of these things [...E]ventually people would talk to me about it, and sometimes it'd be other Cree speakers, and I'd think, "Okay, [...] this is awesome." And then

some people would write to me all in Cree, and so I would write back to them, and sometimes they would write complex sentences, and then I would have to go, "Oh wow, okay," and sit down and parse what was being said to me, which I found incredibly generative because it's the closest you can get to speaking orally with somebody.

*Dallas Hunt, personal communication, December 3, 2019*

Here, Dallas describes Indigenous language as being connection and intimacy with other community members. Learning with community motivates and drives language learning forward. The practice of language learning concerns closeness and developing understandings of others, as is exemplified by the practice of language learning networks on Twitter.

## Relational Pedagogy

Related to the importance of learning one's language within kinscapes, a key theme that emerged in this study was the importance of relational language practices and pedagogy; that is, learning language in relation to the cultural traditions, knowledges, laws, protocols, and landscapes from which the language emerged and continues to live. Throughout the findings, Indigenous language revivalists incorporate into their teachings culturally significant concepts like the worldview that all of creation is in relationship, encompassed in various phrases across distinct Indigenous languages that translate roughly into English as "all my relations." Language itself is often framed as being in close relations with land and place-based, human and more-than-human, and intergenerational knowledge requiring various relational protocols. For instance, the archive contains tweets teaching Indigenous place names and unpacking how the meaning of these place names reveal the ways in which humans, animals, the lands, and waters interact with one another within the place and the laws that should be honored to keep these relationships healthy.

The practice of learning language is therefore embedded within dynamic relations and protocols and necessitates community engagement and relational accountability of individuals to broader relations. This dynamism illustrates that the language is animated in multi-dimensional and many-faceted ways: in the verb sense as living and transforming, in relevance for current and future generations, and in intergenerational community engagement and accountability.

## Place-based Bridging

Indigenous educators have long commented on the importance of land-based pedagogical approaches. Anishinaabe writer Leanne Betasamosake Simpson (2017) says that "Indigenous education is not Indigenous or education from within our intellectual practices unless it comes through the land [...E]ducation comes from the roots up. It comes from being enveloped by land" (p. 154). Thus, Indigenous language learning must be approached through land-based pedagogy. Indeed, our findings point to the importance of considering language learning as a bridge to land-based relations, and point to the ways in which language is always grounded in specific places and peoples.

It is common to think of online spaces as landless (Gaertner, 2016). However, in our conceptualization of digital technologies, we must not overlook or forget that digital technologies and infrastructures are built on and come from the land. Tweets often reclaim Indigenous place-based knowledges and assert that Canada is Indigenous land by sharing the Indigenous place names of various well-known landscapes in Canada: examples from the *#DecolonizingDigital* archive include place names in Tlingit, Sḵwx̱wú7mesh, Secwepemctsin, Anishinaabemowin, and nêhiyawêwin. This is significant because it demonstrates how users utilize technological territories to map and reclaim Indigenous lands in physical and digital spaces. This asserts Indigenous values and sovereignty, carving out space in both real and imagined ways.

Indigenous language revivalists on Twitter often offer teachings that are grounded in place, by using photographs of, teachings from, stories about, and experiences on the land to share and teach the language. The deep connections between online and land-based spaces are powerfully conveyed in a lengthy thread within the *#DecolonizingDigital* archive, which teaches Gwichin words for various types of plant and animal life within Gwichin territory through a series of land-based photos. These photos are shared alongside teachings about the cultural uses of the sacred plants and animals, as well as stories of relationality between the Gwichin and these plants and animals.

The place-based realities of language are also conveyed through tweets that recognize the regional dialects of a particular homeland. Tweets by language teachers and revivalists from different communities show that the same word may be spelled and spoken differently by various communities living in distinct geographical settings. In an interview for the archive, Bryson Syliboy speaks to this aspect of Twitter as well:

> With the Mi'kmaw language too, I'll say a certain word but my other Mi'kmaw followers will be like, "Oh, you can say it this way too." I'm pretty sure we have five dialects in Mi'kmaw. I'm from Cape Breton so it's not necessarily the same word in Quebec. It's continuing learning as well for me, because I got to realize that there are different dialects of my language.
> *Bryson Syliboy, personal communication, April 17, 2020*

The opportunity to engage with regional dialects through Twitter posts brings the place-based life of language into transnational online spaces, thus weaving digital and land together.

## Issues of Access

One of the key tensions regarding Indigenous language learning environments is issues of access to language learning opportunities. Barriers to access include where opportunities are housed, settler dominance within these spaces, and the often-high financial cost to access these opportunities.

Many Indigenous language programs are offered in post-secondary settings. Though this is changing due to the leadership of Indigenous scholars and community members who have been developing language programming in various elementary, secondary, and post-secondary settings, Western institutional environments can often be unwelcoming for Indigenous learners. Hunt articulates this when he states in an interview for *#DecolonizingDigital*:

> [W]hat's lost when they're within these very sanctioned and sanitized white walls of the institution? [...] You're learning your language, and there's this smiling white guy in robes staring down at you in this [...] portrait [...T]hese are all incredibly important, difficult, and sometimes intractable questions of [...] power imbalances or asymmetries.
>
> *Dallas Hunt, personal communication, December 3, 2019*

Hunt's words speak to how, though post-secondary institutions have been working to address their historical lack of diversity and inclusivity, they still continue to celebrate settler colonial perspectives and knowledges and operate, by and large, through settler colonial frameworks.

The discomfort of being in this type of environment is exacerbated when not only the walls of the institution are settler colonial, but the classroom body is as well. Odjick speaks to this issue, stating: "[S]ay, for example, we set up a class in Toronto and [...] the people attending the class were Native and non-Native [...] If, for example, the non-Native people were more proficient with the language than the Native people, it might be weird for Native people to be corrected, for example, by non-Native people" (Jay Odjick, personal communication, November 4, 2019). Odjick's words make clear the importance of Indigenous language learners having a safe and welcoming language learning environment, where they can engage with their languages without the worry of settler incursion. While learning an Indigenous language is a privilege for a settler, it is an inherent right for Indigenous people, and it must be treated as such.

Furthermore, university settings also pose financial barriers to Indigenous language learning. Squamish language revivalist Khelsilem says that "the key to developing a community of language speakers is to make it financially viable for language students" (quoted by McCue, 2016, CBC). Post-secondary based classes tend to be expensive, rendering them inaccessible for too many people who should have priority in these spaces. The often-high fees to take Indigenous language courses at post-secondary institutions bars the next generation of Indigenous people from the opportunity to re-connect.

While it is crucial that institutions of learning continue to create and ensure safe, welcoming, and financially accessible in-person spaces for Indigenous people to learn their languages within community, and while online learning spaces like Twitter language networks cannot and should not replace the opportunity and experience of learning on the land in community, digital language learning environments can offer important and life-nourishing community-based spaces and approaches to language learning that recognize and strive to address some of the issues of accessibility discussed above.

We recognize that language learning within digital spaces raises other issues of access. While many Indigenous language learners are able to access the internet and Twitter on a regular basis, the question of computer access and stable internet access is an ongoing issue, and there are Indigenous people and communities that do not have ready access to stable internet. This is an issue that must be addressed. Especially given how much our day-to-day lives currently rely on ready access to digital infrastructures, widespread access to reliable internet must be seen as a basic human right. Furthermore, Twitter currently lacks syllabics and phonetic features integral to many Indigenous languages, and does not have translation abilities for Indigenous languages at the time of writing this chapter (2021). And, given the publicness of Twitter, Indigenous online community spaces can become targets of threats and racism, when confrontational and discriminatory non-Indigenous people insert themselves into these learning networks. Several Indigenous Twitter users who were interviewed for *#DecolonizingDigital* discussed how they often feel the need to censor what they post on the platform to avoid harassment from non-Indigenous people on Twitter, or how Indigenous people they know have chosen to stop using the platform because of the toxic interactions they have had with non-Indigenous users.

At the same time, and significantly, digital language networks and Twitter-based kinscapes can open accessibility to those who may not live near nor have the financial means to attend in-person classes. Syliboy shares that, as someone living in "an isolated community, not on the reserve," online learning environments like Twitter "bring[…] me closer […] to the community, to the culture. It's nice to see tweets or videos or pictures of my culture […] It makes you feel less isolated" (Bryson Syliboy, personal communication, April 17, 2020). Since a social media space like "Twitter has low financial and technological barriers to entry," (Jackson et. al 2020, p. xxx), anyone who has access to digital infrastructures and technologies is able to join in the online language learning experiences occurring through the platform. Furthermore, since these online language environments are often run by and for Indigenous community members, they enable a focus on community that is not always permitted in settler dominant institutional spaces. This ability to offer culturally centered and land-based approaches to language on Twitter is critical, because it is not always possible or accessible for Indigenous language learners to learn their languages on their homelands. According to the Canadian Census (2016), most registered Indians live in urban areas (45%), while 40% of registered Indians live on reserve. A minority of registered Indians live off reserve in rural areas (14%). Regarding Non-Status Indians, the majority live in urban areas (76%). As such, many Indigenous peoples are physically dislocated from their homelands and language-speaking communities. At the same time, living in urban centers, while representing traditional territories, may also pose risks associated with separation from cultural and linguistic communities. Thus, language learning networks on Twitter especially enable culturally based and land-based learning for those who live physically at a distance from their own home communities.

## Looking Forward: Connecting Indigenous Languages with Youth and Schools

Twitter is a tool and an environment that teachers are incorporating into their classrooms and curricula. There are various reasons why it is an appealing kind of platform for teaching. Educators have utilized the platform to teach students about media literacy, for instance (Twitter and UNESCO). Further, it enables multiple different ways of engaging with material. Students can engage with material through reading and, in that act of reading, listening to and witnessing the teachings, insights, and experiences that people offer through tweets. The platform also enables more active forms of participation. If you are someone who has a Twitter account, then you can actively participate in the knowledge production that is occurring by directly responding to tweets with your own experiences, perspectives, and insights about a topic, and taking on an active role in Twitter-based conversations. This kind of experience enables students to be learners, but also teachers and knowledge sharers. With regard to Indigenous language learning with and through Twitter, the opportunity to actively participate in Twitter conversations in and about Indigenous languages provides Indigenous youth — including those living away from their homelands — the chance to engage in current dialogue with their community, rooted in real-world events and circumstances. This type of active and embodied engagement transcends static memorization of a language and its grammatical structures, illuminating a living language and how it is practiced in day-to-day ways in community and connection with others.

Indeed, when it comes to the teaching of Indigenous languages and Fishman's theory of reversing language shift, it is integral that it is not just grammar, vocabulary, and rote memorization that is taught (Hermes and King, p. 127), but that an embodied and daily relationship with the language is taught through the centering of lived experiences, nation-specific worldviews, cultural knowledge, and place-based knowledge embedded within the language. Studying the #DecolonizingDigital archive illuminates that Indigenous language learning environments on Twitter offer this kind of multifaceted and culturally rooted teaching of language, centered in kinscapes, grounded in homelands, and intertwined with Indigenous laws and epistemologies in the here and now. Thus, Indigenous language learning environments on Twitter offer pedagogical values, practices, and lessons that can augment, enhance, and enrich language learning classes and curricula.

But there are also ethical considerations and responsibilities. Teaching Indigenous languages to Indigenous youth within the Canadian school system is fraught with all the political dynamics of negotiating settler colonial realities. Historically and in contemporary reality, schools are implicated within the settler colonial project. Educators who are interested in incorporating such social media platforms and environments into their classrooms, lesson plans, and curricula must be accountable for the harms of language learning spaces that have been discussed in this chapter, and must work to avoid replicating these cycles: for instance, if your classroom has both Indigenous and non-Indigenous students, be mindful that non-Indigenous students do not trespass into these community-led and community-centered online environments. Within the classroom community, curricula, and teaching/learning etiquette, the principles of Indigenous studies must be at the foreground. These principles are: respect, responsibility, relationship, and reciprocity (Kirkness & Barnhardt, 1991; Pidgeon, 2008, 2014, 2016; Restoule, 2008; Tessaro et al., 2018). A key aspect of honoring these principles is to center an ethics of consent when considering the pedagogical possibilities of these spaces. If we think about the platform of Twitter through colonial ways of knowing, we might think that because Twitter is a largely public space, everyone and anyone should be able to interact with the knowledge publicly posted on it — but that is not necessarily ethical, since not all knowledge sharing and dialogue within the Twitter environment is meant for everyone, even if publicly posted. As Dorothy Kim and Eunsong Kim share in *The #TwitterEthicsManifesto* (2014), when engaging with Twitter as a space of pedagogical possibilities, "[w]e must rethink and consider more radical epistemologies that will push forward an ongoing cycle of consent, credit, citation, and participation." In terms of the ethical practice for the *#DecolonizingDigital* project, we are always in the process of re-thinking and learning, and we are ever-open to shifting our practice to be as responsible, accountable, and ethical as possible: currently, members of the project reach out to Indigenous writers whose tweets we would like to directly cite in our scholarly work, and we share the writing with them throughout the writing process when requested, as well as upon completion and publication of the writing.

Social media is a fraught, complex, and messy place. The public nature of digital environments like Twitter, how rapidly and easily information can be spread across these platforms, and how information posted on these platforms can be reused, recycled, and recirculated, render these digital environments spaces that are filled with power dynamics and ethical complexities. Teaching in relationship with spaces like Twitter requires a nuanced, situational, culturally conscious, and multi-faceted approach to issues of consent, credit, citation, and participation, particularly regarding Indigenous knowledge and especially since digital environments tend to be dictated by colonial copyright and other colonial legal systems. While we cannot adequately address this issue and these complexities in this chapter, we recognize and recommend the writings of Indigenous new media scholars for further information and learning: for instance, Jennifer Wemigwans' book *A Digital Bundle: Protecting and Promoting Indigenous Knowledge Online* (2018). Indigenous language revitalization activists invite us to broaden pedagogical opportunity and educational contexts, and to think about Indigenous educational opportunities through the lens of decolonial justice, by embedding Indigenous self-determinism and kinscapes as the heart of language pedagogy.

## Conclusion

In this chapter, we have sought to highlight how social media environments might be leveraged for new pedagogical possibilities for Indigenous youth language learning. Through a critical examination of the prominent mainstream research on language learning, as well as emerging Indigenous theories of language learning, we have demonstrated that there are various limitations to approaches that do not center culture and relationality to people and place. Overall, there are inequities in Indigenous language learning and resurgence, driven by disparate accessibility and legibility. Our study has made a case for thinking about social media environments like Twitter as uniquely positioned to guide us in imagining inclusive pedagogical possibilities. Our study of a collection of Indigenous language learning and resurgence materials highlights four key themes including: the dynamics of language kinscapes, the value of relational pedagogy, the need for place-based bridging in language learning, and the current limits of language learning programs. These findings emphasize that pedagogical opportunities lay in the zones of relational engagement and accountability, contextually informed and grounded literacy, and the need for decolonial justice in pedagogical practice. Ultimately, the efforts of Indigenous peoples are fueling digital pedagogical possibilities, and this has substantial implications for how we think about educational spaces for Indigenous youth, particularly to ensure that these spaces are inclusive, relational, connected, and full of the vitality of Indigenous self-determination.

## Note

1  The archive was funded by the Social Sciences and Humanities Research Council in Canada. Our study was approved by our university research ethics board, and data use and analysis were conducted in alignment with the Tri-Council Policy Statement on Ethical Conduct for Research Involving Humans, particularly the standards set for research involving First Nations, Inuit, and Métis Peoples in Canada.

# References

Battiste, M. (2017). *Decolonizing education: Nourishing the learning spirit.* Purich Publishing Inc.

Blackstock, C. (2019). Indigenous child welfare legislation: A historical change or another paper tiger?. *First Peoples Child & Family Review, 14*(1), 5–8.

Census of Canada. (2016). *Annual report to parliament 2020.* Retrieved from www.sac-isc.gc.ca/eng/1602010609492/1602010631711

Dion, S. D. (2009). *Braiding histories: Learning from Aboriginal peoples' experiences and perspectives.* UBC Press.

Fishman, J. (1991). *Reversing language shift.* Multilingual Matters.

Fishman, J. A. (2001). Why is it so hard to save a threatened language?(A perspective on the cases that follow). In Can threatened languages be saved? (pp. 1–22). Clevedon, UK: Multilingual Matters.

Fontaine, L. S. (2017). Redress for linguicide: Residential schools and assimilation in Canada. *British journal of Canadian studies, 30*(2), 183–205.

Gaertner, D. (2016). "A Landless Territory? Augmented Reality, Land, and Indigenous Storytelling in Cyberspace." In D. Reder & L. Morra (Eds.), *Learn, Teach, Challenge: Approaching Indigenous Literatures* (pp. 506–510). Wilfrid Laurier University Press.

Galla, C. K. (2016). Indigenous language revitalization, promotion, and education: Function of digital technology. *Computer assisted language learning, 29*(7), 1137–1151.

Haig-Brown, C. (1988). *Resistance and renewal: Surviving the Indian residential school.* Arsenal Pulp Press.

Haque, E., & Patrick, D. (2015). Indigenous languages and the racial hierarchisation of language policy in Canada. *Journal of Multilingual and Multicultural Development, 36*(1), 27–41.

Hermes, M., & King, K. (2013). Ojibwe language revitalization, multimedia technology, and family language learning. *Language Learning & Technology, 17*(1), 125–144.

Hornberger, N. H., & King, K. A. (1996). Language revitalisation in the Andes: Can the schools reverse language shift?. *Journal of Multilingual and Multicultural Development, 17*(6), 427–441.

Iseke, J. M. (2013). Negotiating Métis culture in Michif: disrupting Indigenous language shift. *Decolonization: Indigeneity, Education & Society, 2*(2).

Jackson, S. J., Bailey, M., & Welles, B. F. (2020). *# HashtagActivism: Networks of Race and Gender Justice.* MIT Press.

Justice, D. H. (2018). *Why Indigenous literatures matter.* Wilfrid Laurier Univ. Press.

Kim, D. and Kim, E. (2014). *The #TwitterEthics Manifesto.* Model View Culture. https://modelviewculture.com/pieces/the-twitterethics-manifesto.

Kirkness, V.J. and Barnhardt, R. (1991). First Nations and Higher Education: The Four R's—Respect, Relevance, Reciprocity, Responsibility. *Journal of American Indian Education, 30*(3), 1–15.

Kroskrity, P. V. (2018). On recognizing persistence in the Indigenous language ideologies of multilingualism in two Native American Communities. *Language & Communication, 62*, 133–144.

McCue, D. (2016). *Skwomesh language activist to launch "trailblazing" immersion course at B.C. university.* CBC. www.cbc.ca/news/indigenous/skwomesh-language-activist-b-c-university-launch-immersion-course-1.3404541.

Pidgeon, M. E. (2008). *It Takes More than Good Intentions: Institutional Accountability and Responsibility to Indigenous Higher Education.* University of British Columbia.

Restoule, J-P. (2008). The five R's of Indigenous research: Relationship, respect, relevance, responsibility, and reciprocity. *Wise Practices II: Canadian Aboriginal AIDS Network Research and Capacity Building Conference,* Toronto, Ontario, Canada. Workshop.

Saldaña, J. (2016). The coding manual for qualitative researchers. sage.

Simpson, L. (2017). *As We Have Always Done: Indigenous Freedom through Radical Resistance.* University of Minnesota Press.

Starblanket, T. (2017). "Kill the Indian in the child": genocide in international law. In Watson, I. (Ed.). *Indigenous peoples as subjects of international law* (p. 171–200). New York: Taylor & Francis.

Tessaro, D, Restoule, J-P, Gaviria, P, Flessa, J., Lindeman, C., and Scully-Stewart, C. (2018). The Five R's for Indigenizing Online Learning: A Case Study of the First Nations Schools' Principals Course. *Canadian Journal of Native Education, 40*(1), 125–143.

Truth, & Reconciliation Commission of Canada. (2015). *Canada's Residential Schools: The Final Report of the Truth and Reconciliation Commission of Canada (Vol. 1).* McGill-Queen's Press-MQUP.

Twitter and UNESCO. *Teaching and Learning with Twitter.* United Nations Educational, Scientific and Cultural Organization. https://about.twitter.com/content/dam/about-twitter/en/tfg/download/teaching-learning-with-twitter-unesco.pdf.

Wemigwans, J. (2018). *A Digital Bundle: Protecting and Promoting Indigenous Knowledge Online.* University of Regina Press.

# OUR LANGUAGES HOLD THE PULSING HEARTS OF OUR CULTURES

## Questions for Reflection and Further Applications for Practice

*Amanda Claudia Wager*

The personal is political (hooks, 1994). This phrase signifies a continued awareness of our privileges and oppressions within society. The authors of the *Roots* section describe how culture and language are intimately interwoven, breathe the same air, walk through the same puddles; and how language is deeply rooted in who we are even while colonialism continues to divest Indigenous peoples of lands and languages on a global scale. In these chapters, we hear a deep call to activism through art and language. Activism is more about a world-view or a life-long commitment to community organizing, rather than participation at a protest. Activism is a way of being, a way of thinking, a way of acting (Wager & Goessling, 2020). The same is true of art, which provides myriad channels for activism. It is a part of who we are and a way that we have learned to walk in the world and make sense of it, as with culture. These identities inform our pedagogical choices. We resist through our pedagogy, by practicing what is central to us, in spite of the sociopolitical pressures of the institutions, borders, and governments in which we are embedded.

### *Roots:* Summary of Chapters

Introducing this section, Becky Thiessen, a community artist and researcher, along with Youth Researcher contributors MJ, Charlie, Jaydin, Junior, highlighted a collaboration among an intergenerational group of respected Elders, youth researchers, teachers, facilitators, community members, and artists, who used media creations and local languages to disseminate their findings. Yamila Hussein-Shannan and Khitam Edelbi then discussed the use of Playback Theater to create spaces for Palestinian adolescents to practice intentional listening as they narrated and enacted their and others' stories, expressing how they make sense

DOI: 10.4324/9781003302186-10

of the world around them while cultivating inner and collective strength. From South Africa, Lorato Trok emphasized the importance of Indigenous knowledge systems via the creation of children's books in the original and endangered N|uu language. Next, Maria Schwedhelm Ramirez illustrated and analyzed a university course created ethnodrama, underscoring the value of the arts and performance pedagogies to foster critical ideological awareness, advocacy, and activism for language reclamation in Oaxaca, Mexico. Through dialogue, Cherie Okada-Carlson and Marit Dewhurst reflected on how both Hawaiian language and weaving-specific terminology can be a space for historical, relational, and cultural learning. Joshua Schwab Cartas demonstrated how youth reawaken their relationship with their ancestral language of diidxazá and their Elders through participatory and visual use of cellphilms (short videos shot on a cellphone). Finally, Ashley Caranto Morford, Samantha McCormick, and Jeffrey Ansloos examined how Indigenous communities transform Twitter into a learning environment for their ancestral languages.

## Questions for Reflection

*What are your learners' relationship with the land? What anchors their identity and how can you make that visible and build on it?*

*What is the relationship between the arts, culture, language, family, and community? Why do we need to live in communities? How does the school become a welcoming place for all the learners and their families from diverse communities, cultures, and languages?*

*Why do teachers need to be culturally responsive to each of their learners, families, and communities? And how can teachers use linguistic, cultural, and ethnic diversity as a positive force in promoting equity in effective education for all learners and their families?*

*How do prejudice, discrimination, and invisibility in the curriculum affect people (children, youth, adults) and their perception of their self, families, communities, languages, and cultures?*

*What are the challenges and triumphs you face related to advocating for equity and justice? How might we utilize the arts to infuse these actions with self-care and reflection?*

*Why is it important for antiracism and antidiscrimination to be at the core of education?*

## Applications for Practice

Using art practices to promote social justice in classrooms and educational settings requires intentional planning and preparation (Wager & Goessling, 2020). Pedagogically, begin by identifying the goal of the art practice. Ask and answer for yourself why you are doing this specific practice with this group and what you want it to evoke in participants. Your answers should guide the selection of materials and artform.

### Introductions: Where are You from? Who are Your People?

- Give all learners a piece of paper. For 5 minutes draw the answer to: *Where are you from?*
- In a sharing circle, everybody is given the opportunity to share and explain their drawing to the group.
- Give all learners another piece of paper. For 5 minutes draw the answer to: *Who are your people?*
- In a sharing circle, everybody is given the opportunity to share and explain their drawing to the group.

This activity helps us learn to be able to think more critically about these questions and see, through all participants' drawings, that there are multiple ways that they can be answered. It is important for participants to understand that many learners get asked the first question all the time.

### Warm-up: I Come from a Place That …

Ask learners to complete the sentence "I come from a place that…". For example, "I come from a place that eats rice at every meal." Have them write down their sentence(s). Standing in a large circle with the entire group, one person starts by saying their sentence. If others come from the same place, then they will stomp or clap their hands. This fun activity involves movement and learners share similarities and differences with each other that they may not know. It has the potential to create an initial sense of connection and community.

### Journaling: Personal Vision of the Responsive Classroom

Create a personal vision statement on the culturally and linguistically responsive classroom. As you write your statement consider the following questions:

1. How does your cultural identity influence you as an educator? What characterizes your involvement in the educational process? What have been your challenges and rewards? What advantages and privileges have you received? What barriers have you faced? (see McIntosh, 1988)
2. Which theoretical framework(s) support your understanding of diversity, equity, multicultural education?
3. Which contemporary issue(s) do you feel are most important in education practice?

4.  How will you apply what you have learned thus far to construct a cultur- ally and linguistically responsive classroom? How will you engage family and community members?
5.  What supports will you need?
6.  What does a culturally and linguistically responsive classroom *look* like? Find images that reflect your vision of a responsive classroom.
7.  What are the steps you need to take to work toward that vision?

## Mandalas for Self-Inquiry

Mandala is a Sanskrit word for circle and in the Buddhist tradition symbolizes wholeness or center. Carl Jung popularized the use of mandalas for personal growth and as a tool for consciousness-raising, self-exploration, and wellness. Mandalas have been used in teacher education to address issues of community building through self-discovery that integrate both the head and heart (Young, 2001) and as a tool to facilitate learners' development and growth (Pisarik & Larson, 2011).

Use a three-part process to guide learners or participants through transforma- tive art-making (Wager & Goessling, 2020). First, preparation should entail creating the art-making space, which is important when working in classrooms and non- traditional studio spaces. This process begins with building trust by co-creating a collective space. Once participants arrive, begin with a visualization or meditation and intention setting activity. Explain what you are going to do and allow time for questions. Second, is art-making time. Continue creating the space with music or by using a meditation bell to signal participants to recall their intention. Pay careful attention to how individuals and the group are processing the activity. Third, is writing and reflecting. Translating the non-verbal activity to text format is crucial to the internalization process (Hieb, 2005). In visual art, this involves non-judgmental gazing and observation of the creation. The written reflection or discussion can be scaffolded by a prompt or instructions. Provocations may guide deeper introspection throughout the reflective writing process, advancing from what do you see?, to how did and do you feel? Illustrate this process in the man- dala practice described below.

> *Stage I: Preparation:* Schedule quiet time in a space that allows you to connect to your inner self. Gather artifacts that reflect your values and commitment to your family, culture, language, or whatever topic intrigues your learners. Ponder this question about the topic: what is important to you in the past, present, and future? Gather your art materials and set your intention for the art practice that connects to your identities as language learners—activists— educators—artists, etc.; your "whys"; and possibilities and limitations of this work.

*Stage II: Creation:* Trace a large circle for the mandala on a large piece of paper. Fill the page with lines, colors, shapes, patterns, and symbols guided by your intention and guiding question(s). Let yourself go, follow your intuition, play.

*Stage III: Reflective Writing & Discussion:* Gaze at your creation, how do you feel? Look for meaning and significance in your design: notice the lines, shapes, colors, symbols, sizes of each. What are the relationships (What overlaps? Connects? What is close? Far?)? What does this mean to you and what emotions come up? Share your mandalas in groups or pairs.

### Museum-Curated Autobiography

- Go to a museum with a group/class of learners. Walk through the exhibits.
- Where do you see your experience reflected (or not) in the artifacts? Whose story is visible? What stories are missing? Who is in the museum?
- Find a place in the museum to sit down alone. Write down everything you hear, see, smell, etc., for 20 minutes. Use all of your senses. Write without stopping.
- Take what you have written and connect it to telling a story about yourself, your history, your culture, your language; think about how certain sounds, smells, and senses connect to your memories.
- How would you curate your story in the museum? What artifacts would you include? How would you organize them?
- You can extend this in the classroom by searching for images of historical artifacts, artwork, or family objects of significance. Write the labels on the wall. Learners can create a digital visual autobiography.

### Mapping the Neighborhood Walk(s):

Maps help us make sense of the world. They allow us to visualize things, make connections, document them, represent them. Look at artists that work with maps for inspiration.

Get to know the neighborhood and community of the school you work, especially if you do not live in the community. Walk around, map your trajectory, you can draw a rough map or use an existing map from the web. If possible, visit the neighborhood more than once, walking around, observing, and listening. Try to visit local schools, stores, and health, service, and community agencies. Rework your draft as you go or start a new one; add elements to your map, use symbols, words, colors. Are some places more important than others? Make them bigger. Try to talk with people about their experiences in a specific language-community, broader community-at-large and the school system. How can you represent them in a map? Pay attention to things such as geometric shapes in building designs, kinds of plant life and rocks, kinds of stores, styles of music, kinds of games played by children, etc. Then make a list of things you can use to build upon as examples or lessons.

Make maps of all your findings. Some of you will find a lot of representation of certain ethnicities through local businesses and community centers but some of you will find almost no representation. That's okay. The point is to think about why an ethnic community is represented or why they are not and discuss that. If they are not represented it may be that there is a nearby community that is vibrant in its representation of this group. Or they may have chosen to move away from their ethnic group for certain schools, for convenience to work or other reasons. The main thing is to think about why it is the way it is and how that impacts families and learners. Naturally, refrain from making stereotypical judgments about the neighborhood. Use your experience to re-vision geographies and create subjective maps with your learners.

### Re-visioning Geographies: Mapping Our Experience

Select a population, place, or historical concept to investigate (you may work from a standard or lesson already in your curriculum). Research maps related to what you are investigating. Work with first person narratives and other historical sources. Using existing maps, copy, trace, or otherwise draw from existing maps to re-imagine a map based on a personal or historical narrative. Think about these questions:

- What is the map of your own story?
- How can you represent the physical, cultural, or environmental impact of history on a place?
- Tell a story and map of how it could have been otherwise.
- Tell a story of possible futures. What kind of map could you imagine?

For younger learners, maps can be based on family stories and their imagination. They can map their house, neighborhood, and other significant places. They can track family trajectories or their own. What is their connection to the land?

Other ideas can be based on listening. Think about these questions: What sounds do you hear? Listen to languages around you. What kinds of words are spoken where? When? With whom? What are your spaces? Create a sound map, add symbols to represent meaning. Some may be large, others small, colors can represent ideas.

High school and older learners can research historical, cultural, and or environmental issues. Ask the same questions as above. Create new maps to represent their informed vision of the past, present, and potential visions of the future. Examples of issues can include anything from global warming to forced migrations or shifts in cultural representation.

### Mapping Resources:

West, A. (2011). *Mapping the intelligence of artistic work: An exploratory guide to thinking and writing*. Moth Press.

Ulrich, H. (Ed.). (2014). *Mapping it out: An alternative atlas of contemporary cartography*. Thames and Hudson.

## Collaborative Social Issue Project and Reflection

Investigate a social issue in your community related to language, culture and community. In collaboration with peers, develop a presentation of the issue using multiple art mediums to challenge, question, represent, or advocate for ideas about that issue. Develop an advocacy piece and reflection to document your learning about the role of art in research and advocacy in language, culture, and community.

- DIGITAL: Using a device find at least 10 public domain images that communicate this issue through your lens. Always cite artists.
  - *Share* images with your groups
  - How would this be useful with learners?
- PERFORMANCE (DANCE/MUSIC/DRAMA): Create a skit that presents multiple perspectives of the social issue, using the multiple languages of the learners (if applicable), and perform the skits for each other.
  - *Imagine* how these works might connect with your teaching and learning. How might you learn more about the topic represented?
- MINI LESSON: *Create* a mini lesson in small groups with these works.
  - *Critique* your lesson – how could it be improved with time and additional resources?
  - *Exhibit* or *share* your lesson with fellow learners.

## Wrap-Up: Stereotypes

This activity is useful at the end of a lesson/workshop. Ask learners to silently complete the sentence: "One thing you would not know about me from looking at me is …". They can write down their answers. Then sit in a sharing circle and have learners share their sentences.

> "Language is not a little, airtight, clean, finished container of something. It's permeable, alive. It moves." –Lizette Alvarez

## References

Hieb, M. (2005). *Inner journeying through art-journaling: Learning to see and record your life as a work of art*. Jessica Kingsley Publishers.

hooks, b. (1994). *Teaching to transgress: Education as the practice of freedom*. Routledge.

McIntosh, P. (1988). White privilege: Unpacking the invisible knapsack. Excerpted essay reprinted from Independent School.

Pisarik, C. T., & Larson, K. R. (2011). Facilitating college learners' authenticity and psychological well-being through the use of mandalas: An empirical study. *Journal of Humanistic Counseling, 50*, 84–98.

Wager, A. C. & Goessling, K. P. (2020). Working toward sustainable creative social justice practices: Advancing equity and justice in the academy. In H. Mreiwed, M. R. Carter, & C. Mitchell (Eds.), *Art as an agent for social change* (pp. 252–261). Brill/Sense. https://doi.org/10.1163/9789004442870.

Young, A. J. (2001). Mandalas: Circling the square in education. *ENCOUNTER: Education for meaning and social justice, 14*(3), 25–33.

# PART II
# Routes

# STEP BACK, LEAP FORWARD

*Guy Michel Telemaque and Rocky Cotard*

## Guy Michel Telemaque, born 1966, Queens NY, USA

As a child, Haiti was the place my father came from, but it felt distant to me (see Figure I2.1). In the early 1960s, my parents fled when "Papa Doc" Duvalier's threats to my father's life and family became too much to bear. They moved to Queens, where I was born, and raised me with a clear understanding that they had great pride for where they came from, telling stories of family and society, but our life would forever be in the United States. Haitian was the food we ate and the music we listened to. In 1972, we moved to Miami and I spent a childhood surrounded by immigrant kids from Cuba and Colombia. My days were spent playing sports in the neighborhood and exploring the adjacent construction sites. English was the language of creative adventure. Evenings and nighttime were about family rituals, lived through in French as my parents conversed in Kreyol. Often, we shared experiences that were brought from afar and made commonplace, like the backyard dug-in fire pit, surrounded by onlooking fruit trees planted by my father. Although I was pushed around by bigger kids in school, because I had darker skin and kinky hair, I have always cherished that existence, dramatically marred by the death of my mother to sickle cell anemia when I was 10.

When I was 13 my father wanted my 16-year-old brother and I to go with him to see his homeland. I didn't want to go, but the month we spent traveling throughout the country had a profoundly positive effect on me. I struggled to communicate in Kreyol, but I saw a world so different from anything I knew, and I experienced things I could never have imagined. Everything was striking – the graceful resilience of the people, the creative vibrancy of the culture, and the stunning beauty of the land. Even in the moment, I knew I would never see my life (or anything else in the United States) the same way.

DOI: 10.4324/9781003302186-12

**FIGURE 12.1** Ongoing work from Haiti. The composite design reflects the mis-connectedness I have with my family, my past and Haiti.

In college, I turned to art and photography, worked at the Southeast Museum of Photography, and taught photo in Central Florida. All this led me to the Massachusetts College of Art and Design for an MFA and a teaching position at the Boston Arts Academy (BAA). Throughout, I stayed very close to my father, but increasingly distant from Haiti. As successes came, I was subconsciously becoming more confident as an American.

From his Miami home, while watching the devastating news about the earthquake in Haiti, my father suffered another blow to his heart. In the preceding 20+ years, he had struggled with both cardiac issues and more than one stroke. The images of his homeland crumbling proved to be the beginning of the end of his life. As an artistic-response, to honor his life and greatness, I once again traveled to Haiti to do service work, supporting a rural community center in St. Raphael. Returning to the island reignited everything I had experienced before, but now I was an adult, capable of using this emotional re-stimulation to support others. I spoke more Kreyol in those 2 weeks than I had all my life. Sensing my father's presence as often as I did, I vowed to keep reconnecting with the Haitian culture and people. I didn't know it would be so rewarding.

Upon my return I organized a multi-disciplinary week of Haitian art-centered events, highlighted by an exhibition of three visiting pre-eminent Haitian painters, Gontran Durocher, Ronald Mevs, and Philippe Dodard. Rocky, one of my students at BAA, attended the events. Viewing the exhibition while spending a week with the visiting artists and meeting the ambassador of Haiti made a lasting impression on him. He saw his past reflected in their imagery.

Two years later, while a student at Lesley University College of Art and Design, Rocky contacted me. He said that throughout his studies he had learned about European and American art, but not much about Haitian art. He asked if I knew of any study abroad programs in Haiti. I said I did not, so we created one.

## Rocky, born 1996, Mirebalais, Haiti

Nothing sends me down an existential crisis like the question "Who are you?" In all honesty, the answer is always changing definitions as I am constantly adapting to different parts of life. What has remained constant throughout has been that my name is Rocky Cotard, I make art, I was born in Haiti, and I love the experience of life. Within all of these parts of my being there is a story.

Some of my stories are simple, like my name. I was named Rocky because upon arriving to the United States my father saw one of the Rocky movies. Other stories

**FIGURE 12.2** *Bourik Chaje* (Donkeys Burdern).

**FIGURE 12.3** *Lakou* (Yard).

are complex, like my relation to my Haitian culture while living in the United States. My culture is filled with great examples of courage and leadership; one of the foremost pieces of our history is about our formation. On January 1, 1804 Haitians claimed their freedom by defeating the opposing European forces. That made us the first nation to take form by defeating a European power during the mass enslavement of human beings. This fosters a sense of pride but, even more so, a sense of power.

I was 7 years old when I left Haiti. Arriving in the United States I experienced a sharp cultural shift, but I quickly assimilated. When I began college, I found that a lot of my cultural identity was viewed through one lens, as an impoverished nation. This view was in great conflict with the reality of my experience in Haiti growing up, where love and a sense of community enabled people to continue forward.

With the help of my high school teacher, Mr. Telemaque, I created an opportunity to go to Haiti and redefine my views on my culture. Within the educational curriculum and popular media in the United States, Haiti is described as a place stricken with poverty and disaster. Working with amazing Haitian artists I was able to dispel any encroaching doubt on the variety of beautiful experiences in Haiti. This led to a sort of awakening to reclaim my identity through my art (see Figures I2.2 and I2.3). I learned that the image of Haiti intersects between distance and time, that the Haiti that I left when I was 7 years old has physically changed, but the pillars remain. From that point forward my work shifted focus to instilling a sense of Haitian cultural pride through my artwork for those viewers who may not have the opportunity to visit the country.

# 7

# REIMAGINING LANGUAGE CURRICULUM

## Black Language and Literacy Education Through Hip-Hop and Rap Inclusion

*Chelsea Jimenez*

> *I was hip-hop outside the classroom and student inside it. There was no space for both at once. As well-versed as I could be in the language of hip-hop, that knowledge did not provide me with any source of power or access inside academic spaces. While I saw myself in hip-hop, I did not see myself in classroom texts. Ultimately, I was only marginally involved in my own education.*
>
> Kelly, 2013, p. 52

## Introduction

We are currently living in a time where culturally and linguistically diverse student populations are at an all-time high (NCES, 2021). Yet, U.S. public schools are failing to engage and educate these pupils in culturally relevant or sustaining ways, as the national and state level standards, curriculum, and teaching practices are often based in Eurocentricity. This is especially evident in language curriculum, known as English Language Arts (ELA) education. While there are many variations of English, standardized English is the variety that is expected and utilized within social mainstream, professional, and educational spaces (Gottlieb & Slavit-Ernst, 2014; Wheeler & Swords, 2006; Wolfram, Adger, & Christian, 1999). In maintaining standardized English as the language of academia, canonical texts, such as *Romeo and Juliet*, *Frankenstein*, and *Ulysses*, are the basis for instruction and curriculum. For students who do not speak standardized English in their homes and communities, being immersed in such spaces may be difficult to navigate. This is the case for many Black students who speak African American Language (AAL). Despite Black students making up a significant proportion of the public-school student population, their cultures, arts, literacies, and ways of being are not reflected within the curriculum. AAL is the home language of the majority of

DOI: 10.4324/9781003302186-13

Black American people; however, it is not taught or supported in classrooms across the country. While AAL is celebrated across the globe by people of all races and backgrounds through the streaming of Hip-Hop and Rap music, it is often not seen as a relevant or valuable resource in academic achievement or advancement. Being juxtaposed with standardized English, AAL is often reduced to a colloquial variety, one relegated to the ghettos, not one for the scholars. However, rappers, songwriters, singers, and artists of many mediums have continuously shown the intricacies of how the speech of Black America can be used to teach, transform, and test our understanding of language and communication.

While Hip-Hop and Rap are typically thought of as entertainment, they can also be used as educational resources to support students in reading, writing, listening, and speaking through poetry writing (regular or slam), storytelling, narrative writing, songwriting, spoken word, and cyphers. While students have been taught how Shakespeare used form, flow, rhyme, and other language features to write lines of verse and sonnet, students can also be taught about the ways J Cole, for example, used the same practices in modern day to talk about race, gender, class, and power. When we see aspects of a culture as acceptable only for entertainment purposes, we miss out on the rich brilliance of knowledge that is housed in our students' minds and communities. In addition, when Hip-Hop and Rap have been used in curriculum, it has often been used in comparison to texts from the literary canon. By juxtaposing Hip-Hop and Rap as a bridge or a supplement to existing curriculum, we are failing to remedy the cultural inequity that is occurring in ELA classrooms across the country.

Shifting the power for whose cultures and languages matter is essential for our Black students to feel welcomed, supported, and appreciated in academia. What if we challenged the way we view and interact with Black languages in K-12 educational spaces? What if highlighting a language such as AAL could center the brilliance of Black literacy, as well as expose non-Black students to a linguistic resource of wealth and community? What if Hip-Hop and Rap songs could be viewed as texts, and artists as educators and culture bearers? In this chapter, I propose that we as educators have an opportunity to reimagine our approaches to language curriculum, through interrogating our biases, challenging our existing ways of knowing, and opening the door for learning, embracing, and uplifting Black language and literacy in our classrooms. This chapter will provide a historical and current context of language and culture in schools and society in the United States, with a focus on AAL, standardized English (SE), Hip-Hop culture, and the Rap genre. Finally, I share some resources and methods that teachers can use to supplement the inclusion of AAL, Hip-Hop, and Rap in their language curriculum.

## African American Language: A Language of Black Struggle, Beauty, and Heritage

The language of Black America, a speech variety used in the majority of Black homes and communities across the nation, is known as African American

Language, or AAL. It has been known by many names, such as Ebonics, Black English, African American Vernacular English (AAVE), and more. Delpit (1998) beautifully described AAL as

> …the language spoken by many of our African American children. It is the language they heard as their mothers nursed them and changed their diapers and played peek-a-boo with them. It is the language through which they first encountered love, nurturance, and joy.
>
> *p. 17*

It is the first language of the majority of African Americans, regardless of class differences. While some may describe it as a variation rather than its own language system, its deep-rooted history provides context as to why the evolution of AAL cannot be attributed solely to the English language. AAL combines the aspects of European English vocabulary with West African cadence, flow, pronunciations, and grammar in many aspects (Jackson, 1997). However, it is important to understand that the language did not evolve into what we know it as today by chance. The horrific linguistic experience of the enslaved African in the United States differs from that of any other cultural immigrant background by two major distinctions. First was the intentional grouping of people. During the transatlantic slave trade, African people were kidnapped, beaten, and tortured to be owned and used as working chattel. The colonizers were strategic in their efforts to sort and separate people through what is known today as language planning. Language planning was the calculated, insidious practice of separating Africans of the same tribes, communities, and linguistic backgrounds (Baker-Bell, 2020; Baugh, 2015). Colonizers enforced this practice through physical and fatal punishment when African individuals communicated amongst each other, whether through utilizing the same verbal language or other means of body language. Baugh (2015) described this deliberate act of silencing:

> …slave traders routinely separated slaves by language whenever possible upon capture. This practice, of isolating recent captives who shared a common language, was intended to minimize uprisings; if slaves had a harder time communicating, they were less likely to be able to organize revolts. This form of "language planning" was intended to isolate the enslaved African captives from the language(s) they knew and used. Moreover, this linguistic isolation began in West Africa prior to the Atlantic crossing, and as a result of these efforts, no African language survived the Atlantic crossing completely intact.
>
> *p. 293*

Secondly, and incredibly relevant to the academic standing of Black American children today, it was illegal to teach the enslaved African how to read and write upon arrival to the United States. By law, Black bodies were denied access to literacy for any reason (Baugh, 2015). Other immigrant groups that arrived in the United States had the opportunity to speak their native languages with others who arrived from their home country, as well as the opportunity to attend school and learn English as a second language. However, for the enslaved African, this was not the case as they were not only racially segregated, but they were also "linguistically segregated" (Baugh, 2015). This did not stop them however, as the restrictions created the space for new mediums and communications to be formed. AAL became a counter-language, and evolved into mutual means of communicating amongst groups of different tribes and languages, while also creating means for double meanings when outsiders listen to the language. It is the meshing of these language varieties that have shaped AAL into the language system we know today, one of resistance, of community, of solidarity. It has been demonstrated and supported by linguists and education scholars alike (Baker-Bell, 2020; Baugh, 2015; Delpit, 1998; Rickford & Rickford, 2000; Smitherman, 2000) that AAL is a structured, rule-governed language. Whether this language is used by literary greats such as Toni Morrison or by lyrical artists such as Common, AAL is a language of Black artistic expression.

### AAL to Hip-Hop, Peanut Butter to Jelly

AAL is the mother tongue of Hip-Hop and Rap. In explaining the relationship between AAL and Hip-Hop, Smitherman (2000) stated, "It is critical to keep in mind that the racialized rhetoric of Rap music and the Hip-Hop Nation is embodied in the communicative practices of the larger Black speech community. The language of Hip-Hop is African American Language" (p. 271). If Hip-Hop is the finished product, AAL is the medium in which it is delivered. Smitherman (2006) detailed AAL's significance to Hip-Hop:

> The language of Hip Hop originates with Black working and unworking class youth who take patterns and styles of AAL and play with them. The major and most significant changes taking place in AAL today are those generated by [Black urban youth] who are masters of the Word. The best Hip-Hop artists in this group of language pace setters are conscious linguistic innovators who forge new thought in fast forward meter, renewing AAL with syntactical and rhetorical reinventions. These innovations that come out of urban hoods are transforming their linguistic landscape of the English language, contributing not only new, dynamic "slang" words and expressions, but also restructuring and enriching the grammar of English.
>
> *p. 101*

Hip-Hop music is one of the main ways that these linguistic nuances have spread across Black and non-Black communities around the globe. All over the world, there are people who do not speak English yet are able to Rap and sing entire Hip-Hop songs. While AAL is typically not allowed in K-12 academic spaces, it is celebrated every time it is spoken played outside those classrooms. Like other languages, its speakers (primarily the youth) continually produce new phrases and "slang" that become part of the language variety through mainstream spread. This popularized slang of the youth is typically what people may recognize as AAL on commercials, movies, and displays. Unfortunately, the use of AAL as a medium of entertainment has caused the language to be viewed as a deficit, rather than a respected medium of communication and cultural identity. In direct connection to the public stigma surrounding the legitimacy of AAL, academia has also discredited its relevance within educational praxis. It has been argued in education law and policy that AAL is a legitimate home language, separate from Standardized English (the language of mainstream American society), of many Black students across the country and could be immensely useful in the curriculum and instruction of these students in the ELA education, as well as to support their own cultural, racial, and linguistic identities (Perry & Delpit, 1998; Ramirez et. al, 2005; Smitherman & Baugh, 2002; Sung & Allen-Handy, 2019). However, AAL still is not largely accepted, welcomed, or supported in schooling spaces, although Black children make up 15 percent of all public-school children (NCES, 2021). These students may find themselves working overtime to reach a linguistic standard that white students enter the school with.

## Inclusive or Exclusive Education: Monolingual Academia Today

While an official national language has never been formally established, English has become the standardized language variety in U.S. society. The U.S. education system boasts of its inclusive environment with statutes such as the No Child Left Behind Act (U.S. Department of Education, 2022), yet monolingual language curriculum across the nation does not align with this vision. Regarding Common Core standards, there is an explicit expectation that students are to learn and become proficient in using "standard English grammar and usage when writing or speaking" (Common Core, 2021). Based on the full immersion language model in U.S. public schools, all subjects, coursework, homework, interactions, and materials are taught in SE. White students who are native speakers of SE enter schools with knowledge from home that is seen as valuable, simply because their histories, literacies, and languages are the standard. On the other hand, Black students often enter these spaces seeing themselves, their cultures, languages, and histories as irrelevant, nonexistent, or deficit.

Currently, public schools continue broadly to use canonical texts that often reflect Olde English patterns. Within the ELA curriculum, the texts that are used tend to be written by white authors that shape what we know as the western literary canon. Such writers, such as Shakespeare, Charles Dickens, Homer, and Geoffrey Chaucer, and their works are seen as literary brilliance. Works such as

*Othello*, *The Odyssey*, and *Great Expectations* are only a few of the popular titles used in high school ELA instruction to teach reading and writing skills. In many cases, they are upheld as the standard for students learning to use and manipulate the English language to their needs. These writings have been used to teach young students how to utilize grammar, syntax, rhyme, flow, alliteration, similes, metaphors, and many other literary strategies and tools.

For students that do not speak SE in their homes or communities, the full immersion education model can often present academic difficulty in classroom spaces, as well as a cultural disconnect between the students' home languages and the expected language of school. Linguistically diverse students, especially those within urban settings, may be less likely to be engaged or motivated to participate because there is not a reflection of their own languages and literacies within the curricula. For example, some Black students may find themselves compromising their identities within the classroom for the sake of academic success. Black students may find that they are balancing in limbo, floating between dual identities, an academic self, and the real self. As Kelly (2013) elaborated, these students may feel that "they must shed their true selves to be successful academically; those who refuse to shift personas, resist education, since they find that it conflicts with their own identities" (p. 52). The goal is to support both of these identities, as these students have been forced to compromise for far too long. AAL is typically not included in the language curriculum, yet when it is, teachers may use it as parallel to SE instruction. Many educators know this as the code-switching or contrastive analysis method (Wheeler & Swords, 2006).

## Code-Switching: Tool for Accessibility or Respectability?

Code-switching is the action of verbally switching between "codes" or language varieties in the same conversation, as a speaker deems fit or appropriate for different settings, audiences, etc. Some people find that code-switching allows them to alternate between codes so they can accommodate the listener(s) or avoid miscommunication. For those that speak many languages, dialects, and variations, this can be beneficial to know how and when to switch codes as different scenarios will have different expectations for communication. While the process itself can be like the act of translation, code-switching can diverge by acknowledging respectability politics and language ideologies. As explained by Woolard (2020), ideologies about language are "morally and politically loaded representations of the nature, structure, and use of languages in a social world" (p. 1). While any spoken language should be seen as a legitimate structure and method of verbal communication, assumptions and biases are made about varieties and the speakers themselves. As a result, languages such as AAL are then seen as "bad English," and this is often reflected in how its speakers are viewed or acknowledged as less intelligent and capable. Baker-Bell (2013) explained that many students may even begin to internalize these perceptions, causing them to reinforce negative attitudes about AAL and themselves. Because of this, speakers of nonstandard varieties may consciously choose to switch the code they speak to avoid correction, silencing, assumptions, and biases.

In many schools, teachers use code-switching methods to teach language with Black students. While this may be well-intentioned in trying to prepare their students for higher education, employment, legal, professional, and other social spaces that expect SE to be used for access and participation, it could potentially be harmful. Depending on the approach, teachers can be complicit in maintaining a linguistic hierarchy, where AAL is a substandard, inferior language and SE is the standard, superior language. The issue with code-switching approaches is that they tend to "re-create a politics of place that keeps Black people out of white spaces by insisting that they are not welcome into white spaces unless they have assimilated into standardized English" (Saeedi & Richardson, 2020, p. 148). While being in school, students that speak AAL have recalled experiences of being silenced, corrected, ignored, spoken over, and told to reserve their language for personal/ social settings (Alim, 2007; Baker-Bell, 2013; Kinloch, 2010). As a result, many of these speakers are then taught to code-switch with the intention that they must speak only SE in school to be successful. This silencing then relinquishes any agency for the speaker to independently make the decision for when they deem code-switching appropriate. While it can be beneficial for speakers of non-standard varieties to know *how* to code-switch, it can be damaging for teachers to tell students *which* code is expected in certain spaces. As Saeedi and Richardson (2020) argued, when this happens, "there is a simultaneous inclusion and exclusion of Black students that happens at the heart of the code-switching methods; respecting Black individuals while relegating their languages to their 'homes' in the most essentialist and dehumanizing way" (p. 150). Black students who speak AAL may find that they are being asked to abandon their mother tongues in hope for success and access. U.S. educational spaces are losing far too many students this way. This reality must be disrupted – schools and educators of culturally, racially, and linguistically diverse students have a responsibility to utilize methods of including, legitimizing, elevating, and supporting the home languages of their students. Hip-Hop and Rap are avenues for this disruption and reimagination.

### Hip-Hop and Rap: Mediums of Black Resistance, Strength, and Community

Whether the definition is given by a high school teen, a rapper who's been in the game for 10 years, or one of the originators of the cultural movement, Hip-Hop cannot be reduced to solely a musical genre. Smitherman (2006) detailed that it has been defined by many as "Breakin' (Breakdancing), Emceein' (MC/ Rap), Graffiti art (aerosol art), Deejayin' (DJ), Beatboxin', Street Fashion, Street Language, Street Knowledge, and Street Entrepreneurialism" (p. 84). Hip-Hop is layered; it can be thought of as an umbrella term for many different arts. Hip-Hop can be seen, heard, and felt – it is interdisciplinary. It is a lifestyle, a culture, a way of being for many people of color and urbanized peoples. While Hip-Hop got its start in Black neighborhoods, you can hear it beating through Latinx, Asian, and White communities alike. Smitherman (2006) explained that at least 70 percent of all Hip-Hop music record sales are made in white suburbia, as it's used to market products from sneakers to fast food. Baker-Bell (2020) detailed this through recalling the popularized phrase "Lovin' it" by McDonalds.

Further, it is a culture that many non-Black, non-urban people have made a healthy living from. Its definition is continually evolving as the youth continues to morph new ways of cultural expressions through the identity and culture that is hip-hop. Hill (2009) eloquently summarized the shapeshifting of it:

> Since its birth on the streets of New York in the 1970s, hip-hop culture has been transformed from a local youth movement to an international phenomenon. From the iPods of suburban American teens to revolutionary movement in the Global South, the sites, sounds, and spectacles of hip-hop have become a central feature of an increasingly globalized cultural landscape. Despite its roots within U.S., Caribbean, and African diasporic traditions, hip-hop has been consumed and refashioned in ways that respond to the experiences, traditions, imaginations, and desires of young people throughout the world. Such developments speak to the significance of hip-hop not only as a popular culture text, but also has a rich site for complex forms of identity work.
>
> *p. 1*

This characterization of Hip-Hop details that while its culture started in Black American communities, it has become one that is praised and celebrated all over the world.

### The Need for Hip-Hop and Rap Curriculum

Hip-Hop culture is dope, cool, fun. It has spread to every sector of social life. Described by Bruce and Davis (2000), Hip-Hop "is where many of our students live – the music they listen to, their traditions, the language they speak, the clothes they wear, the way they interact in the streets" (p. 122). The commodification and mass-production of Hip-Hop as a culture has led Black culture and AAL to become world-renowned. It is time for educational spaces to use it as a resource for scholarly instruction and investigation. Belle (2016) explained that by including Hip-Hop as a literary resource, educators can then set the tone within their own classroom to challenge existing ways of knowing, while reimagining the possibilities for excellence. Through implementing Hip-Hop and Rap into the curriculum to teach and learn with Black students, educators will be able to support complex identity affirmation and formation, in addition to fostering safe spaces for teaching about students' cultural and linguistic backgrounds.

## *Shifting Power in Curriculum: Black Linguistic Brilliance*

During Fall 2018, I conducted research in a central South Carolina elementary school with a small group of four Black first-grade students. My goal in this case study was to learn about how these students may respond to lessons focused on Black languages and histories. I worked with them two times a week over a 15-week period through introducing lessons about topics such as AAL, Africa as a continent, and Black historical figures that were typically not taught in schools. Usually, we would read a book, or view a slideshow I created, which was followed with a writing activity. During the first few lessons that I worked with them, there were moments where the students did not seem engaged. I assumed that they would be motivated to work because the lessons were about Black topics, but I was mistaken. I did not realize how small minded this was until much later. The methods that I used to teach about these topics failed to connect with the students in a meaningful way. Following a lesson one day, Isaac[1] stayed behind to talk after the other students left. He said, "Ms. Jimenez, I like learning about Black stuff but some days it's kinda boring. Can we maybe have some videos or music?" I was shocked at his blunt statement, and I initially could not figure out why it left me speechless. I responded, "Wow, I didn't realize you felt that way. I can definitely add in some music and videos. I'll try to think on what to include for our next lesson." I returned with the next lesson, eager to share a video of what I thought would be an interesting read aloud for the students. This still was not received well, but Isaac did not stay behind for another chat.

It took a few days to go by before I arrived at two revelations. First, I failed to ask the students which artists or songs they would like to see and hear. I assumed that I could handle it myself, because I was the teacher, the "expert in the room." As a result, I was dismissive of the knowledge that the students could bring to lessons and classroom space, so I did not invite them for contribution. Second, I was surprised by Isaac's straightforward nature because I had been socialized and trained to believe that adults, and specifically teachers, are the authority. It was uncomfortable to feel challenged by someone much younger than me, and to feel like all my training and education still was not enough to meet their needs. However, I was humbled by the interaction. I chose to skip a day of lesson time to instead interview the students about what they would like to see, hear, or engage with. I explained that my goals in working with them were to 1) teach them about Black culture and Black languages that are typically not included in schools, 2) collect student work, and 3) conduct interviews to learn about how the lessons were received, and if they were impacted by the lessons through increased positive racial identity or increased academic achievement. Amongst the four students, their interview responses resulted in two requests, 1) to include a video with all lessons, and 2) to include music in lessons OR allow music to be played during work time following the lesson. They explained that their main classroom teacher and their parents/guardians often used technology to teach things and that it was difficult to be engaged or motivated to work when lessons did not include things they liked. I learned through the interviews that they would enjoy videos with animation of the stories and topics we discuss, as well as music that was tied to the lesson or that they liked to listen to in their homes and communities. While I had some ideas for videos to include moving forward, I was not exactly sure how and who to include for music. The students were eager to also tell me some artists they liked, such as Beyoncé, Drake, Kendrick Lamar, Cardi B, and Childish Gambino. Conveniently, these were people that I listened to in my own free time. I was eager to switch my practices up.

I felt more prepared the next time we met for small group time, as the new lessons I created seemed to have more potential. I prepared a lesson about a grammatical rule in AAL, which is called the Habitual Be. Many speakers of AAL use the Habitual Be to replace words such as "always, regularly, consistently," with the word modifier "be" to show the verb as an act that is done habitually. For example, if a speaker of SE wants to tell someone that they regularly eat at a restaurant, they may say, "I always eat at the café nearby." However, if a speaker of AAL were to describe the same sentence, they may say, "I be eating at the café nearby."

Following this introductory discussion, I read aloud the book *Flossie & the Fox,* which is a story about a young Black girl who speaks AAL and uses the language to outwit a sly fox. The students enjoyed this and began to make connections immediately. They discussed how they use Habitual Be regularly in their communities, and that they didn't realize they were speaking different varieties of language.

This was a perfect segue into discussing how some of their favorite Hip-Hop and Rap artists use the Habitual Be. As AAL is fundamentally the language of Hip-Hop, it is expected that the inclusion of Hip-Hop would also lead to an inclusion of its language. Since I heard two of the students singing the song "Bodak Yellow" during the week prior, I mentioned that the artist of that song, Cardi B, regularly uses Habitual Be. The students had a puzzled look on their face, so I tried singing some lyrics to see how they would respond. They jumped in and finished the lyrics with me ("Cardi B, you know where I'm at, you know where I be"). We discussed how in that line, Cardi was explaining how she is regularly frequenting the same places.

After this conversation, I asked students to write 2-3 sentences using the habitual rule and to draw a picture with it. One student, Ayanna★, decided to write much more than the amount the assignment required. When I inquired about what made her fill both the front and back of her paper, she said that she speaks like this all the time, so it was "fun and easy" to do. Figures 7.1 and 7.2 are some examples of her work.

This specific recollection was only one moment of many where the students and I connected with each other and the curriculum. Through listening and reimagining, the students helped shape what and how we learned together, while still having opportunities to learn language and writing skills. Teaching Hip-Hop

FIGURE 7.1 Example 1 of student work for "Habitual Be" lesson.

was a humbling experience because my preservice education and degree did not train or prepare me to include this type of art and way of knowing in my teaching practices and curriculum. I was forced to reimagine how we as educators can engage students in innovative ways. I was challenged to interrogate my biases of how Hip-Hop and Rap are viewed in society and how we can instead view them as resources. I found myself having to unlearn "best practices" from my training and professional development sessions that limited my ability to see the possibility in nontraditional, yet culturally and linguistically relevant practices. Using Hip-Hop and Rap brought a wealth of knowledge, culture, and beauty into the classroom. Finding ways to include these artistic mediums in the curriculum has…

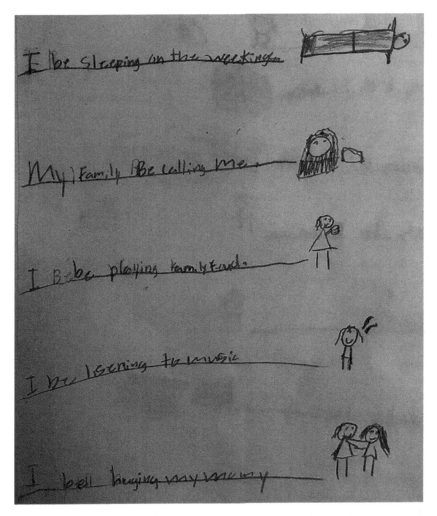

**FIGURE 7.2** Example 2 of student work for "Habitual Be" lesson.

- Provided an opportunity for me to connect my students' interests and hobbies to required coursework.
- Opened the door to providing a safe, supportive space where my students can trust that their identities and interests are validated.
- Provided me with cultural competence to include the latest artists and works of the community I serve.

I believe that all educators have the opportunity and power to make this a reality, to center Black voices, languages, histories, and cultures for students of all ages.

## *For the Educators: Hip-Hop & Rap as Curriculum*

There are many educators and schooling spaces that already include Hip-Hop curriculum and practices. In some cases, this is focused on comparing it to the texts of the literary canon. Studying and teaching aspects of Hip-Hop and Rap on its own can meet those same state standards and expectations for learning. Some teachers have taught about the parallels between Shakespeare and a Rap artist, such as Tupac. While in some cases, it may be well-intentioned, it further pushes the notion that Black literacy must be compared to European works to be seen as legitimate. Hip-Hop and Rap are so powerful on their own, but we reduce them to mediocrity when we include them only for supporting canonical texts. We as educators can shift our approach and practices to uplift those cultures and art forms that have been silenced and excluded to reimagine how we listen and engage.

Another occurrence that is present within current methods of Hip-Hop and Rap inclusion is the recycling of pre-existing lessons. The culture is constantly evolving, so the curriculum should reflect this as well. YouTube is flooded with popular Hip-Hop songs that have been recreated for the purpose of educational learning, but those songs will only be popular for so long. Learning who your students are and what their current interests are will go a long way in meeting their needs academically, but also always for bonding with them on a personal and emotional level. This may take a level of vulnerability on educators' part first as you may need to be instructed, rather than to instruct. Centering student voice and interest will help reimagine new ways of knowing. It also creates a bond.

When we bring our whole selves to the classroom, students see this, and they allow themselves to become more vulnerable and open. Much of this starts with a question, who do you like to listen to? What kind of music do you like? What do you like to do in your free time? Students are often eager to answer when given the opportunity. By learning more about your specific class of students, you can learn and then decide which artists, songs, or other forms of text are useful and appropriate for the lessons in mind. While a generation ago, students may have wanted to hear Biggie and Tupac, the kids today are likely to tell us their favorite artist is someone you've never heard before. It is then our job to do research and incorporate it in a meaningful way by using our experience as a trained educator.

While Hip-Hop is popular in mainstream culture, there are still many people who do not interact with its culture. Teachers can recognize and acknowledge their students, their families, and their communities as resources for understanding how to support them academically and emotionally. While educators may be trained and prepared to support students in many ways, there will be humbling moments where we must be willing to learn and listen, so our students can lead the way based on their existing knowledge, interests, and needs. For teachers who are unfamiliar with Hip-Hop culture, we can take a note from our pupils as they may be the experts in this field of learning and growing. The students themselves, their cultures, and their lived experiences should be viewed as resources within the academic space as they contribute to the learning space through the dialogue of their experiences, belief systems, and realities. Alim (2007) further elaborated, "It is one thing to view the culture of our students as a resource for teaching about other subjects, and it's quite another thing to see our students as the sources, investigators and archives of varied and rich bodies of knowledge rooted in their cultural-linguistic reality" (p. 17). Seeing students as valuable and needed in creating and shaping the classroom culture is mandatory if we are to shift in recognizing Black students and their cultures as brilliant and necessary to educational advancement and excellence.

## Hip-Hop and Rap as Practice

While educators may ask how time will allow for any extra lessons, Hip-Hop can be integrated into the existing curriculum and meet existing state standard expectations. By substituting Hip-Hop and Rap texts for canonical texts, we have an opportunity to reinforce how we can teach required standards with new, culturally relevant methods. Based on the current Common Core standards for ELA, there are four focus areas: reading, writing, speaking, and listening (Common Core, 2021). Teachers can first review the specific state-, district-, and school-level standards that students are expected to meet for the year. As Hill (2009) suggested, teachers can frame music as "authors" and the songs and other mediums of art that they produce can be considered as "texts." Based on the writing, speaking, and reading standards, teachers can find nontraditional texts, such as songs, poetry, movies, podcasts, or any other artistic medium that they deem academically fit, to still teach the expected standards.

As students are required to be taught about poetry, teachers could use Hip-Hop or Rap artists to talk about the different types of poems, how to write them, and how to identify them. Hip-Hop and Rap lyrics are poetry, and vice versa; we see this in Tupac's book *The Rose That Grew From Concrete*. Like canonical texts, Hip-Hop texts can address figurative language, assonance, alliteration, metaphor, and similes, to name a few. Hip-Hop texts can be song lyrics, graffiti art, spoken word, poetry, or other mediums. Such Hip-Hop texts can be used to allow for students to practice both AAL and SE in reading, writing, speaking, and listening through poetry writing (regular or slam), spoken word, storytelling, narrative writing, songwriting, and cyphers. Artists such as Tupac, Nas, Jay-Z, Lauryn Hill, Jill Scott, and TLC utilize rhyme, flow, similes, metaphors, double and triple entendres, and much more within their music. However, instead of discussing the grammatical parallels between AAL and SE, teachers can acknowledge the language of Black America through music as rule-governed, culturally conscious, and legitimate on its own accord through dual language instruction.

Teachers can use Hip-Hop and Rap songs to facilitate dialogues about language, power, class, race, and other topics that may be relevant to the students' learning experiences or personal of the classroom. Artists such Jay-Z, Nas, Biggie, J Cole, and Common make music and poetry about poverty and divestment in the Black community, the gatekeeping of jobs and resources, gender roles, societal expectations, and the realities of living while Black in the United States. Their lyrics can be utilized to talk about critical issues, while also facilitating methods to use language in creative ways. These artists use figurative language such as alliteration, triple entendres, flow, rhyme, irony, personification, and puns. Students can listen to the music and look at the lyrics on paper to learn about rhyme and flow. Through using Hip-Hop and Rap works, teachers can work with students applying similar skills in their own writings through building vocabulary, spelling, building, and constructing sentences, and grammatical rules. Below are some potential ideas of inclusion of AAL, Hip-Hop, and Rap in ELA coursework.

Reading:

- Poems and Lyrics as Texts: Students use lyrics and poems to work on comprehension with multiple language varieties, as well as to learn more about code-switching in practice.

Speaking:

- Cyphers: Students write and prepare raps and poems to participate in a "verbal battle" amongst classmates, to practice vocabulary, flow, and rhyme.
- Varied Assignment Submission: Teachers provide students with an opportunity for completing assignments through performance, spoken word, Rap, and song instead of only written submissions. This is useful for students who need practice with speaking in front of audiences.

Writing:

- Narrative Writing: Students use Hip-Hop and Rap songs to learn about narrative writing and creating their own. Many Hip-Hop and Rap songs tell personal stories, including characters, setting, conflict, resolution, metaphors, personification, etc. (La Di Da Di by Doug E. Fresh).
- Analytical Writing: Given the chance to make and defend an argument on a topic they are well-versed on, students are motivated to think critically and argue soundly. An example activity would be, if students watch Straight Outta Compton and are questioned on the morality of certain characters, such as the music manager or others in the music industry, then students analyze and defend this claim in an articulate and coherent manner.
- Expository Writing: In expository writing within public school education, many of the prompts are not culturally relevant to Black students. This may

make it difficult for students to write an informed piece about an idea or theme if it is outside their realm of interest. Another example activity could be to ask students to describe something of interest with regard to music, such as a music genre, an artist, aspects of the Hip-Hop culture and community, then write about these topics with detailed and eloquent understanding and clarity.

- Persuasive Writing: While this can be a writing lesson explicitly, there is also an opportunity to do an integrated lesson, combining ELA and visual arts. For students who may not be confident in writing but are very good at art, this may be enjoyable as teachers can suggest different prompts where students respond by creating persuasive advertisements or arguments. For example, teachers could ask students to make ads promoting artists, or themes within different artists' music. As graffiti is a powerful form of art within Hip-Hop culture, students may create visuals with other classroom safe materials. Students can make a persuasive argument for why they believe an artist should be listened to.

## Conclusion

Hip-Hop culture is a major aspect of the youth's homes, communities, backgrounds, and interests and utilizes AAL as a key component from its origination to its continued success today. Including Hip-Hop within the curricula and instruction of classrooms not only shows inclusion of Black students' cultural backgrounds and knowledge, but also it will also allow for direct integration of AAL into lessons. The inclusion of the art form and culture known as Hip-Hop legitimizes Black youth. As Kelly (2013) argued, "for students to truly engage in learning, they must be able to see a space for themselves within it" (p. 52). Fostering a classroom space in which students can know that their interests and identities are valued and welcomed allows for students to participate more, be more academically successful, and hopefully, to learn more about themselves and other cultures.

Further, Hip-Hop culture is deeply ingrained in the interests, music preferences, and identities of non-Black youth across the country and world. Most students of color spend their entire K-12 experience learning about white histories, cultures, and languages, and white students are rarely exposed to cultures beyond their own within academic settings. Students of all backgrounds will benefit from the inclusive nature of these suggested practices, but it will especially impact white students to connect with other backgrounds who they may otherwise not be exposed to on a personal level. Yes, Hip-Hop is innately Black at its inception and core, but it has become a culture for all people. Through advancement of the culture, languages, and histories of the Black community, we can advance such for all people through our connection of humanity and desire for inclusive education.

## Note

1 All names for students are pseudonyms.

## References

Alim, H. S. (2007). "The whig party don't exist in my hood": Knowledge, reality, and education in the hip-hop nation. In H. S. Alim & J. Baugh (Eds.), *Talkin Black talk: language, education, and social change* (pp. 15–29). New York, NY: Teachers College Press.

Baker-Bell, A. (2013). "I never really knew the history behind African American language:" Critical language pedagogy in an advanced placement English language arts class. *Equity & Excellence in Education, 46*(3), 355–370. DOI:10.1080/10665684.2013.806848.

Baker-Bell, A. (2020). Linguistic Justice: Black Language, Literacy, Identity, and Pedagogy. Routledge, Taylor & Francis Group.

Baugh, J. (2015). Use and misuse of speech diagnostics for African American students. *International Multilingual Research Journal, 9*(4), 291–307. https://doi.org/10.1080/19313152.2015.1082416.

Belle, C. (2016). Don't believe the hype: Hip-Hop literacies and English education. *Journal of Adolescent & Adult Literacy, 60*(3), 287–294. https://doi.org/10.1002/jaal.574.

Bruce, H. E. & Davis, B.D. (2000). Slam: Hip-Hop meets poetry – A strategy for violence intervention. *English Journal, 89*(5), 119–127. https://doi.org/10.2307/822307.

Common Core State Standards Initiative. (Retrieved April 2021). Frequently Asked Questions. www.corestandards.org/about-the-standards/frequently-asked-questions/.

Delpit, L. (1998). What should teachers do? Ebonics and culturally responsive instruction. In T. Perry & L. Delpit (Eds.), *The real Ebonics debate: Power, language, and the education of African-American children* (pp. 17–26). Boston, MA: Beacon Press.

Gottlieb, M., & Slavit-Ernst, G. (2014). *Academic language in diverse classrooms: Definitions and contexts.* Thousand Oaks, CA: Corwin.

Hill, M. L. (2009). *Beats, rhymes, and classroom life: Hip-hop pedagogy and the politics of identity.* New York, NY: Teachers College Press.

Jackson, J. J. (1997). On Oakland's Ebonics: Some say gibberish, some say slang, some say dis den dat, me say dem dumb, it be mother tongue. *The Black Scholar, 27*(1), 18–25. DOI:10.1080/00064246.1997.11430836

Kelly, L.L. (2013). Hip-Hop literature: The politics, poetics, and power of hip-hop in the English classroom. *English Journal, 102*(5), 51–56.

Kinloch, V. (2010). "To not be a traitor of black English": Youth perceptions of language rights in an urban context. *Teachers College Record: The Voice of Scholarship in Education, 112*(1), 103–141. https://doi.org/10.1177/016146811011200101.

National Center for Education Statistics (NCES). (2021). Racial/Ethnic enrollment in public schools. https://nces.ed.gov/programs/coe/indicator_cge.asp.

Perry, T., & Delpit, L. (1998). What is the standard English proficiency program? In T. Perry & L. Delpit (Eds.), *The real Ebonics debate: Power, language, and the education of African-American children* (pp. 154–155). Boston, MA: Beacon Press.

Ramirez, J. D., Wiley, T. G., De Klerk, G., Lee, E., & Wright, W. E. (Eds.). (2005). *Ebonics: The urban education debate* (2nd ed.). Tonawanda, NY: Multilingual Matters.

Rickford, J. R., & Rickford, R. J. (2000). *Spoken soul: The story of Black English.* New York, NY: Wiley.

Saeedi, S., & Richardson, E. (2020). A Black lives matter and critical race theory-informed critique of code-switching pedagogy. In V. Kinloch, T. Burkhard, & C. Penn (Eds.), *Race, justice, and activism in literacy instruction* (pp. 147–161). New York, NY: Teachers College Press.

Smitherman, G. (2000). *Talkin that talk: Language, culture, and education in African America.* New York, NY: Routledge.

Smitherman, G., & Baugh, J. (2002). The shot heard from Ann Arbor: Language research and public policy in African America. *Howard Journal of Communications, 13*(1), 5–24. DOI:10.1080/106461702753555012

Smitherman, G. (2006). *Word from the mother: Language and African Americans.* New York, NY: Routledge.

Sung, Kenzo K. & Allen-Handy, Ayana. (2019). Contradictory origins and racializing legacy of the 1968 Bilingual Education Act: Urban schooling, anti-blackness, and Oakland's 1996 Black English Language Education Resolution. *University of Maryland Law Journal of Race, Religion, Gender and Class, 19*(44). https://advance-lexis-com.pitt.idm.oclc.org/api/document?collection=analytical-materials&id=urn:contentItem:5WFD-SNY0-0198-F0TJ-00000-00&context=1516831.

U.S. Department of Education. (Retrieved March 2022). Every Student Succeeds Act (ESSA) U.S. Department of Education. www.ed.gov/essa.

Wheeler, R. S. & Swords, R. S. (2006). *Code-Switching: Teaching standard English in urban classrooms.* Urbana, IL: National Council of Teachers of English.

Wolfram, W., Adger, C.T., & Christian, D. (1999). *Dialects in schools and communities.* Mahwah, NJ: Lawrence Erlbaum.

Woolard, K. A. (2020). Language ideology. In J. Stanlaw (Ed.), *The International Encyclopedia of Linguistic Anthropology* (pp. 1–18). Wiley-Blackwell. https://doi.org/10.1002/9781118786093.iela0217.

# 8

# THE COMPLEXITIES OF CHINESE CHILDREN'S MEANING-MAKING REVEALED THROUGH ARTISTIC PRACTICES, TALK, AND SOCIAL INTERACTION

*Ling Hao and Sally Brown*

## Introduction

> *Art is not the possession of the few who are recognized writers, painters, musicians; it is the authentic expression of any and all individuality.*
>
> *Dewey, 1934*

After reading the wordless picturebook *Hello* (Ikegami, 2019), Anna drew four pictures about the two main characters playing together in different seasons (see Figure 8.1). Then, she stuck the four pictures together to tell the whole story she created. As she explained, "第一个是冬天，第二个是秋，第三个是春天，第四个是夏天. (The first one is Winter. The second one is Autumn. The third one is Spring. The last one is Summer.)" Her drawing was an extension of the book's plot using a variety of colors to represent each season. These rich details in her drawing helped us understand her complex meaning-making process.

Many schools are places where monolingualism dominates, and students are forced into print-centric practices to showcase their language and literacy learning. Unfortunately, a restricted view of meaning-making restricts learning opportunities and marginalizes the academic progress of multilingual students (Brown & Hao, 2022; Suárez-Orozco & Suárez-Orozco, 2015). This chapter highlights the voices of Chinese learners to show the power of art, multilingual talk, and culture in speaking about the world we live in.

Meaning-making for young bilingual composers is a complex process involving multiple modes within specific classroom contexts. Each learner brings their culture, languages, and experiences to the authoring process while drawing upon their linguistic repertoires (García, Johnson, & Seltzer, 2017). According to Baroutsis, Kervin, Woods, and Comber (2019), a child's drawing

DOI: 10.4324/9781003302186-14

**FIGURE 8.1** Anna's Response to *Hello.*

cannot offer a complete picture of learning. Instead, it must be coupled with other modes like talk, especially creative blends of languages. Talking and drawing are a parallel process that results in a semiotic ensemble, or cohesive text (Kress, 2010). We investigated Chinese emergent bilinguals' meaning-making processes and multimodal literacy practices in response to picturebooks and explored the following research questions: How do Chinese children use artistic practices and resulting artifacts to (a) understand picturebooks and (b) tell their own stories using a blend of languages and cultural backgrounds as a foundation? The term picturebooks is used as a compound word to capture the interdependence of words and images in the selected books (Arizpe, 2013). In particular, we want attention to be paid to the illustrations designed by the illustrator.

## Multimodal Meaning-Making Practices

Language is only one resource for meaning-making and needs to be studied within the context of other modes and the social practices during which it occurs. Speech, writing, gesture, the creation of art are also resources for navigating the communicational landscape (Jewitt, Bezemer, & O'Halloran, 2016). Children actively make signs and blend forms and meanings based on available resources. When listening to and responding to read alouds, emergent bilinguals draw not only from their cultural and linguistic resources, but also from what occurs within interactions with peers, teachers, and other adults. For example, if children are given material affordances like paper, markers, and scissors, these may be used within specific modes to make meaning based on the surrounding learning activity (Kress, 2010). In one instance, a pencil drawing of a star was transformed into fireworks as the child traced the lines with blue and orange crayons while seeing fireworks in an illustration during a read aloud.

This process positions children as active as they assume the role of decision maker as they design responses when choices are offered (Kress, 2010) including linguistic forms in various languages. In order to truly understand children as multimodal meaning makers, there must be an examination across modes to understand the relationships and cohesiveness of the ensemble or cohesive product as a result of the process (Bezemer & Kress, 2016).

## Translanguaging as a Multimodal Engagement

According to García, Ibarra Johnson, and Seltzer (2017), translanguaging is a system of complex language practices where multilingual people draw from their linguistic repertoires using their own perspective where creative infusions of meanings occur. This process ignores boundaries set by standards and society. Translanguaging is not only a multilingual process, but also a multimodal one, where numerous language resources are combined to make sense of the world (Vogel & García, 2017; Wei, 2018). This process differs from code-switching, which tends to have a limited focus on the use of two languages during a conversation as opposed to translanguaging that incorporates a more holistic approach. Translanguaging draws from the assumption that emergent bilinguals have one linguistic repertoire, not two, and the construction of interrelated discursive practices (Bhatt & Bolonyai, 2019; García & Wei, 2014). Multilingual children take control of their learning as they make choices to create new forms of language as communicative resources (Bengochea, Sembiante, & Gort, 2018). The unique linguistic combinations intertwine with other modes to impact learning.

Further, this approach opens spaces for creativity especially in terms of visual or artistic practices. Insight about the ways children understand stories can be gained by listening to their word choices and viewing the images they create. Therefore, positioning translanguaging as an art form. Viewing translanguaging as an art form draws from the notion that users create unique ways of mixing and melding their linguistic repertoires. Each person creates a remarkable way of using language. Just as no two artists paint a landscape in the same way, the same applies to languaging. No two users bring their resources together to respond to a question or discussion in the same manner. It is an art form guided by the individuals' use of resources.

## Artistic Responses to Reading

Compared to the traditional responses like oral or written responses, artistic responses open spaces for students to respond to the texts freely without worrying about being right or wrong, thus encouraging students' reading and responding. Children communicate their ideas about books and demonstrate thinking and emotions through their drawings. Sometimes that takes the form of a greater degree of care, control, and accuracy regarding the details in their drawings (Rabey, 2004).

In addition to drawing, children also showcased their interpretations through other artistic forms, such as song and dance (Enriquez & Wager, 2018), drama performance (Adomat, 2010), and clay sculpture (Carger, 2004). These different forms included various modalities that stimulated young children's imagination and creativity. For example, Adomat (2010) argued that performative responses stimulate children's imagination, give children agency, enable children's active meaning-construction, and promote collaboration among children as they read books.

## Culture as a Vehicle for Literacy Learning

Creating spaces for children to become multimodal authors of their own understandings of story requires a multimodal approach that accepts (and utilizes) culturally diverse ways of meaning-making. Ladson-Billings (1995) and Gay's (2018) culturally responsive approach to teaching places culture at the center of learning. This goes beyond the surface level and encompasses the intentional weaving of rich cultural practices into everyday events. Thus, requiring educators to have in-depth conversations with their students and seeking out their own understandings of cultures different from their own.

Paris and Alim's (2017) work extend the focus to culturally sustaining practices, meaning not only fostering these practices but sustaining them to a point that results in social transformation. The desired result being additive views of children rather than deficit ones that damage the identities of children and their life trajectories. Cultural ways of knowing must be understood as complex practices rather than simple notions of student assets. This includes seeing culture as fluid and emerging with a dependence on the way people live. Blending a focus on culture with a multimodal view of translanguaging can inform the literacy work of young emergent bilingual children.

## Building on Culture: Multimodal Engagement with Stories

The sociocultural knowledge of emergent bilinguals has a long history of being unrecognized and devalued (Cummins, 2009), highlighting the need to push educators to forefront cultural and experiential knowledge (Gay, 2018; Paris & Alim, 2017). This requires a flexible space where children can build meaning by telling narratives drawing from background knowledge (Clark, 2020). Rich oral language may originate from teachers' thoughtful use of culturally relevant texts. This is also true as young emergent bilinguals engage with wordless picturebooks with their mothers (Hu, Liu, & Zheng, 2018). The cultural and linguistic lives of the children tend to inform children's narratives about the images in the books. Multilingual storytelling opportunities are often supported by the joint use of languages guided by conversational scaffolds.

The combination of art and writing are frequently used by children to make sense of stories (Martens et al., 2018; Pantaleo, 2020). Picturebooks can be the inspiration for bringing together elements of color, form, and shape to tell stories in their own voices through design choice. Dialogic elements of communication are also enhanced through the addition of visual modes particularly when children are drawing, cutting paper, and writing (Alvarez, 2018; Chang & Cress, 2014). Visuals along with conversational elements assist in helping children to understand their world. However, this requires a conversational element. In order to fully understand the power of children's artwork, there needs to be probing in order to discover the implicit meanings the child embedded. Many times, this information is shared among peers within situated practices (Kim, 2016) and in families at home (Louie & Davis-Welton, 2016).

## Methodology

This qualitative case study provides a rich description of the experiences of eight emergent bilingual children who engaged in virtual book club discussions focused around culturally responsive texts. The children used multiple modes to process the new information they were learning and to tell their own stories. Both Mandarin and English languages were used in fluid ways during the learning process. The trustworthiness of this study is addressed through thick description about the children's meaning-making processes, prolonged engagement with the children and their families, and multiple sources of evidence, including the researchers' observations, video transcripts, children's artifacts, and reflections.

### Book Club Community

The participants were eight Chinese American emergent bilinguals studying Chinese at a local Chinese Heritage School in southeastern United States, which offered a language immersion experience. The majority of the children were four to six years old and spoke Chinese as their first language. Grace (all names are pseudonyms) was the only participant who spoke English as her first language. In addition, Ken was a nine-year-old who volunteered to join the book club after listening to his little brother Mack's first session. When the school closed during the Covid-19 pandemic, the children participated in a virtual book club once per week over the course of four months via Zoom where Ling and Sally guided an English read aloud of picturebooks. The virtual format differed from a face-to-face book club in a couple of ways that were actually beneficial for the children and families. First, parents sat next to their child during the read alouds given their age and need to navigate technology. This allowed a space for parents to join the interactions. For example, parents frequently added cultural comments to extend what was being read in the stories. This information was based on historical accounts of Chinese culture as well as their personal and familial experiences. This would have never happened in a classroom because the parents would not have been there. Second, during the read alouds, some students left the screen to gather artifacts in their homes. This allowed them to share and connect with their home environments. For example, Anna showed the group red envelopes given to her during the Chinese New Year.

## Instructional Procedures

Each session contained a pre-reading, a during-reading, and an after-reading phase. During pre-reading, the children engaged in activities to build background information about the book. In addition, each week Ling taught the children Chinese characters and provided space for their attempts at writing the characters. During reading, a culturally relevant picturebook was read aloud in English and the children were asked to talk about various pages of the book in either language using open-ended questions. After reading, the children responded to the book through drawing or making artifacts. The students were encouraged to respond freely to the books using multimodal artistic practices like papercuts, drawings, cards, and a mix of languages. The children had many physical resources available in their homes that included playdough, markers, crayons, paper (white and colored), scissors, and paint.

## Book Selections

Culturally relevant picturebooks were selected to build a foundation for extending learning about Chinese characters and culture. Appendix A presents the books read during the ten weeks.

## Data Analysis

The meaning-making processes, drawings, artifacts (e.g., paper-cuts, Lego creations/toy bricks), and talk were analyzed using both visual and verbal discourse analyses to understand the perspectives of the children (Kim, 2018). The analysis revealed the rich ways multiple languages, pictures, and artifacts were used as mediational tools for cultural constructions of personal experiences and the use of imagination (Khimji & Maunder, 2012).

## Findings

The following sections present findings that offer insight into specific pedagogical strategies for supporting multilingual students' multimodal literacy development. First, the hidden meanings contained in children's artwork go unnoticed. By combining modes, it is possible to gain a richer understanding of what emergent bilinguals know and can do. Second, book selection is critical in order to provide texts that offer cultural connections. However, this may not be possible especially when the texts are not in their first language. This calls for supplementary resources (i.e., short poems, pictures, photographs) to be embedded in the read aloud experience. Last, translanguaging is a central piece in the learning puzzle. Valuing translanguaging as an art form shows the challenges children engage in as they select the appropriate words in multiple languages to convey exactly what they mean. Translanguaging is not simply the use of two languages, but incorporates highly complex thought processes where emergent bilinguals make informed decisions (Wei, 2018). For example, Rena used a unique mixture of her linguistic resources as she commented on an illustration in *Pancakes for Breakfast* (dePaola, 1978). 小猫都等不及吃 pancake 了，小狗也等不及吃 pancake 了。他们在玩捉迷藏。 (Kittens can't wait to eat pancake, and puppies can't wait to eat pancake. They are playing hide and seek.) This example shows the emphasis on the English word pancake while using Chinese to talk about the details occurring around the cooking session.

### Hidden Meanings

A child's artwork cannot be understood by a single view. A more extensive approach must be employed to include a look at the surrounding social interactions during the creative processes along with verbal explanations. In addition, attention must be paid to the ways modes like color, layout, size, etc., are used to make meaning.

After the reading of *Goldy Luck and the Three Pandas* (Yim, 2014), Grace created a response using pencil, crayons, and paper (see Figure 8.2). There were multiple aspects of meaning-making represented in her drawing. A quick, initial examination of the image revealed very basic elements. One of the pandas was presented along with the main character (girl dressed in red) and the bed where she slept. This left many unanswered questions about the remaining objects and their significance. Upon completion of the artwork, Grace shared these hidden meanings offering insight into the cultural ways of being that influenced her interpretations of the story and connections with her life. Below is a vignette of Grace's talk that extended our understanding of Grace as a learner.

Smiling, Grace held up her paper in front of the Zoom camera and replied,

> "Well, that's a little panda (pointed to the top of the paper) … I also draw the dumpling bed. (The mid-sized bed in the story folded up like a dumpling.). The dumpling bed is the one right here (pointed to the bottom left).

**FIGURE 8.2** Grace's Response to *Goldy Luck and the Three Pandas.*

The green and pink. I really wanted to draw the dumpling bed, but I didn't know how (laughed). Well, I kinda like the blue one (circle representing another bed) just because I could use that because it's a little bit like the color of winter. I also draw snowflakes because it's almost Christmas. I made a gift." (Earlier during the drawing process, Grace asked, "How much weight is a panda? 100 or more. A panda because he's really heavy.") The numbers represented the weight of her panda.

Taken together, the image and dialogue, the two modes extended what Grace knew about the story. This suggested she had a blend of fictional information about the characters in the story and the setting with factual information about the weight of pandas (a cultural connection about pandas from China in an earlier story, *Giant: A panda of the enchanted forest*). *Goldy Luck* was read in December, which explained Grace's connections to winter, coldness, snow, and Christmas. It was as if the drawing contained dual meanings that extended beyond the story itself.

Hidden cultural meanings arose in many other artistic responses including Rena's drawing. After engaging in a read aloud of *Dim Sum for Everyone* (Lin, 2003), Rena immediately began drawing (see Figure 8.3). She created a salient image of a table similar to one represented in the book with three dishes. When she was asked about her use of color, she replied, "这三个都是盘子的颜色啊. (All three are the colors of the plates.)" In this case, Rena's drawing reflected details from the story where the small dishes were green, orange, and purple. A use of color was hidden but showed the close attention Rena paid to the story. She did not simply choose her favorite colors, but recreated what she saw as essential elements from the book.

Further, Rena's talk about her drawing revealed some personal and cultural elements unclear to the naked eye. The word "Gorge" is noted at the top of the page, which was significant to her food story. According to Rena, "有一天，我的弟弟 George 回家发现桌子上面摆满了吃的，他就，而且没人，他就觉得有点奇怪. (One day, my brother George came home and found that the table was full of food, then he , and there was no one, he thought it was a bit strange.)" Thus, explaining George's facial expression. Rena explained, "摆满了包子，豆腐，蛋糕，还有饼干. (It was filled with buns, tofu, cakes, and biscuits.)" While the book mentioned various foods such as fried shrimp, coconut milk, carrots, and egg tarts, Rena selected foods to include in her drawings as she constructed her responses. These were the specific foods with cultural relevance for her Chinese American family. She continued, "对啊，是我弟弟，不是哥哥。他比我小两

**FIGURE 8.3** Rena's Response to *Dim Sum for Everyone*.

岁。他还刚三岁呀. (Yes, it's my younger brother, not my elder brother. He is two years younger than me. He is just three years old.)" Here, Rena painted a portrait of her own family mealtime just as the storyline presented. She included her younger brother who is a significant part of her life and frequently sat next to Rena during the read alouds.

## *Supplementing Culture*

The book club was designed to include different pre-reading activities to supplement texts and build cultural relevance for the children. One of the challenges was to locate Chinese relevant picturebooks for young readers. To adapt the existing texts, the theme of the picturebooks was connected with Chinese characters and poems in the pre-reading phase. For example, *The Farmer* (Abadia, 2019) was used as a read aloud that described a farmer's hard work and perseverance. While this book did not have direct connections with Chinese culture, it was selected because it was a wordless book that would allow students to author their own story based on personal experiences with farming within the Chinese culture. The illustrations were highly open to multiple interpretations. Ling taught the children a classic Chinese poem 悯农 *(The Peasants)* that also described farmers' hard work. Ling selected two images of the poem presenting Chinese farmers, taught the children to read *Min Nong,* and explained the meaning of this poem to the children. The children gained insight into the hard work of farmers through reading the poem and looking at the images of the poem.

Another way texts were adapted was to teach Chinese characters and use Chinese images in the pre-reading phase. For example, before reading *Thanking the Moon: Celebrating the Mid-Autumn Moon Festival* (Lin, 2012), Ling taught the Chinese character 月 for moon through pictographic characters. The children had prior experiences learning from pictographic characters in their Chinese class. Learning the Chinese character for moon helped the children to connect with the picturebook content (e.g., admiring the moon and eating mooncakes). Some children also wrote 月 in their drawings and built connections with their family's cultural practices in the Moon Festival (see Figure 8.4).

When the picturebooks contained Chinese cultures and traditions, it was emphasized in the pre-reading activities. For example, *Goldy Luck and the Three Pandas* had a page introducing the Chinese Zodiac at the end of the book. Ling presented the Chinese Zodiac page in English in the pre-reading phase and explained it in both languages to link it to the children's cultural knowledge. During reading, the children saw the Chinese Zodiac rug embedded in the story, which they immediately recognized, and ultimately caused excitement. After reading, Mae made paper cuttings about the Chinese Zodiac (see Figure 8.5).

**FIGURE 8.4** Mack's Response to *Thanking the Moon: Celebrating the Mid-Autumn Moon Festival.*

When the picturebooks contained Chinese characters, the children were taught writing and recognizing Chinese characters as a means to connect to their experiences. *The Pet Dragon: A Story about Adventure, Friendship, and Chinese Characters* (Niemann, 2008) used pictographic characters and presented many Chinese characters. When Ling read the book, she also taught the children about the structure of the Chinese characters that appeared in the picturebook. In another book, *The Magic Brush: A Story of Love, Family, and Chinese Characters* (Yeh, 2011), Ling asked the children to recognize the Chinese characters while reading. When the Chinese character 朋 (friend) appeared in the book, the children were excited to find it consisted of two 月 (moon) that they had learned earlier. The children consistently made connections among the content of the sessions.

## Translanguaging as an Art Form

The creative intermixing of multiple languages can be considered an art form in itself. It requires a delicate balance of selecting just the right words and language to communicate meaning. Children used translanguaging when they

**FIGURE 8.5** Mae's Paper Cuttings about Chinese Zodiac.

encountered unfamiliar English words and when they negotiated meanings as a whole class.

### Unfamiliar English Words

The children used translanguaging to express their ideas and discuss unfamiliar terms. For example, when Cindy saw the panda image, she described it as very dirty. However, she did not know how to say dirty in English. Thus, she said "He's very 脏 (dirty)," an instance where new language practices were emerging for Cindy. Another form of translanguaging occurred when English words were unknown. Choices were made by the children to respond using their family language resources. The following shows an example of Rena's translanguaging practices to express her ideas when she encountered unfamiliar terms in English. Here, Rena responded to Ling's question about the chicken in the story *Pancakes for Breakfast* (dePaola, 1978), which was extended to include Rena's personal preferences for eggs.

> *Ling:* To eat something. 小鸡在房里做什么呢？ (What is the chicken doing in the house?)
> *Rena:* 它要下蛋。 (The chicken is going to lay eggs.)

*Cindy:* Eggs.
*Ling:* Eggs. Yeah eggs.
*Grace:* Yeah. I love eggs.
*Rena:* I like eggs even more. 我喜欢炒蛋，我喜欢煮蛋，我喜欢煎蛋。 (I like scrambled eggs. I like boiled eggs. I like fried eggs.)

The translanguaging process allowed Rena to provide more details and express her inclination to different kinds of eggs in their conversation. Rena's decision to use Chinese was purposeful because it was about communicating knowledge regardless of language. In this space, Rena knew that a response in Chinese would be equally valued. Equally important here was Ling's use of both languages that may have solidified the acceptance of multilingualism.

## Negotiating Meaning

The children also used translanguaging to communicate and negotiate meaning as a large group. The translanguaging process reflected creative ways of blending languages for specific purposes. In addition, the children relied on particular words they knew in each of the languages and supplemented them with words in the other language. This process may be considered an artform given the unique form of communication. For example, when Ling presented a picture from *Pet Dragon* and asked the children about their thinking, the children used translanguaging to negotiate meaning.

*Ling:* So, what's happening here?
*Grace:* He went to the castle.
*Rena:* He went to the mountain.
*Cindy:* 不是 castle. (It's not a castle.)

While Grace described the image as a castle, Cindy did not agree with her. She selected the Chinese phrase 不是 (not) to emphasize her perspective. This was coupled with the English word castle. The result was a collaborative storyline.

In another example, the children attempted to make sense of the storyline in the book *The Farmer*. There were minimal words in the book, which left much to be discovered through the children's interpretations. In the transcript below, Ling positioned the children as authors of the story by asking them to predict based on the images in the book and their background knowledge about farming.

*Ling:* So, what do you think will happen? What's going to happen next?
*Rena:* I don't know.
*Grace:* People will be running out of the farm and trying to drink. Maybe not just people. Animals.
*Anna:* 我觉得他没有水了。 (I think he ran out of water.)
*Ling:* 没有水了，嗯。 (Ran out of water. Uh-huh.)

*Rena:* 会不会着火啊？ (Will it be on fire?)

*Ling:* 会着火吗？ (Will it be on fire?)

*Anna:* 会不会浇水啊？ (Will he water the plant?)

*Grace:* He can make more water.

*Rena:* 他怎么 make water? (How can he make water?)

*Grace:* He can use the water from the sea.

*Cindy:* Yeah.

*Ling:* Oh.

*Rena:* 那个water, 那个海上的水没了，怎么办呢？ (The water, what if he used all the water of the sea?)

*Anna:* 后面的。 (Behind.)

*Grace:* But if he used all the water of the sea, then he doesn't have, can't have any more water.

Grace started the storyline with her English comment about the farm running out of water and the need for both animals and humans to drink. The conversation continued in Chinese as Anna agreed, and Ling restated. This was followed by two inquiries in Chinese from Rena and Anna about a possible fire and watering the plants. Grace pushed the group's thinking forward by proposing he get more water from the sea. During the middle of this Rena asked a question by mixing the two languages. Grace responded in English and did not pause in crafting a response to a Chinese-English question. The languages continued to be used fluidly while a pondering of a larger question arose – what if the sea ran out of water.

In these instances, translanguaging extended the children's semiotic repertoire as an avenue for ways of being, knowing, and doing. The children represented here established new language practices in spaces where there were no threats to their unconventional ways of using language. Instead, the children were in continual states of becoming as they experimented with language forms in response to picturebooks (García & Wei, 2014).

## Discussion

Throughout the findings, there were multiple examples of children as social agents where dynamic interactions with others shaped and enhanced their lives. The semiotic efforts of the children presented learning opportunities revolving around culture and language. The artistic creations offered insight into what they were learning about their world. In many instances, the dialogue and artwork showed the children as agentive meaning makers. In other words, they actively sought and used available resources as decision makers (Fisher, 2010). The multimodal interactions around the read alouds revealed the consideration of alternative possibilities and the potential of collaborative text making whether the text be a storyline or an artistic representation (Mavers, 2011).

Within the children's explorations (linguistic and physical art), there was evidence of extended cultural understandings. In the case of translanguaging, the children experimented with linguistic resources in playful ways that increased their use of both Chinese and English words regardless of the dominant language. This was not only true in the dialogue examples, but also in the rich writing that occurred across languages (Leung, 2019). Therefore, it is essential to create learning invitations, respond in open-ended ways, and allow for the expansion of the initial invitation. Placing value on shared thinking and problem solving are critical components of supporting diverse cultural and linguistic practices (White, 2016).

In addition, Davies' (2014) concept of emergent listening assists in rethinking listening. Within her definition, it means opening yourself up to new possibilities. Instead of listening with preconceived notions of what children might say, emergent listening requires paying attention to each moment and the multiplicity of differences. In other words, being open to the unknown. It is through this frame that educators see new ways of being and doing literacy as they are performed by children. The Chinese American children in this research were able to continually reinvent themselves as the researchers remained open to new possibilities and learning from the children.

## Curricular Recommendations

The results highlight several ways that educators can adapt classroom literacy practices to better support multilingual children from various cultural backgrounds.

1. Integrating Multiple Modes into Daily Instructional Activities
   As learning opportunities are planned, be sure to think multimodally. Offer students more than one way to show and create knowledge. Additionally, use multimodal practices in your own teaching, so that new information is presented in more than one mode. This may mean that you use a series of Google images to pre-teach vocabulary prior to reading a story. The examples in the findings highlight the importance of visuals in picturebooks coupled with a space for in-depth dialogue. The dialogue should not be limited to questions from a textbook, but arise from the children. Pose questions that require pondering and possibilities. Even better, allow students to ask their own questions and push for peer responses. The students should have an agentive role in expanding the conversation (Darling-McQuistan, 2017; White, 2016). Further, offering artistic spaces for responses to books reveals new insights into the knowledge students have about read alouds. Providing a wide variety of resources for multimodal responses enhances learning. Consider drawing materials and other resources like Legos, scissors, paint, staplers, etc. Application of the visual arts helps students bridge links between stories read to them and their own lives (Kim, 2016).

2.  Supplementing Culture

    When struggling to locate authentic cultural resources, think about supplementing some existing resources that you already have as in the case when Ling paired *The Farmer* with a Chinese poem and cultural images of farmers. Try searching nontraditional publishers for culturally relevant texts across a broad base. The following is a list of recommended sites:

    Language Lizard – www.languagelizard.com/Default.asp
    Lee and Low Books – www.leeandlow.com/
    Lantana Publishing – https://lantanapublishing.com/

    Families are also a great resource. Get to know the families of the children you teach in order to understand their home resources. For example, a father might be a great storyteller and can share cultural stories with the class. Other family members might have expertise in areas such as music, drawing, and cooking. The use of culturally relevant texts cannot be overstated (Gay, 2018; Ladson-Billings, 1995; Paris & Alim, 2017). Be creative with the ways you put together resources to build connections to students' cultural lives. Teaching online sessions offers a great opportunity to get to know the families since they may sit beside the child.

3.  Supporting Translanguaging

    It is critical for both multilingual and monolingual teachers to open classroom spaces for translanguaging practices. Allow for moment-to-moment interactions to adapt from one language to another including the writing process. A holistic view of the student is needed to see the interdependence of resources used in concert with one another to make sense of the world (Clark, 2020; Cummins, 2009; Wei, 2018). Accepting student work that contains multiple languages is part of the process. Move beyond an English-only curriculum to value the home languages of students. If you are a monolingual teacher, technology resources supporting translation can be very helpful. For example, Google Translate (https://translate.google.com/) offers a means to translate written work, and Talking Points (https://talkingpts.org/), a free app, supports verbal communication in multiple languages. Note that forcing children to adhere to only one language when they use multiple languages at home every day may stifle learning for some students (Hu, Liu, & Zheng, 2018).

## Conclusion

The virtual book club was an out-of-school experience for these children where they were able to be supported and engage in culturally meaningful ways that sustained and revitalized their connections to Chinese culture. We make the call to open spaces like this within the confines of schools and classrooms. García and Wei (2014) state, "Translanguaging enables us to imagine new ways of being and languaging so that we can begin to act differently upon the world" (p. 138).

This is only possible when multimodal practices become a routine staple in early childhood practices.

We also invite you to continue thinking about translanguaging and the ways in which emergent bilinguals use it as an artistic expression. It is easy to see a drawing or painting as artistic because of the visual nature of the product. However, more of a concerted effort must be made to think about language use as art. The beautifully complex ways in which children utilize their linguistic repertoires to explain their understanding of the world is also art, but we must take the time to notice and value it.

## References

Adomat, D. S. (2010). Dramatic interpretations: Performative responses of young children to picturebook read-alouds. *Children's Literature in Education, 41*(3), 207–221. https://doi.org/10.1007/s10583-010-9105-0

Alvarez, A. (2018). Drawn and written funds of knowledge: A window into emerging bilingual children's experiences and social interpretations through their written narratives and drawings. *Journal of Early Childhood Literacy, 18*(1), 97–128. https://doi.org/10.1177/1468798417740618

Arizpe, E. (2013). Meaning-making from wordless (or nearly wordless) picturebooks: What educational research expects and what readers have to say. *Cambridge Journal of Education, 43*(2), 163–176. https://doi.org/10.1080/0305764X.2013.767879

Bengochea, A., Sembiante, S. F., & Gort, M. (2018). An emergent bilingual child's multimodal choices in sociodramatic play. *Journal of Early Childhood Literacy, 18*(1), 38–70. https://doi.org/10.1177/1468798417739081

Bezemer, J., & Kress, G. (2016). *Multimodality, learning, and communication: A social semiotic frame.* Routledge.

Bhatt, R. M., & Bolonyai, A. (2019). Code-switching and translanguaging. In J. Östman and J. Verschueren (Eds.), *Handbook of Pragmatics: 22nd Annual Installment* (pp. 59–78). John Benjamins Publishing Company.

Brown, S., & Hao, L. (Eds.). (2022). *Multimodal literacies in young emergent bilinguals: Beyond print-centric practices.* Multilingual Matters.

Carger, C. L. (2004). Art and literacy with bilingual children. *Language Arts, 81*(4), 283.

Chang, N., & Cress, S. (2014). Conversations about visual arts: Facilitating oral language. *Early Childhood Education Journal, 42*(6), 415–422. https://doi.org/10.1007/s10643-013-0617-2

Clark, A. (2020). Cultural relevance and linguistic flexibility in literature discussions with emergent bilingual children. *Bilingual Research Journal, 43*(1), 50–70. https://doi.org/10.1080/15235882.2020.1722974

Cummins, J. (2009). Pedagogies of choice: Challenging coercive relations of power in classrooms and communities. *International Journal of Bilingual Education and Bilingualism, 12*(3), 261–271. https://doi.org/10.1080/13670050903003751

Darling-McQuistan, K. (2017). Beyond representation: Exploring drawing as part of children's meaning-making. *International Journal of Art & Design Education, 36*(3), 281–291. https://doi.org/10.1111/jade.12158

Davies, B. (2014). *Listening to children: Being and becoming.* Routledge.

Enriquez, G., & Wager, A. C. (2018). The reader, the text, the performance: Opening spaces for the ferforming arts as reader response. *Voices From the Middle, 26*(1), 21–25.

Fisher, R. (2010). Young writers' construction of agency. *Journal of Early Childhood Literacy, 10*(4), 410–429. https://doi.org/10.1177/1468798410382407

García, O., Johnson, S. I., Seltzer, K., & Valdés, G. (2017). *The translanguaging classroom: Leveraging student bilingualism for learning.* Caslon.

García, O. & Wei, L. (2014). *Translanguaging: Language, bilingualism and education.* Palgrave McMillan.

Gay, G. (2018). *Culturally responsive teaching: Theory, research, and practice* (3rd ed.). Teachers College Press.

Hu, R., Liu, X., & Zheng, X. (2018). Examining meaning-making from reading wordless picture books in Chinese and English by three bilingual children. *Journal of Early Childhood Literacy, 18*(2), 214–238. https://doi.org/10.1177/1468798416643357

Jewitt, C., Bezemer, J., & O'Halloran, K. (2016). *Introducing multimodality.* Routledge.

Khimji, F., & Maunder, R. E. (2012). Mediational tools in story construction: An investigation of cultural influences on children's narratives. *Journal of Early Childhood Research, 10*(3), 294–308.

Kim, H. (2018). Towards a dialogic understanding of children's art-making process. *International Journal of Art & Design Education, 37*(1), 101–112.

Kim, S. J. (2016). The role of peer relationships and interactions in preschool bilingual children's responses to picture books. *Journal of Early Childhood Literacy, 16*(3), 311–337. https://doi.org/10.1177/1468798415577874

Kress, G. (2010). *Multimodality: A social semiotic approach to contemporary communication.* Routledge.

Ladson-Billings, G. (1995). Toward a theory of culturally relevant pedagogy. *American Educational Research Journal, 32*(3), 465–491. https://doi.org/10.3102/0002831203 2003465

Leung, S. K. (2019). Translanguaging through visual arts in early childhood: A case study in a Hong Kong kindergarten. *Asia-Pacific Journal of Research in Early Childhood Education, 13*(1), 47–67. http://dx.doi.org/10.17206/apjrece.2019.13.1.47

Louie, B. & Davis-Welton, K. (2016). Family literacy project: Bilingual picture books by English learners. *The Reading Teacher, 69*(6), 597–606. https://doi.org/10.1002/trtr.1444

Martens, P., Martens, R., Doyle, M. H., Loomis, J., Fuhrman, L., Stout, R., & Soper, E. (2018). Painting writing, writing painting: Thinking, seeing, and problem solving through story. *The Reading Teacher, 71*(6), 669–679. https://doi.org/10.1002/trtr.1668

Mavers, D. (2011). *Children's drawing and writing: The remarkable in the unremarkable.* Routledge.

Pantaleo, S. (2020). Slow looking: "Reading picturebooks takes time." *Literacy, 54*(1), 40–48. https://doi.org/10.1111/lit.12190

Rabey, K. (2004). Thinking aloud: looking at children drawing in response to picturebooks. In Arizpe, E., & Styles, M. (Eds.), *Children reading pictures: Interpreting visual texts* (pp. 117–143). Routledge.

Suárez-Orozco, M., & Suárez-Orozco, C. (2015). Children of immigration. *Phi Delta Kappan, 97*(4), 8–14.

Vogel, S., & García, O. (2017). *Translanguaging.* Oxford University Press.

Wei, L. (2018). Translanguaging as a practical theory of language. *Applied Linguistics, 39*(1), 9–30. https://doi.org/10.1093/applin/amx039

White, E. (2016). *Introducing dialogic pedagogy: Provocations for the early years.* Routledge.

## Children's Literature Cited

Abadia, X. (2019). *The farmer*. Holiday House.
dePaola, T. (1978). *Pancakes for breakfast*. Clarion Books.
Lin, G. (2012). *Thanking the moon: Celebrating the mid-autumn moon festival*. Knopf Books for Young Readers.
Lin, G. (2003). *Dim sum for everyone*. Dragonfly Books.
Niemann, C. (2008). *The pet dragon: A story about adventure, friendship, and Chinese characters*. Harper Collins.
Yeh, K. (2011). *The Magic Brush: A story of love, family, and Chinese characters*. Walker Childrens.
Yim, N. (2014). *Goldy Luck and the three pandas*. Charlesbridge.

## Appendix A

| Week | Book | Author / Illustrator |
| --- | --- | --- |
| 1 | Thanking the Moon: Celebrating the Mid-Autumn Moon Festival | Grace Lin |
| 2 | Hello | Aiko Ikegami |
| 3 | Dim Sum for Everyone | Grace Lin |
| 4 | The Pet Dragon: A Story about Adventure, Friendship, and Chinese Characters | Christoph Niemann |
| 5 | The Magic Brush: A Story of Love, Family, and Chinese Characters | Kat Yeh / Huy Voun Lee |
| 6 | Giant: A Panda of the Enchanted Forest | Xuan Loc Xuan |
| 7 | The Farmer | Ximo Abadia |
| 8 | Pancakes for Breakfast | Tomie dePaola |
| 9 | Round is a Mooncake: A Book of Shapes | Roseanne Thong / Grace Lin |
| 10 | Goldy Luck and the Three Pandas | Natasha Yim / Grace Zong |

# 9

# MY STORYTELLING JOURNEY

## From Rural Settings in Haiti to Urban Settings in New England

*Charlot Lucien*

*Krik?* I shouted!

*Krak!* They responded. But not loud enough to my taste. I went on:

*KRIK-KRIK?* I shouted louder.

*KRAK-KRAK!!* They shouted back powerfully. Now, I knew I had my audience's attention.

*So do tell me, those of you who have some cats and some dogs at home, how much do they love each other? Not at all? Guess what! In Haiti, we know why! And since you are such a good audience, I will tell you.*

*Once upon a time, Brother Cat and Brother Dog, who back then lived like brothers, were sitting under the mango tree discussing the affairs of the village, when Dog barked: "Ruf! Ruf! Ruf! So bad in the village, no one is feeding me anymore, and I have been going hungry! What's a dog got to do to survive? Maybe I should ask Papa God to bring dead people back on earth, and I will have more meat, more bones to eat?"*

*Brother Cat explained that there wasn't enough space on earth to receive all the dead, but Brother Dog wouldn't have it, pointing out how those humans were all crying whenever someone died.*

*"They will make room in their living rooms for dead people."*

*"But how would you get dead people back alive"?*

*Ruf! Ruf! Brother Dog barked joyfully. "I'll have to convince Papa God to bring them back so I can eat more. God made me without teaching me a trade and I depend on humans. He owes me that. I will visit him tomorrow."*

The story sets the stage to explain to my general audience why cats and dogs have not been friends since Brother Cat betrayed Brother Dog's plans to Papa God and why dead people are no longer back on earth. In the process, I get my audience to meow, bark, or snore as powerfully as Papa God, a task the younger members of my audience usually participate in with contagious enthusiasm.

#######

DOI: 10.4324/9781003302186-15

## The Storyteller's Beginning: Spirited Folktales

My storyteller's journey starts on a dark night in Charlette, one of these remote hamlets in Southern Haiti, where I spent my summer vacations in my grandparents' house back in the early seventies. Some 500 souls lived in small houses with no electricity by a dirt road that barely saw a truck drive in four times a year. Visiting from the capital, I would join others at night around a campfire to enjoy some spirited sessions of riddles, listen to frightening folktales featuring great devils that gobble up unruly children, gigantic monsters (Barthélemy, 1995), blank-eyed zombies, and other fantastic creatures in Haitian mythology identified by Charles Asselin (1980).

The traditional Haitian storytelling moment, known as *"tire kont"* – "to fire stories" – starts with an animated call-and-response. A vigorous *"Krik?"* call from the storyteller is expected to be met with a resounding *"Krak!"* from the audience. The storytelling itself is usually preceded by pointed riddles to rouse the audience.

I joined enthusiastic children singing along when a story included a song or eager adults competing to showcase their mastery of a folktale or the latest riddles. In the process kids learned about community norms: respect for the elderly, taking turns, sharing, etc. They also sharpened their wit and debating skills as we had to at times justify the validity of a response to a riddle.

The setting and the intent of these outdoor sessions, similar in format to many held in various African villages for centuries, are a far cry from the settings and the intent of storytelling sessions staged under the bright lights of an academic hall in Boston, Montreal, Florida, in a barely lit café in Massachusetts, or arranged via Zoom –one of the latest options for sharing stories since COVID-19.

## Traditional Haitian Storytelling: Intergenerational Gifts

Traditional storytelling is an inherent societal and cultural oral practice, particularly in Haiti where the adult literacy rate has fluctuated around 62% depending on the period or the reference source (uis.unesco.org). From a literary perspective, one would have to refer to the abundant volume of scholarly works available to fully appreciate the richness of the Haitian oral tradition and its various components: proverbs, riddles, folktales, and the more recently named *lodyans*, a distinct type of short story that relies on observation of social facts, humor, and vocal abilities.

In rural Haiti particularly, children and adults are raised practicing le *"tire kont"* – literally "fire folktales" – as part of their nighttime ritual. Folktales have entertained families or kept unruly children in check by instilling the fear of the bogeyman or the great devil, and taught them wit and resourcefulness thanks to certain folk characters. These stories, some dating back to slavery times and rooted in African traditions, have been passed from generation to generation through gifted storytellers known as *"mèt kont"* ("master of stories"), the equivalent of the African "Griot" (Wolkstein, 1993).

Many Haitian folktales frequently evoke tigers, monkeys, and lions…wild animals that do not exist in Haiti. It is then fair to speculate that survivors who made the slave trade journey between 1503 and 1793 (the abolition of slavery in Haiti) would have brought their memories across the Atlantic and evoked visions of such wildlife creatures with their children during slavery times. Haitian folktales that feature French or Spanish kings or other European characters stem from the interaction between the Africans forced into servitude and the European colonizers.

In her research, Fatoumata Seck observed: "When millions of Africans were taken to the Americas, their oral literature, encapsulated in their memories, was one of the few belongings they were able to bring with them to this new land and life" (Seck, 2018, pp.76–78). Evidence of such transfer can be found in the Haitian Bouki/Ti Malis, Jean Sot/Jean Lespri dyads where a trickster (Ti Malis, Jean Lespri) routinely outsmarts a slow character (Uncle Bouki, Jean Sot). Research suggests that these stories often mirror folktales involving the hyena and the devious jackal, two characters often found in traditional South African folktales

In *The Magic Orange Tree*, there is an elaborate compilation of Haitian folktales. Anthropologist and storyteller Diane Wolkstein (1993) also observed, "Many of the tales I recognized at once because of their European or African counterparts. Mother of the Waters is a version of the German "Mother Holle" collected by the Grimm brothers."

Riddles are known to be integral parts of the Haitian storytelling session and usually precede the formal storytelling in a rapid series of calls-and-responses (Préval, Guerdy-Jacques, 2021).

*Storyteller: Tim-tim?* (The call for a riddle.)
*Audience: Bwa Chèch!* (The response to the call.)
*Storyteller: I have four feet, I get dressed every day, but never leave the house?*
 After various attempts, the answers might come: *"the bed"!*

Aside from the display of wit, the riddles bring into light established traditions and serve as norm-reinforcement tools. The daily making of the bed is part of the morning routine that children ultimately assimilate. Riddles integrated into the storytelling sessions affirm for children certain normative social practices and values: specific placement of household items, respect for elders, gratitude, appreciation of the environment, etc.

James Ivy's (1941) observed, "One African tradition which flourished in Haiti was the African knack of creating proverbs and traditional metaphors. Moreover, the tradition still lives; hence Haiti today is rich in proverbs" (p. 197). A trademark of the Haitian oral tradition, proverbs express popular wisdom, community, or individual experiences. They are used not just for their colorful or witty evocations, but also as educational tools, public health guidance, wisdom recipes, or plain survival guide. Some resort to metaphors or allegories that may be unique to Haitian culture, which make them at times challenging to translate or convey to the non-Haitian audience.

*Dèyè mòn gen mòn. ("Behind mountains are more mountains.")*

The basic literal translation says little about the depth of this proverb, which Haitians use to express that the country has always had to climb through hardship (mountains) after hardship since its independence including regular invasion attempts or sustained waves of natural disasters or political turmoil.

A particular brand of written storytelling emerged at the end of the 19th century and flourished at the beginning of the 20th century, the *lodyans*. "In recent years, microfiction, the art of brevity in literature, has blossomed in the French Antilles. From modern folktales to Haitian "lodyans," these stories are meant for laughing, smiling, grinning, grimacing, pondering" (Saint-Fort, Hugues & Spring, 2013, pp. 317–318). The *lodyans* features real-life stories shared to seemingly entertain revelers at social gatherings while in fact the stories ridicule, denounce social aberrations, unbecoming personal behaviors, or political misdeeds.

In the Gwo Moso lodyans, master storyteller Maurice Sixto features a loud-mouth character who brags about teaching respect to and beating up people who challenge him. He relishes in the fear his stories seem to inspire in his audience. Out of nowhere, a policeman who felt provoked by Gro-Moso's repeated tirades about beating up "anyone" arrests him and threatens to break his teeth, to the delight of the crowd. The lodyans ends with Gwo Moso whispering, "So, if that's what you want, I will walk to the precinct chief with you; you know, jails are built for humans you know? Not for dogs; but let me tell you, as soon as we get there… I know people, people who know me too…" A woman in the crowd praises the policeman, and concludes with a string of proverbs: *Chak boutèy gen bouchon li; ou jwenn pa ou.* (To each bottle, its cap; he found his) (Sixto, 2001). Author Georges Anglade summed up the concept, "We are dealing with the art of voicing stories, with a way to tell stories that provides an angle to appreciate Haitian humor, exactly as one refers to British or to Jewish humor" (Lévy, 2004, p. 205).

Wakes have been prevalent settings for traditional *lodyansè* and *mèt-kont* to compete for audiences' attention according to Carey Cardompre who presented a thesis on lodyans at the Sorbonne University (Cardompre, 2018). However, the oral manifestation of the *lodyans* blossomed on Haiti's radio waves in the mid-1970s and the 1980s, thanks to contemporary Haitian storytellers –*lodyansè* – such as the late Maurice Sixto (Otilien, 2018), Jean-Claude Martineau, (Toussaint, 2021) and later, Charlot Lucien (Comeau, 2002), while its written version found public praise in published stories by contemporary authors such as Gary Victor and Yanick Lahens, to cite a few (Nzengou-Tayo, 2010).

## The Immigrant Storyteller: Negotiating Challenges

My journey as an immigrant in Massachusetts started in my late twenties and could have been a story in itself. In my attempt to integrate various circles, within and outside my community, I found myself negotiating – or unable to negotiate – a host of challenges: language barriers, cultural barriers, the value of money, the changing weather, new holidays, friends and relatives' new norms that made some into unrecognizable compatriots.

Having been engaged in storytelling as an artform all my life, first as an eager listener-consumer in my childhood and for the past 25 years as a performing storyteller, I am now able to retrospectively appreciate some highlights of my trajectory (i.e., major lessons learned and mistakes made). An immigrant storyteller performs in a new environment characterized by different cultural norms, new technologies, pragmatic considerations (the grant, the stipend, the reports), multiculturalism, and lingering effects of racism that they may not have experienced in their native country.

My first public appearances as a storyteller came through live community radio programming in the mid-1990s, a departure from the communal setting I knew in Haiti. Through word of mouth, and with some of my *lodyans* being aired on various radio programs in the US Diaspora, I found myself invited to several US states and later to Guadeloupe, Canada, and France. However, such recognition had its limitations since the target audience was essentially my Haitian compatriots.

Two opportunities would take me to a wider English-speaking audience, increasing my visibility and my awareness of the cultural differences. I was hired in 2007 by Revels Theater company, based in Watertown MA, to work with about 15 non-Haitian children age 7 to 15 as part of the annual Summer Revels Theatre at the Boston Children's Museum. They were to perform Haitian children's songs in Creole and mime the two Haitian folktales that I would narrate. A musical director coached them practicing the songs I had transcribed in some unorthodox Haitian Creole phonetic spelling with my children Malaika and Sebastien who had previously mastered the lyrics. A few days later I experienced a powerful cultural moment when the children delivered an almost flawless Haitian Creole rendition of the songs *Ti Zwazo* and *Zanmi Mannmannan*. The lesson was simple: children involved in storytelling are significantly incentivized and overcome cultural and language barriers when supported by qualified teachers and enthusiastic peers.

My journey took another leap after the devastating 2010 Haiti earthquake that left more than 250,000 people dead. I was invited to contribute with stories at fundraising events for the victims. Two storytelling organizations, Massmouth and the League for the Advancement of New England Storytelling (LANES), reached out and I found myself in the company of dedicated storytellers brought together by an unprecedented tragedy. Interaction with these networks and my collaboration with their members prompted me to revisit my concepts of storytelling. I was no longer *sharing* a story in a familiar rural setting. I was to *perform* for sitting crowds trained in a certain way of experiencing formally introduced *performances* – unlike "tire-kont/firing stories" – while casually chewing on a mango, sharing a piece of fried goat with others.

To present stories in a new language brings both challenges and retooling opportunities. It is about threading carefully the terminology and awareness of linguistic pitfalls, and pondering potentially revisionist adaptations to account for cultural differences or sensitivities:

- How would my young audience grasp a character in my story who goes hungry for one day, sucking on a piece of sugarcane to quiet his hunger? What is sugar cane anyway?
- Should I adjust my stories to substitute some Haitian fruits (mango) with local American fruits (apple) to make my story more relatable for some students in Massachusetts?
- How do I negotiate gender-stereotyping stories? (Wolkenstein, 1978)
- How do I properly translate some colorful expressions such as *Lave men siye atè* (literally "to wash your hands and wipe them in the dust") to describe a useless endeavor?

Over time, with the support of fellow storytellers – Norah Dooley, Andrea Lovett, Sharon Kennedy, Cheryl Hamilton, Michael Anderson, Arnie Danielson, and my own children, Malaika and Sebastien, who took on storytelling at a young age – I developed the confidence to turn such challenges into opportunities. I became more creative in my approach. My audience could not always rely on my storytelling skills to "visualize" my "yuca" or the "sugar cane." I needed to give them a chance to view, touch, and smell by adding a tridimensional aspect to my craft. Young audiences are willing to stomp their feet along with the Great Devil, bark while chasing the cat in "Cat and God and the return of the Dead," or sing along with the horse in "Horse and Toad" as it happened in my most recent April 2022 session in Winthrop, Massachusetts.

Storyteller Jo Radner commented after I performed the story "The Kissing Round" at the North East Storytelling conference in 2017: "You lifted us out of that hotel ballroom, out of our manufactured chairs and tired conference-weary bodies, into a new country, a new way of thinking about and feeling story, a welcome delight in the word and the tale. I loved the way you presented the riddles (and tossed the mangoes!). Your personal stories showed us much about Haiti – and about the USA." (www.nestorytelling.org/charlot-lucien/). Further opportunities to appreciate Haitian riddles presented themselves in some academic settings.

*Storyteller's call: Tim-tim?*
*Audience's answer: Bwa-chèch!*
*Storyteller: Born in water, made of water, if I fall in water, I "die," I disappear?*
*Audience member: Ice!*

The response appears to be correct. However, if the session was introduced by contextualizing the geographic and economic reality of Haiti, we would undoubtedly find a student questioning the validity of such an answer. Does "ice" meet the parameters established for an underdeveloped island surrounded by the ocean? Do most people have a fridge? With enough prompts, some students usually come up with the accurate answer: "the salt!" With trained storytellers, riddles, folktales, and proverbs bring awareness about geography, other countries' cultural practices, economic differentials, the importance of the flora or the wildlife in ways that turn them into innovative learning tools. This is in line with an observation shared by Haitian author and educator Evelyne Trouillot who actively promotes the concept of Social and Emotional Learning (SEL) in the classroom. "Trouillot believes that while it will not be easy to maintain, Haitians must thrive to keep storytelling alive. In fact, she notes that teachers can even leverage storytelling in the classroom to improve student litteracy." https://iei.nd.edu/initiatives/global-center-for-the-development-of-the-whole-child/news/the-intersection-of-haitian

## Bearing Witness: A Transformational Cultural Act

As an immigrant storytelling within a Western context, choosing and delivering a story remains a balancing act. While some traditional stories rooted in ancient times may have no agency over a community's contemporary identity, for the uneducated audience they may easily trigger stereotypes about such identity. All immigrant communities have gone through their share of prejudice and stereotyping often exacerbated by pop culture (Maan, 1974). How they handle the prejudice and the stereotyping will often determine their social network and their standing in their host environment.

Are all Haitians "Boat people"? Are all Italians mafia associates? Do all Latinos eat "arroz con pollo?" As a storyteller, should I modify my characters' identities to avoid controversy? Should I avoid "scaring young audiences" by steering clear of "great devils gulping unruly children"? Should I remove the misogynistic aspects of a story? Or do I embrace the story's ethnological features and engage the audience in learning moments?

Without the proper framing, the uncontextualized, raw delivery of a story may generate cultural or emotional trauma and become counterproductive as we pursue mutually beneficial cross-cultural relationship-building. Not all audiences, nor all educators realize that in a new environment, the immigrant storyteller at times becomes self-conscious and over-processes the disposition of the audience, which potentially impacts the performance or the authenticity of the delivery. Ultimately storytellers bear witness to their surroundings and their times. Bearing witness, feeling the responsibility to represent (Toussaint, 2012) becomes a transformational cultural act in the face of many prevalent issues of the 21st century, including racism, environmental disasters, and a worldwide public health crisis created by COVID.

## Storytelling: Opening Doors to Unexpected Fields

On January 11, 2018, President Trump called Haiti and other developing countries "s...hole countries." With the realization that the racism was being either more overt or better recorded, I retooled history – that is, Haitian history – to tell stories, while also using stories to tell Haiti's history. The film industry successfully uses storytelling to sell otherwise little known, but crucial historical events

(Spartacus, 1960; Gladiator, 2000). Haiti's unique history can also leverage super-heroes, epic battles, unique local gods and malevolent spirits (Dayan, 1995) that can be packaged for diverse audiences. Thanks to technology, I have presented storytelling remotely to educators and students in London, Boston, and Florida during the COVID-19 pandemic and the responses prompted me to explore – or *storytellize* – other Haitian historical characters and events https://mit-ayiti.net/res ous/entevyou-ak-lodyanse-charlot-lucien/

Storytelling in fact has been opening doors in unexpected fields – theology, narrative medicine, communication, narrative management – to cite a few points made by Joseph Daniel Sobol (Sobol, 2008). Additional testimony came from New York City-based storyteller and author Laura Simms who traveled to Haiti after the devastating 2010 earthquake to work with distressed youth. She attests to the proven therapeutic value of storytelling in helping victims of disasters regain a sense of normalcy and connections with others (Simms, 2012). Author Jocelyn Trouillot who experienced Haitian storytelling in her childhood, and education expert Anasthasie Liberiste-Osirus, make the case for integrating storytelling as a Social and Emotional Learning (SEL) tool in literacy campaigns for any age group (Global Center for the Development of the Whole Child, 2021).

With a bit of creativity, other doors can still be opened. As the visual artist interacting weekly with some 40 other artists over more than 20 years, I am real-izing the fascinating evocative power of both arts and the opportunity to connect them by bringing to life through storytelling, both the trajectory of the inspiration and the final artwork. If anything, the lives of Frieda Kahlo, Dali, Da Vinci, or the immigrant journey of 30 Haitian painters residing in Massachusetts are powerful storytelling materials, in addition to their artworks. Of all the artistic genres, visual art is the one that remains silent in its exchange with its audience. Storytelling can change this dynamic and I believe in undertaking such a challenge to expand the educational and cultural experiences of all stakeholders. The omnipresence of drums and women in my artworks has been a reminder that through their evolu-tion Haitians have remained rooted in their culture to give meaning to their exist-ence and withstand political turmoil, international ostracism, and environmental disasters. Representations of cultural symbols and historical figures matter.

## Conclusion: The Call-And-Response Exchange

Ultimately, I have learned from this journey that storytelling is an efficient tool to get audiences to experience the challenging and extraordinary journey of immigrants. This journey, told by those who have lived it, usually carries an emo-tional charge and an authenticity level that resonates with audiences, whether elementary school students, educators, politicians, or legislators enacting policies.

The challenges are real, however the beauty and richness of storytelling, as a performing art form and an instrument of awareness, empowerment, and ultimately change, will continue to reside in the realization that the immigrant storytelling con-struct is constantly negotiated over time in a call-and-response exchange between the storyteller and the audience, between educators and storytellers, between agency and structure. The dynamics of such exchange provide as much learning opportunities as the stories themselves. Understanding and respecting the journey of immigrant storytellers will elevate our ability to properly make use of storytelling in educational settings that are currently challenged by the dual impact of a public health crisis and the cost of education. Open-minded and receptive partners willing to assume their agency and push the structural boundaries of creativity will make room for more powerful stories and real system change in the future.

## References

Barthélémy, M. (1995). *Contes diaboliques d'Haïti*. KARTHALA Editions.
Charles, A. (1980). Voodoo Myths in Haitian Literature. *Comparative Literature Studies, 17*(4), 391–398.
Comeau, L. (2002). Littérature Orale Haïtienne: Analyse d'un Nouvel Apport. *Journal of Haitian Studies*, 80–97.
Dardompré, C. (2018). *La lodyans, un romanesque haïtien perspectives historique, poétique and didactique. Perspectives historique, poétique and didactique: La lodyans, a Haitian literary genre. Its historical background, poetics and use as didatical approach* (Doctoral dissertation, Sorbonne Paris Cité).
Dayan, J. (1995) Haiti, History and the Gods. University of California Press, Oakland, California.
Global Center for the Development of the Whole Child (2021) https://iei.nd.edu/initiatives/global-center-for-the-development-of-the-whole-child/news/the-intersection-of-haitian
Ivy, J. W. (1941). The Wisdom of the Haitian Peasant: Or Some Haitian Proverbs Considered. *The Journal of Negro History, 26*(4), 485–498.
Lévy, J. J. (2004). Entretiens avec Georges Anglade. L'espace d'une génération. *Montréal: Liber.*
Maan, A. (1974). Immigrants in American Life. Houghton Mifflinc Company, Boston, MA.
Nzengou-Tayo, M. J. (2010). The Haitian short story: an overview. *Journal of Caribbean Literatures, 6*(3), 37–52.
Otilien, E. (2018). Maurice Sixto ou le phénix de l'oraliture haïtienne. JEBCA Editions.
Préval, G.J. (2021). Les 175 devinettes illustrées les plus savoureuses d'Haïti (The 175 Most Enjoyable Haitian Riddles); Editions Histoires Nouvelles, Montréal, Canada.
Saint-Fort, H. (2013). La Famille des Pitite-Caille; Zoune chez sa ninnaine, par Justin Lhérisson by Léon-François Hoffmann. *Journal of Haitian Studies, 19*(1), 317–325.
Seck, F. (2018). Crossing the atlantic: bouqui and malice, a caribbean counterpoetics. *Journal of Haitian Studies, 24*(1), 76–100.
Simms, L. (2012). Passport to Joy: The Journey of a Haitian Tale in a Tent in Haiti. *Storytelling, Self, Society, 8*(3), 202–207.
Sixto, M. (2001). Gwo Moso, Fresco Productions. Pétion-Ville, Haiti.
Sobol, J. D. (2008). Contemporary storytelling: Revived traditional art and protean social agent. *Storytelling, Self, Society, 4*(2), 122–133.
Toussaint, E. (2012). Another Face of Haiti, Tanbou Magazine on-line. UNESCO's Institute for Statistics (uis.unesco.org). Data as of September 2020.
Toussaint, E. (2021). https://lenouvelliste.com/article/229667/jean-claude-martineau-an-vedet-nan-livres-en-folie
Wolkstein, D. (1978). *The Magic Orange Tree, and Other Haitian Folk Tales*. Knopf Books for Young Readers.

# 10

# IDENTITY, VOICES, AND AGENCY OF ASIAN FEMALE GRADUATE STUDENTS THROUGH VISUAL SELF-INQUIRY

## An Interdisciplinary Study of Art, Literacy, and Language

*Bokyoung Jo and Yixuan Wang*

### Introduction

The authors, Bokyoung and Yixuan, first met each other during the international student orientation at a university in the southeastern U.S. Having similar cultural backgrounds and hobbies, the friendship developed through the sharing of our respective cultures, food, and research interests. As two East Asian female international students, we have experienced micro-aggressions, racism, and xenophobia on and off the campus. However, these negative experiences have caused more fear and anxiety since the outbreak of the COVID-19 pandemic, due to the rising levels of anti-Asian hatred around the world. As we went through this fear and stress, we started creating visual journals as auto-ethnographies so we could record our unprecedented experiences as Asian female international students in the United States. In this chapter, our stories will unfold through both narratives and visual journals.

### Collaborative Process

In Fall 2020, Bokyoung created a group space for Asian international doctoral students from South Korea and China to share and explore our unique experiences through the online meeting platform, Zoom. During our weekly two-hour meetings, Bokyoung led lectures that guided the group to explore a focused topic/emotion by showing artwork from different artists and asking prepared questions. The meetings asked participants to reflect on their daily experiences and identities through their artwork (Berriz, 2005). The explored topics included but were not limited to memories, hoarded items, and personal fears. After the synchronous

DOI: 10.4324/9781003302186-16

meetings, the group members spent the week creating new visual journals, a combination of drawings and essays/narratives, that either centered on a given topic or documented their daily lives of the week. The newly created journals would then be shared and discussed at the next group meeting.

## Context

The term, "Asian American," according to the U.S. Census Bureau (2000), is used in the United States to define "a person with origins in any of the original peoples of the Far East, Southeast Asia, or the Indian subcontinent" (as cited in Asian Pacific Institute on Gender Based Violence, n.d., para. 1). Another term, "Native Hawaiian and Other Pacific Islander," includes Native Hawaiian, Samoan, Guamanian or Chamorro, Fijian, Tongan, or Marshallese people eliminate 's' and encompasses the people within the United States' (?) jurisdictions of Melanesia, Micronesia, and Polynesia. Therefore, the combined term Asian/Asian American and Pacific Islander (AAPI) describes a diverse and fast-growing population that has heritage from more than 40 countries.

Incidents of hate crimes, racism, discrimination, and xenophobia against AAPI communities have increased since the beginning of the COVID-19 pandemic in 2020. According to the research released by the reporting forum, Stop AAPI Hate, nearly 3,800 incidents of discrimination were reported in a one-year span from March 2020 to February 2021. Within these incidents, women reported 2.3 times more frequently than did men (Stop AAPI Hate, 2021). The pain and anger of the AAPI community reached its peak after the tragic spa shootings in the Atlanta metropolitan area in March 2021. The shooter's comments on his sex addiction drew society's attention to the intertwined issues of sexism and racism that Asian females continue to face in the United States. Although most of the victims in the spa shootings were Asian immigrants who worked in the service industry, harmful stereotypes, racism, and sexism against Asian females exist in many other professions.

In U.S. higher education, whether American-born or not, both AAPI male and female educators, students, administrators, and policymakers have been viewed as a homogenous group of foreign, non-native English speakers, regardless of the diversity of ethnicities, cultures, home languages, and individualities. While being subjected to many stereotypes such as being quiet, docile, exotic, as well as hardworking and successful, the AAPI communities' experiences are still invisible in higher education. As has been noted, "Stereotyping as an inscriptive act of temporal deprivation or imaginary desiccation is not only metaphysically delimiting but psychically damaging … In the land of stereotype, no one escapes her/himself" (Lee, 2013, p. 92). However, in recent years, scholars, educators, and students of Asian descent have pushed back against stereotypes and advocated for Asian/Asian American students, educators, and scholars to amplify Asian voices (Housee, 2010; Hsieh & Nguyen, 2020; Ifitikar & Museus, 2018). In light of the social movement of Stop Asian Hate and increased attention on Asian females' experiences and voices, we aim to showcase our experiences and voices as two East Asian international doctoral female students through the approach of visual journals, with the guidance of translanguaging, Asian Critical Race Theory (AsianCrit), arts-based educational research (ABER), and feminism. The visual journals and stories we present in this chapter focus on our identities, resilience, and healing offered by visual art-making and multilingual storytelling to combat the pain and trauma caused by racism, sexism, and xenophobia during the COVID-19 pandemic.

## Literature Review

### Translanguaging

Situated in the context of Welsh-English bilingual education, Williams (1994) conceptualized translanguaging, also known as "trawsieithu," as the pedagogical practice that allows students to code-switch in language input and output in bilingual classrooms. García and Li (2014) state that code-switching and translanguaging are different, although both are positive bilingual practices. Code-switching is seen as a process of changing languages, while translanguaging is constructing multilingual speakers' complete linguistic and cultural repertoires. Lewis et al. (2012) point out that code-switching may be used to practice the notions of separating languages in classrooms or conversations, but translanguaging emphasizes learning and using both languages as a holistic linguistic practice. The notion of translanguaging has since been further refined as a discursive and simultaneous process when multilingual and multicultural speakers use their entire linguistic and cultural repertoires in all the processes of meaning making in their multilingual worlds, even beyond the educational settings (García, 2009; García & Li, 2014). The recent literature emphasizes meaning making as an ongoing process of meaning negotiation in multilingual speakers' knowledge construction, which extends beyond multilingualism and includes multimodal, multisemiotic, and multisensory practices (Li, 2018). Translanguaging offers a holistic and dynamic perspective to approach bi/multilingualism and multiculturalism. This framework also expands the understanding of multilingual speakers' dynamic, creative, and strategic selections of linguistic, cultural, and semiotic repertoires to make meaning in different communicative contexts (Anzaldúa, 1987/2012; Stavrou et al., 2019; Otheguy et al., 2015).

### Arts as Translanguaging Multimodal Practices

Art has been closely related to language development that focuses on fostering multiple symbolic meanings (New, 2007). However, art is a means of exploring and expressing all people's experiences, which goes beyond the role of supporting children's and adults' language learning and actively forms a creative translanguaging space. This, in turn, forms a hyperverbal community discourse space while providing multilingual learners with new translations and discourses (Dewey, 2005). According to Yoon-Ramirez's study (2021), using the term "inter-weave" emphasizes the collectiveness and coordination of community programs that bring bilingual or multilingual adults and families together "to create a translanguaging space through art" (p. 24). The author has been working with the Immigrant Resource Center in Springdale, Arkansas to host her own art-making program since 2018. This study captures the active changes and movements in linguistic repertoires by exploring the possibility and pedagogical potential of translanguaging community spaces based on art. The study explores art as multimodality and demonstrates "how art constitutes a key part of the translanguaging practice." (p. 24). In addition, a study by Lark (2005) proposes introducing an art-based process to elicit racial and hyper-cultural discussions to combat racism. Lark demonstrates that arts-based learning can contribute to transforming the power dynamics within a group by breaking down the assumption that English is an equally accessible language and providing rich voices and channels to members of different cultures and backgrounds.

The theory of translanguaging also offers more pedagogical, educational, and social possibilities. In the multilingual spaces, translanguaging invites bi/multilingual speakers to bring knowledge developed in diverse repertoires into intellectual and social conversations and development. When combined with multimodal and multi-semiotic approaches, meaning making and meaning negotiation can also be embodied and achieved through visual, audio, and kinesiological elements (Stavrou et al., 2019; García & Kleyn, 2016). Through the larger lens of social contexts, translanguaging also disrupts the long-standing and monolithic linguistic and social standards set by White monolingual English native speakers in and beyond academic contexts. Translanguaging perceives bi/multilingual speakers as capable learners and participants who are competent in flexible, fluid, dynamic, and creative language uses.

## Asian Critical Race Theory (AsianCrit)

Drawing on the original framework of Critical Race Theory (Crenshaw, 1989), Chang (1993) proposed Asian Critical Race Theory (AsianCrit) to conceptualize the racial realities faced by Asian Americans. Building on the works of the original works of CRT and Chang's proposal of AsianCrit, Muses (2013) developed seven specific tenets of AsianCrit, which are Asianization; transnational context; (re)constructive history; strategic (anti)essentialism; intersectionality; story, theory, and praxis; and commitment to social justice. The first tenet, Asianization, explicitly explains the paradoxical stereotypes that Asian Americans face. On the one hand, Asians are collectively racialized as "forever foreigners" who have not desired to be Americanized (Tuan, 2005). This discriminatory ideology has been the "common cause for historical and contemporary anti-Asian violence, oppression, and discrimination" (An, 2017, p. 133). In the meantime, Asians are also praised as the model minorities who become successful in the United States through their hard work, without much complaining. However, such emphasis on Asians' success overlooks and denies the systemic injustice that Asians and other people of color still face. The myth of the model minority further divides East Asians who tend to be successful and other AAPI communities that are less privileged and affluent. The paradoxical stereotypes have been used to maintain and perpetuate systemic injustice against Asians and other racially minoritized communities.

Since most Asian Americans have an ancestral history of immigration, AsianCrit highlights the national and international contexts of Asian experiences in the United States. Aligning with the original CRT's anti-essentialism, this framework also suggests that an examination of Asian American history in the United States is necessary to fully understand the unique historical backgrounds of Asian voices and experiences, while acknowledging the intersections of systemic injustice. The goal of AsianCrit further aligns with CRT's justice-oriented goals through its specific critical analysis of racism against Asian communities.

AsianCrit provides scholars with social sciences and other disciplines a powerful theoretical and methodological framework to challenge and transform research in pursuit of a broader goal of justice. With a strong focus on the intersectional experiences of Asian females, many scholars have also further explored feminism from a transnational and Asian perspective, in collaboration with the third wave of global feminism.

## Asian Women's Experiences in the United States and the Third-wave Transnational Feminism

During the era of the Chinese Exclusion Act of 1882, Chinese women, specifically, were viewed as threats to U.S. public morality and were presumed to be prostitutes. As a part of the exclusion act, anti-prostitution legislation was signed and passed to disproportionally keep Asian female immigrants from entering the United States (Chang, 2015). Korean women in the United States faced similar historical obstacles. From 1903 to 1924, U.S. immigration law restricted Koreans from immigration (Oh, 2017). Negative associations between Korean women and prostitution emerged in the popular American imagination by military brides in U.S. Forces Korea (USFK) camps or GI towns ("kijichon" in Korean) since the 1940s (Lee & Lee, 2007; Doolan, 2019; Yuh, 2002). Other factors that caused the discrimination included the political relationship and transpacific circuits between the United States and Korea, which implied the military prostitution business. The legitimate military brides who immigrated to the United States with their American husbands often settled in places such as Kansas and New York (Lee & Lee, 2007; Kim, 2012; Doolan, 2019). At that time, Korean women not only faced language barriers and socio-cultural challenges in adapting to the unfamiliar land but also, within the Korean community, a social stigma—they were called "yanggongju" (yankee princess; foreigner's whore) by the Korean communities in both countries. Thus, they were considered a shame and became a taboo subject in both their native and adoptive homes (Doolan, 2019, p. 36). Since the 1950s, the racial and sexist stereotype of Asian women being prostitutes further evolved into the prostitute-turned-wife/mail-order-bride stereotype. Asian women were, once again, targeted as "morally problematic transgressors requiring oversight and regulation, and they were portrayed as engaging in a new type of prostitution: sexual services in exchange for immigration benefits" (Chang, 2015, p. 247).

Often portrayed as threats to U.S. public morality and society, Asian women now have been perceived as hypersexualized objects with the desire of White men. To better assimilate and survive in the United States and Canada (Park, 2011), Asian women were pushed to adopt paradoxical stereotypes. Specifically, Asian women were expected to be quiet and submissive, yet simultaneously exotic and hypersexual. Other stereotypes that are linked with Asian motherhood portray Asian women as bossy and controlling (e.g., tiger moms).

To fight back against such discriminations, Asian/Asian American feminism forms a kind of particular and "ever-evolving mode of knowledge, politics, practice and approach to social justice" (AAFC, 2018, p. 1). Asian feminism is influenced by various factors such as the perspective of Black feminism and the Third World feminist movements in the 1960s and 1970s. The critical factors of women-of-color feminism and xenophobia enable Asian feminism to examine the long-standing reality of racial, gender, and colonial violence in history and to create voices (AAFC, 2018). Asian feminism has scrutinized "anti-immigration reforms, the dismantling of reproductive rights, increased U.S. militarization at home and abroad, and environmental policies that disproportionately target poor people of color and reductions to federal land protections that impact Native sovereignty" (AAFC, 2018, p. 2). Furthermore, it pursues "gender equity, justice for poor and working-class people, justice for queer and trans people, the movement for Black Lives, immigrant justice, and a need for movements that do not rely on divide and conquer tactics" (AAFC, 2018, p. 2).

In the 1980s, in the women's news journal, *Off Our Backs*, two articles titled "Asian Feminism" by Cad (1988) briefly addressed the socio-cultural challenges faced by single women in Chinese society and the characteristics of feminism in Japan. Douglas (1989) further discussed the case of the Philippines, along with issues concerning physical, economic, and social authority of Chinese women. Additionally, some studies explored feminism in Singapore to reveal that consensus must be socially requested to embrace feminism that had not been included in the Asian feminism research (Lyons, 2000). Other studies have included various socio-political contexts, fragmented topologies, and historical legacies of feminism in Korea and Japan (Kim & Kang, 2001; Pak, 2006; Kitagawa, 2010; Lee & Chan, 2019).

Joining with other women of color in the world in the emergent new paradigm of the third-wave feminism, Asian feminism highlights transnational experience, decenters, and rejects the focus on Western White females' voices and experiences that exclude other women around the world. As the third wavers try to address concerns that the previous waves of feminism failed to consider, "they also recognize their relationship to their 'motherland' communities and how these relationships enrich their understanding of 'feminism'" (Yu, 2009, p. 11). Rehman and Hernández (2002) also express their strong eagerness to be connected with their motherland and heritage,

> [f]eminism should have brought us closer to our mothers and sisters and to our aunties in the Third World. Instead, it took us further away. Academic feminism didn't teach us how to talk with the women in our families about why they stayed with alcoholic husbands or chose the veil.
>
> *p. xxii*

As the third wavers move forward to embrace both their heritage and motherland beyond the foundations set by Western-centered White feminism research practices, more and more decolonizing research methods have been adopted by feminist researchers in order to conduct studies centering on women of color's voices and experiences.

The concepts of transnational feminism, Asianness, and being Asian women in the West are embodied through multiple layers of individual, social, and institutional structures (e.g., race, gender, social class, languages, and cultures). All these relations are intertwined in and embodied through Asian women's lives. Thus, the transnational feminist framework "allows one to see the blind spot or discrepancy in the discourse of 'multilingualism', 'differences and diversity', 'democracy', and 'human rights'" (Mayuzumi, 2008, p. 179). The tight connection between women of color, their homelands, and native languages calls for a necessary understanding and collaboration with translanguaging, which is a critical factor in the process of expressing voices, making meaning, and telling stories. Following the theoretical frameworks discussed above, in the next section, we present our transnational, multilingual, and multicultural stories through visual journals.

## Our Visual Journals

### Bokyoung's Stories

I was born and raised in Korea, but my journey of visual journals did not begin until the fall of 2018, when I started my life as a first-year international doctoral student in the United States. I had a particularly challenging time adjusting to the language. Embarking on all the journeys I faced—challenged by the classroom environment, the new academic culture, and the basics of being a Ph.D. student in a second language—was a struggle far beyond what I expected. Tired of everything, whether in Korean or English, I wanted to run away, and felt depressed every day. At the time, blaming only myself for all my hardships and failures, visual journaling was a reliable shelter for me. I was mesmerized by the feeling of capturing the difficulties that could be expressed in verbal or written words and a third form, art. As a doctoral student and international student, I created drawings in a small notebook to capture unforgettable and impressive moments that I encountered and wanted to remember in my daily life. Then I collected those snippets and interwove them with my writing. In this way, I have uploaded my episodes and narratives to my blog and social media for almost 5 years. My visual journal is a sort of drawing-essay, in which drawings and texts are interwoven together. With art, I was able to transcend language barriers.

I met Yixuan for the first time during an orientation for international students provided by the university. While our friendship blossomed instantly, I believed it was my visual journaling that allowed me to form a full-fledged bond with her. She empathized with my struggles as a newcomer, and she liked my unique way of blending playful drawings and verbal wit to express my experiences. She also encouraged me to express my voice through artwork continuously. I was able to overcome that mentally difficult time through visual journaling and the bonds I developed with my colleagues, especially her.

This experience has convinced me of the power of visual journaling to transcend national and linguistic barriers, form empathy and solidarity with myself and others, and broaden my experiences and understanding. At first, I thought that I could just relieve my own stress through art, which would be enough. However, the more I experienced, the more I wanted to share the art-embodied power with other international graduate students. Then, I planned a pilot study. This study involved weekly meetings, and I focused on themes that could enable international graduate students to share their stories and reflections of their daily lives, socio-cultural experiences, and academic adaptations weekly, and I collected works of art that supported these themes. In addition, I developed a platform for dialogues with the participants by posing pertinent questions that could evoke solidarity and prompt them to reflect upon and confess their own experiences. Yixuan was interested in my research and participated in this art class and meetings. As a participant, she shared her adaptation process as an international graduate student, focusing on the topic of the microaggressions that Asian women could face and describing detailed experiences that I had not previously recognized very well in my limited community. While we were exchanging dialogue based on our visual journals, we discovered further acts of discrimination and microaggressions in different areas that we had not noticed until that moment. This caused a great awakening inside both of us. In particular, art has subtleties that delicately capture ideas that cannot be fully expressed in English. These characteristics of art can alleviate the misunderstandings that may occur when one is speaking publicly in a foreign language, and lessen the difficulties of communication that may arise between people with different socio-cultural backgrounds. Through the study, Yixuan and I, as Asian female international graduate students, shared our unique senses of solidarity and awareness of problems, and our conversations and works emerged as acts of counter-storytelling that amplified our voices.

Ever since I came to the United States, I have tried not to think about myself as an Asian woman. This is because I thought it would allow me to be free of the pressure to live up to the stereotypes and make my best efforts for my personal growth instead. I used to turn off many of my "switches" inside to not care about any negative signals I received. Nevertheless, the friendly attempts of people interested in my existence as a Korean student have embarrassed me at times, even when they were being gentle. As I mentioned earlier, the vast category of "Asian" is often provoked by non-Asian people's frequent quick generalization, which lacks awareness of nuanced differences among Asians. For example, one of the classmates recommended a Japanese sushi restaurant to console my homesickness and desire for Korean food, and yet another friend was completely disappointed and lost interest in talking with me since I did not know much about K-pop or how to play Baduk.

Furthermore, I had to ignore the giggles as people laughed at my English behind my back. I could not quickly address all these situations and my feelings at the time. I just laughed it off and tried to be kind. I acted like the stereotype of "a kind Asian woman." There were words I should have said then, but I missed my opportunity and could not say what I felt back in English. Those words lingered in my mind for a long time for me to ponder back and forth, in both languages. There were words that I could not say due to the gap between English and my native language, Korean, and words that I could not resist and swallow because I was stuck in my own box of being kind and polite as an Asian. The art-making process enabled me to make connections between my numerous languages, experiences, and identities.

## Cute Mask Design

*Cute Mask Design* captures the school-life changes that I experienced as I began my self-quarantine in mid-March of 2020 (see Figure 10.1). This piece was designed to look fancy and pretty at the first glance. However, the pretty masks, with their cute arrangements of round mandarins, reflect the defense mechanisms I mounted to protect myself from my own fears in the wake of intensifying hatred against AAPIs during the COVID-19 pandemic in the United States, where wearing masks is not common. During spring 2020, I went grocery shopping, and while I was immersed in choosing green onions, a stranger approached and asked me, "Do you know this news in your country?" He suddenly showed his phone to me, which displayed news about COVID-19 spreading in Korea. His sudden behavior was abrupt and seemed aggressive to me. I felt that he was telling me that my country was the main culprit behind this pandemic, and my country, and even myself, must be responsible for it. Whenever I took an Uber, the drivers I encountered during that time would ask me, "Where are you from?" Already prepared for such a question, I would answer, "Don't worry. I'm from Korea, and

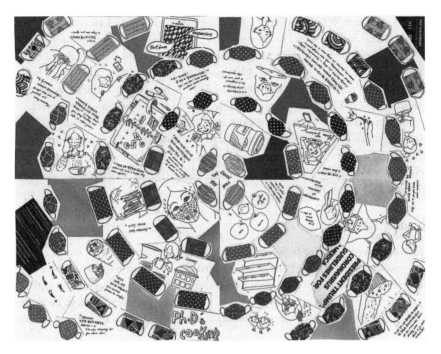

**FIGURE 10.1** A collage of cute mask design.

I haven't left the United States in two years. I've never visited Korea during that time." As soon as I responded, they were at ease.

More than two years have passed since those early pandemic days. I have been studying myself as an Asian woman and had the opportunity to contemplate feminism. I first began this research because of my close conversations with Yixuan and an emerging sense of responsibility to tell my truth as an Asian woman. Now, I realize and acknowledge that my research, contemplations, and practice reflect much more closely the racial reality I face: the Atlanta spa shootings that happened just about one hour away from where I live. I feel everything I have been struggling with, studying, and reflecting upon is now more painful than ever.

Currently, my university has a Korean student community. Through the Korean messenger app KakaoTalk, Sometimes students share eliminate this anecdotes about the hate crimes, attacks, and assaults they have experienced as a result of being Asian. We are terrified, and therefore share and ponder upon ways to defend and protect ourselves. For instance, we check if the area we live in permits us to carry pepper spray or take actions for self-defense.

When my close friends asked me if I had experienced anything related to discrimination or hatred against Asian women due to the COVID-19 pandemic, I used to answer cynically, as if it was a joke, "I have not had a chance to experience any kind of discrimination after the pandemic was declared since I was stuck in my apartment. Where would I go?" I feel appalled when I now recall what I said casually at that time. The answer I gave led me to ask myself the following questions. For Asians to live safely, it feels like we must be completely isolated from society and the community, like babies in incubators, to protect us from racism. Do we really have to live like this? Do we have to push ourselves to this extreme corner? This series of thoughts led me to the beginning of my grief.

The brighter the light, the darker and deeper the shadow becomes. The brighter colors and playful atmosphere exude from the surface of my artwork. Ironically, the more of my voice, experience, and the insecure and precarious feelings that I could not reveal from the outside, the more of these feelings were demonstrated in my artwork.

## Yixuan's Stories

Resonating with some of Bokyoung's experiences in our weekly meetings, in my four-year stay in the United States as an international graduate student, I have had multiple encounters in which people asked me for an English name to replace my name since pronouncing my name is a challenge for non-Chinese speakers. Figure 10.2 depicts one of the encounters that I had, which was similar to many

**FIGURE 10.2** A I Got a New Name from Starbucks?

other international students, on and off campus. My name in Chinese means artistic jade/gemstones, and thus when people only see the spelling and pronunciation as weird, the beautiful meaning of my name is denied and disgraced. After several similar encounters, I started using the English name "Annie" whenever I needed to offer a name for my orders at places, such as restaurants, to avoid the uncomfortable situation of people asking me for an English name. When creating this visual journal, I realized that the art-making process helped me reconfirm the great meaning of my name, as well as the profound value of my culture and native language.

Such experiences related to non-English names not only apply to international students, but also the U.S.-born AAPI community since many of them are named in their heritage languages. However, the meaning of their names that are given by their parents and families may be perceived as foreign and non-native by the monolingual English-speaking mainstream. This problematic ideology that views AAPI names as foreign keeps shaping the racial reality of the AAPI community in U.S. society, even though many of us have perfected our English and forced us into the stereotype of a model minority. Whether we are willing to anglicize our names or are pushed to do so, the sacrifice is not just our names, but also our cultures, heritage languages, and identities. Nonetheless, even when we offer an English name to represent ourselves, often White mainstream names, the question "What's your real name?" always follows. These encounters and questions situate AAPI in a dilemma.

For me, making my visual journal and sharing it with Bokyoung is not only an individual space that truly embodies these experiences and creates a conversation with myself in both languages, but also a powerful translational and translanguaging community space that encourages us to learn and discuss racial and gender injustice, which we might not have learned to discuss in our native languages, especially when we come from racially homogenous Asian countries like South Korea and China.

Under the increased anxiety and fear of unpredictable legislation changes against international students, as well as the increased racism, discrimination, and xenophobia in 2020, I gradually became insomniac, unable to concentrate, and easily losing my temper. I did not pay attention to finding solutions, because I was so occupied by the fear about the possibility of the death of my family on the other side of the world and my own safety in the United States. I started having nightmares about death constantly, dreaming about whether one of my parents died in China and I was not able to go back, or if I died in the United States alone. Later, I also dreamed that I was verbally and/or physically attacked due to my ethnicity in grocery stores, parks, or my apartment complex. Starting from August 2020, I had several panic attacks that I had never heard of or experienced before.

The accumulated stress and negative emotions finally pushed me to the peak of the panic attacks in which I could not help crying, trembling, having problems breathing, and thinking about the last words I should put on a piece of paper to my family and friends to let them know that I felt guilty to be so far away from home without many accomplishments so far. Every time I found myself trembling in my bed, I imagined that I was a tree, withering, and all the colorful and happy memories were dying. The only feelings left were fear, nausea, anger, and embarrassment.

Growing up in a national and domestic culture that perceives mental health issues as taboo, I tried to deal with the anxiety and stress by myself. The mental issues were not possible for me to share since I was not even equipped with the vocabulary in my native language. Then, I decided to start getting professional counseling help. After several months of counseling and treatment, I finally understood that the silence that I tried to keep did not help solve racism, discrimination, and xenophobia that I had to face. The embarrassment that I imposed onto myself only contributed to the false image of AAPIs. The silence that each individual in the AAPI community strives to maintain can no longer keep us "safe," because the inner pain, stress, and loss can only be solved when we speak up and when society starts to listen. My visual journal helped me describe my symptoms to my therapist, and in turn, my therapist helped me learn how to talk about these issues in both languages. The combination of visual journal, languages, and counseling enabled me to find artistic and bilingual ways to discuss the injustices that I face. The drawings keep the memories alive to me and are expressive to others. Every time I tell stories based on my visual journals, my languages along with them add another layer of meanings and details. The combined narrative and arts reveal that the myth of the model minority has been used to divide AAPI from other communities of people of color in the United States. It is time for us to express our voices for solidarity among communities to heal the pain that we have endured not just during the pandemic but for centuries. My journey of keeping the visual journals led me to learn the beauty of the union of arts and languages.

## Discussion and Implications

Methodologically, our process of creation adopts the frameworks of autoethnography, translanguaging, arts-based education research (ABER), arts-based research (ABR), and arts-integrated study. Art, the research methodology we chose, is also a way to perform and practice visual methodologies in qualitative research. The emergence of arts-based multilingual storytelling and research began to be recognized as a world formed by researchers' interpretation and semantic composition (Kang, 2009), which has led to the acknowledgment that written language is insufficient to reflect the creators' intentions and thoughts. The integration of art and language can better emphasize the marginalized voices and form an interactive relationship and engagement with the audience (Kang, 2009).

The creating and meaning-making process entails that selecting and creating images based on the power of visual and translanguaging can amplify expression when discussing our intersectionalities and lived experiences. This multilingual and multimodal practice builds our own perspective of the world and allows us to think about the social features, corresponding responsibility, effects of images, and dissemination of the meaning (Rose, 2016).

Visual methodology in social science research coincides with critical sociocultural approaches and the values of anti-oppressive methods, social justice, social practice, political integration, and emancipation (Brooks & Poudrier, 2014; De Lange, 2012). It aims to achieve a thick and broad "repertoire" of exploring our "being and doing" through multiple modalities and opportunities (Mitchell, 2008, p. 367). Therefore, in social science research, visual methodology values social responsibility as the researcher goes beyond pursuing superficial images to form a voice and discourse (Mitchell, 2008). The social responsibilities of researchers and educators who want to explore the possibility of visual methodologies is the creation of new knowledge that helps shed light on the various problems and challenges in society (De Lange, 2012). This approach also centers the active value of envisioning that encourages practice and creates change, not just a wait-and-see attitude in the community, society, and the world surrounding us beyond the constrained boundaries of classrooms and academia (Metcalfe, 2016; Rose, 2016).

Although our visual journals were created under the context of being graduate students and researchers, numerous studies have discussed that drawing is "essential, and it points to arts-based ways of working not as separated activities reserved for artists, but fundamental literacies that everyone can bring to bear on their own thinking and ways of working" (Sousanis, 2018, p. 198). Therefore, drawing and visual arts provide benefits for language learners of all ages, especially bi/multilingual learners who aim for academic success while developing diverse linguistic and cultural repertoires. For K-12 students, teachers and researchers have found that visual literacies and drawing assist language learning through vocabulary development and metacognition (Cappello & Lafferty, 2015). As multilingual and multicultural learners navigate the process of academic development, arts-based activities, especially drawing, in language and literacy classrooms offer the space and potential "for students to experience deep structures of meaning where they emotionally connect with the content and sustaining learning" (Zoss et al., 2010, p. 136). Likewise, Newland's (2013) study that integrates drawing with language learning of young children suggests that "students should understand the world outside of the school building is not segmented into 45-minute blocks. Students need to see connections between subjects" (p. 49). Students should be able to see beyond the rectangular classroom space and be aware that education, society, and the world are holistically intertwined, regardless of their ages. From his implementation of comics in language classrooms and research, Sousanis (2018) concludes that comics created by students demonstrate "an extremely sophisticated understanding of the comic form and it powerfully speaks to how working in visual ways allows us to make discoveries and understand things about our subject and ourselves that we couldn't without it" (p. 109). Our chapter encourages educators and researchers in all grades to include drawing and visual journals to help students learn through visual ways and form multimodal, multilingual, and multicultural communities.

This study, which uses the methodological lens of ABR/ABER, follows this entanglement between visual methodology, translanguaging storytelling, and educational research. In addition, this study is based on the art meetings designed and led by Bokyoung incorporating the individual and collaborative autoethnographic storytelling strategy. This suggests that through sharing our stories, we can truly share the various types of chaos and alienation we face as Asian women international graduate students in the United States, particularly in our local context. Simultaneously, it plays an important role in creating and criticizing the dominant discourses and systems that monolingual and monomodal structures have maintained. Therefore, visual and other artistic approaches allow artists to share their intimate experiences using the lens of artistic and autobiographical/autoethnographic self-inquiry (Leggo, 2008). These methods are practice-led and motivational, and can be delivered to the audience regardless of linguistic and cultural backgrounds. These creations also capture subtleties in the experience and create new knowledge in an interdisciplinary approach and intuitive visual form (Kay, 2013). In particular, the process of observing and exploring our own experiences is not just a conversation with ourselves, but also a significant bridge to achieve liberating politics and language practices through a profound reflection of our own social positions.

## Conclusion

While we both identify as Asians, we also recognize that our voices as East Asians (i.e., Korean and Chinese) cannot represent the diverse ethnicities, languages, and cultures from Asia. We also acknowledge that East Asians are usually prioritized in the discourse of Asian voices. In general, East Asians are portrayed as successful, while other AAPI paths of life are not equally valued and discussed. Therefore, for future studies and collaboration, it is important to include AAPI voices beyond East Asians (i.e., Chinese, Korean, and Japanese) to better understand the nuanced and diverse perspectives and different experiences as discussed in our review of AsianCrit earlier in the chapter.

This chapter was written in the midst of the painful loss of lives in hate crimes against people of color and the COVID-19 pandemic. As we conclude this chapter, we must recognize that pain, trauma, and loss still happen on a daily basis worldwide. Our visual journals cover several shared experiences that AAPI and possibly other communities have experienced prior to and during the pandemic. The visual and written narratives we include in the chapter aim to exemplify the racial, gender, social, and academic reality that we both face as Asian female international students. The process of creating our visual journals not only attempts to record our daily lives but also serves as healing and resistance during these challenging times when we are away from our families and home countries. The combination of arts, languages, and storytelling filled the void that written texts cannot fully offer for creative multilingual and multicultural speakers who have been through pain and trauma.

# References

An, S. (2017). AsianCrit perspective on social studies. *Journal of Social Studies Research, 41*(2), 131–139.

Anzaldúa, G. (1987/2012). *Borderlands/La Frontera: The new mestiza.* Aunt Lute.

Asian American Feminist Collective (AAFC) (2018, September). Building an Asian American Feminist Movement, Making Asian American Feminist Politics, New York University, https://steinhardt.nyu.edu/ihdsc/on-the-ground/making-asian-american-feminist-politics

Asian Pacific Institute on Gender Based Violence. (n.d.). Census data and API identities. www.api-gbv.org/resources/census-data-api-identities/#:~:text=Definitions, Asia%2C%20or%20the%20Indian%20subcontinent.

Berriz, B. R. (2005). *The emergent cultural identity of Puerto Rican and Dominican third-grade students and its relation to academic performance.* Harvard University.

Brooks, C. M., & Poudrier, J. (2014). Anti-Oppressive Visual Methodologies: Critical Appraisal of Cross-Cultural Research Design. *Qualitative Sociology Review, 10*(4), 32–51.

Cad. (1988). Asian Feminism. *Off Our Backs, 18*(8), 17.

Cappello, M., & Lafferty, K. E. (2015). The roles of photography for developing literacy across the disciplines. *The Reading Teacher, 69*(3), 287–295.

Chang, R. S. (1993). Toward an Asian American legal scholarship: Critical race theory, post-structuralism, and narrative space. *California Law Review, 81*(5), 1243–1322.

Chang, S. (2015). Feminism in yellowface. *Harvard Journal of Law and Gender, 38*(2), 235–268.

Crenshaw, K. (1989). Demarginalizing the intersection of race and sex: A Black feminist critique of antidiscrimination doctrine, feminist theory and antiracist politics. *University of Chicago Legal Forum, 1989*(1), 139–167.

De Lange, N. (2012). Editorial: Visual Methodologies in Educational Research. *South African Journal of Education, 32*(4), 1–3.

Dewey, J. (2005). *Art as Experience.* A Perigee Book.

Doolan, Y. W. (2019). Transpacific Camptowns: Korean Women, US Army Bases, and Military Prostitution in America. *Journal of American Ethnic History, 38*(4), 33–54. https://doi.org/10.5406/jamerethnhist.38.4.0033

Douglas, C. A. (1989). Asian Feminism. *Off Our Backs, 19*(8), 13.

García, O. (2009). Bilingual education in the 21st century: A global perspective. Wiley/Blackwell.

García, O., & Li Wei. (2014). Translanguaging: Language, bilingualism and education. Palgrave Macmillan.

García, O., & Kleyn, T. (2016). Translanguaging with multilingual students. Routledge.

Housee, S. (2010). When silences are broken: An out of class discussion with Asian female students. *Educational Review, 62*(4), 421–434.

Hsieh, B., & Nguyen, H. T. (2020). Identity-informed mentoring to support acculturation of female faculty of color in higher education: An Asian American female mentoring relationship case study. *Journal of Diversity in Higher Education, 13*(2), 169–180.

Ifitikar, J., & Museus, S. (2018). On the utility of Asian Critical (AsianCrit) Theory in the field of education. *International Journal of Qualitative Studies in Education, 31*(10), 935–949.

Kang, E.Y. (2009). A Study on Arts-Based Educational Research Methodology. *The Korean Journal of Arts Education,* 7(1). 45–59.

Kay, L. (2013). Visual Essays: A practiced-led Journey. *International Journal of Education through Art, 9*(1), 133–138.

Kim, H. M., & Kang, S. M. (2001). Achievements and challenges of an Asian women's studies project. *Asian Journal of Women's Studies, 7,* 106–121.

Kim, S. J. (2012). *"We shouldn't be forgotten": Korean military brides and Koreans in Kansas.* [Doctoral dissertation, University of Kansas]. https://kuscholarworks.ku.edu/bitstream/handle/1808/10252/Kim_ku_0099D_12209_DATA_1.pdf;sequence=1.

Kitagawa, S. (2010). Japanese Feminism in East-Asian Networking. *Diogenes, 57*(3), 35–40.

Lark, C.V. (2005). Using Art as Language in Large Group Dialogues: The TRECsm model. *Art Therapy, 22*(1), 24–31, DOI: 10.1080/07421656.2005.10129458

Lee, A., & Lee, J. T. (2007). Korean military brides in New York. *Inter-Asia Cultural Studies, 8*(3), 458–465.

Lee, K. (2013). Why Asian female stereotypes matter to all: Beyond Black and White, East and West. *Critical Philosophy of Race, 1*(1), 86–103.

Lee, M. P., & Chan, S. (2019). *Quiet Odyssey: A Pioneer Korean Woman in America.* University of Washington Press.

Leggo, C. (2008). Autobiography: Researching Our Lives and Living Our Research. In S. Springgay, R. L. Irwin, C. Leggo, & P. Gouzouasis (Eds.), *Being with A/r/tography* (pp.3–23), Sense Publishers.

Lewis, G., Jones, B., & Baker, C. (2012). Translanguing: Developing its conceptualisation and contextualisation. *Educational Research and Evaluation, 18*(7), 655–670.

Li, W. (2018). Translanguaging as a practical theory of language. *Applied Linguistics, 39*(1), 9–30.

Lyons, L. (2000). Disrupting the Centre: Interrogating an "Asian Feminist" Identity. *Communal/Plural: Journal of Transnational & Crosscultural Studies, 8*(1). https://doi.org/10.1080/13207870050001466

Mayuzumi, K. (2008). "In between" Asian and the West: Asian women faculty in the transnational context. *Race Ethnicity and Education, 11*(2), 167–182.

Metcalfe, A. S. (2016). Educational Research And The Sight of Inquiry: Visual Methodologies before Visual Methods. *Research in Education, 96*(1), 78–86.

Mitchell, C. (2008). Getting the picture and changing the picture: Visual methodologies and educational research in South Africa. *South African Journal of Education, 28,* 365–383.

Muses, S. D. (2013). *Asian American students in higher education.* Routledge.

New, R. S. (2007). Children's ART as symbolic language: Action, representation, and transformation. *Visual Arts Research, 33*(2), 49–62.

Newland, A. (2013). Engaging students through image and word. *Art Education, 66*(2), 47–51.

Oh, Y. (2017). Korean picture brides in Hawaii: Historical and literary narratives. *Journal of Literary and Art Studies,* 7(12), 1632–1644.

Otheguy, R., García, O., & Reid, W. (2015). Clarifying translanguaging and deconstructing named languages: A perspective from linguistics. *Applied Linguistics Review, 6*(3), 281–307.

Pak, J. H. C. (2006). *Korean American women: Stories of acculturation and changing selves.* Routledge.

Park, H. (2011). Migrants, minorities, and economies: Transnational feminism and the Asian/Canadian women subject. *Asian Journal of Women's Studies, 17*(4), 7–38.

Rehman, B., & Hernández, D. (2002). Colonize this! Young women of color on today's feminism. Seal Press.

Rose, G. (2016). Visual Methodologies: An Introduction to Researching with Visual Materials (4th edition), SAGE.

Sousanis, N. (2018). Thinking in comics: An emerging process. In M. Cahnmann-Taylor & R. Siegesmund (Eds.), *Arts-based research in education: Inquiry and pedagogy across diverse contexts* (2nd ed., pp. 150–199). Routledge.

Sousanis, N. (2020). Thinking in comics: All hands-on in the classroom. In S. E. Kirtley, A. Garcia, & P. E. Carlson (Eds.), *With great power comes great pedagogy: Teaching, learning and comics* (pp. 92–167). University Press of Mississippi.

Stavrou, S., Charalambous, C., & Macleroy, V. (2019). Translanguaging through the lens of drama and digital storytelling: Shaping new language pedagogies in the classroom. *Pedagogy, Culture & Society, 29*(1), 99–118.

Stop AAPI Hate. (2021). Stop AAPI Hate national report. Retrieved from https://securese rvercdn.net/104.238.69.231/a1w.90d.myftpupload.com/wp-content/uploads/2021/03/210312-Stop-AAPI-Hate-National-Report-.pdf

Tuan, M. (2005). Forever foreigners or honorary whites?: The Asian ethnic experience today. Rutgers University Press.

Williams, C. (1994). Arfarniad o Ddulliau Dysgu ac Addysgu yng Nghyd-destun Addysg Uwchradd Ddwyieithog, [An evaluation of teaching and learning methods in the context of bilingual secondary education]. Unpublished doctoral thesis, University of Wales.

Yoon-Ramirez, I. (2021) Inter-weave: Creating a translanguaging space through community art. *Multicultural Perspectives, 23*(1), 23–32, DOI:10.1080/15210960.2021.1877544

Yu, S. (2009). Third-wave feminism: A transnational perspective. *Asian Journal of Women's Studies, 15*(1), 7–25.

Yuh, J.Y. (2002). *Beyond the shadow of Camptown: Korean military brides in America.* New York University Press.

Zoss, M., Siegesmund, R., & Patisaul, S. J. (2010). Seeing, writing, and drawing the intangible: Teaching with multiple literacies. In P. Albers & J. Sanders (Eds.), *Literacies, the arts, and multimodality*. National Council of Teachers of English.

# 11

## ITS

## Identity, Technology, and Storytelling

*Lina Maria Giraldo*

### Starting with Me

How is an algorithm connected to identity? How can being a maker help you understand who you are? What is essential to hold an intergenerational class? Why is coding necessary to find a neutral platform to improve learning and self-esteem? What is the common ground in a room where all the participants speak different first languages, like English, Haitian Kreyōl, or Spanish? To try and answer these, I start with myself. It is always said that we are more than the sum of our parts. In my case, I am an immigrant, a mother, a wife, a daughter, a sister, a designer, an artist, and a professor. Each of these parts has many challenges, successes, tears, and smiles. Something that always remains constant, though, is the lack of belonging. I am not entirely American or Colombian, and sometimes I feel I am not here or there. I struggle to understand my identity, and I am not alone. When you leave your land of origin, it does not matter what the reason is, identity becomes a fussy combination of worlds. The food, history, and language from where I grew up were forcibly combined with new dishes, words, beliefs, and education. Finding yourself in the middle of this tension turns into a journey of survival. I am always aware of the challenges that I have had to overcome, and because of this, I am a proud Latine immigrant. But not everyone feels the same. There is also a narrative that dismisses us, makes us believe we do not belong here, and treats us as less, or even worse, makes us invisible.

### The Boston Artist in Residence Program

As an Artist in Residence at The Boston Artist In Residence Program (AIR) (City of Boston, 2018), I was assigned to work in the Hyde Park neighborhood, situated

DOI: 10.4324/9781003302186-17

7.9 miles south of Downtown Boston, Massachusetts. During this residency, I had the opportunity to develop Identity, Technology, and Storytelling (ITS) (Giraldo, 2019), a project that was carried out in collaboration with the Hyde Park Boston Center for Youth and Family (BCYF) (City of Boston, n.d.). The goals of ITS focused on changing the narrative of an underserved community of color by amplifying their voices from a maker's perspective, creating a safe and inclusive environment within an intergenerational group, and learning coding and electronics to encourage critical thinking while exploring Identity. The project aims to rewrite the misrepresentation of the narrative of minorities. Coding and electronics become tools for writing their own story. Its objective is to learn from the community members and hear their childhood stories, their difficulties with speaking a new language, and how society is recognized and categorized by origin and skin color. Only by working directly with the community is this possible for future generations. We achieve a strong sense of community as we build our stories, collect, and share them, helping us create identity and ownership of our history as immigrants.

Prior to AIR I had just finished a project called City Journalists, working with the Latine Community at Egleston Square. In this project, we explored collective storytelling looking for new ways to preserve cultural roots and grasp the memories and heritages that were being erased. Boston AIR was the perfect extension of this work. As a Latine immigrant and a new mother, I had been trying to come to terms with my Identity, so the AIR proposal opened up an opportunity for me to explore and enhance my self-understanding.

## The Hyde Park Boston Center for Youth and Family

Unfortunately, I knew little about the Hyde Park community, although I knew for sure that the BCYF would reflect the demographics of the larger community. Before submitting the final proposal for the Boston AIR project to the City of Boston, I spent three months researching the neighborhood demographics and spent the most time possible immersed at the center. In the late 1980s and 1990s, a significant percentage of the Haitian community immigrated there, shifting demographics. By 2010 the race and ethnicity of Hyde Park had changed (Analyze Boston, n.d.)

Helped by Mr. W, the Programs Administrator, I learned about the different programs and services. The most popular services were aftercare and afterschool programs from Pre-K to middle school. They also offered ESL for non-English speakers and had a robust senior center. The members were mainly African Americans, Haitian, Dominicans, and Puerto Ricans. The exception was the center director, who was of Irish descent. From this initial research stage, I learned that even though all the services offered centered on families and included different age groups, they worked as silos. There was no connection among them. It was essential to connect the different generations in the same place to create a bond between middle schoolers, teenagers, and elder members. Even though they attended the center simultaneously, they never interacted with each other. BCYF was a second home for the middle schoolers to spend time after school, a refuge for teenagers to do their homework and play basketball, and for the elders, a place to share time with other elders. I needed to be flexible and create a welcoming space for all to connect and create together.

## Listening to the Elders

I spent time with and interviewed many elderly members, the teachers at the community center, middle school and high school students, and administrative staff. After better understanding the services offered, the next step was crucial for critical success: Listening. I spent the first few months having conversations with the members. First, I met the elder participants and sat with them during the Senior hour, an event where all the elders get together, to get feedback about their needs, share stories, play games, and receive guidance on how to use a computer or transportation. They shared many stories, photos, and challenges with me. They struggled from being isolated and found themselves in a community that had changed exceedingly fast in the last 50 years. The memories that kept them moving forward were fading fast too. Technology was also a huge obstacle. Transportation was not accessible, and the community they grew up in did not exist anymore. They were alone in a bubble of memories that they were eager to share, but they did not know how to. They had difficulty communicating using new technologies, such as sending emails or doing tasks online and filling out forms. The overall feeling for the elders was a shared sense of frustration and loneliness.

## Listening to the Young People

I did a few icebreaker workshops with a culturally diverse group of teenagers. Even though participants spoke many languages at home, the common language was always English inside the classroom, and small talk sometimes happened in other languages amongst them. We had a conversation about how they perceived and connected with Hyde Park. While creating participatory activities with the youth, the concept of identity surfaced: What does it mean to be you? What food represents you? What makes you unique? Who is your network? Where was your family born? Where are you from? I created a series of activities based on "horizontal and vertical identity" (Merchant, 2018). Vertical Identity refers to cultural roots, family, beliefs, and language; horizontal Identity refers to your daily interactions with your community, media, school, and friends.

Many first and second generations did not find any connections with the community. We discussed their favorite restaurants and foods, like empanadas from downtown, the church they went to every Sunday, or the absence of art in the community. However, one thing was the same for all: the lack of a sense of belonging. Interestingly, Hyde Park was perceived as a temporary place. It didn't feel like home. Especially for the youth, Hyde Park's history did not define them.

I explored accessibility, ownership, trust, listening, and experimentation. I wanted to create a safe space to explore ideas and learn from each other. We could talk and listen while building and creating trust, experimenting, failing, and creating together. I established this space by setting ground rules of respect, listening, and non-judgment. The number of participants varied and eventually ended up with a smaller but steadier group. I created flyers and spread the invitation to different staff members. The only requirement that I had for participating was consistency.

## Intergenerational Learning: The Project Structure

The final group was an intergenerational collection of participants, four middle schoolers, three teenagers, and an elder member, all with different cultural backgrounds spanning from American, Haitian, Barbados, and the Dominican Republic. The computer lab in the center was made available to us on Tuesdays and Thursdays, and we met during the after school program hours. The project's structure supported core concepts of storytelling and technology under the umbrella of identity from the maker's perspective. I refined the curriculum based on these two perspectives:

> 1- Storytelling: How to tell community stories, learn to do interviews, and handle video and semi-professional Single-Lens Reflex (SLR) cameras. And how to co-create questions that help us learn from each other and our community from a storytelling perspective.

> 2- Technical: How to learn Coding and Electronics. This part of the workshop was focused on learning coding with open-source software called Processing, an accessible language to code in the context of visual arts. I also created learning modules to learn and explore electronics using Raspberry Pi, (Rasberry Pi Foundation, n.d.), an affordable, open-source electronic prototyping platform. It was vital for me to work with open-source, accessible, and affordable software because commercial software can cost thousands of dollars, while open-source software can be downloaded for free.

I was able to find an organization that donated laptops for each student. I put together inexpensive electronic kits that contained resistors, capacitors, Light-Emitting Diode (LED), breadboards, switches, buzzers, and a Raspberry Pi (see Figure 11.1). It was essential for me that each group member had a complete kit to build ownership in the process.

During the 38 weeks that the workshop ran, I divided the session into three modules, concentrating on community members being makers while improving

**FIGURE 11.1** Testing Electronic Kits.

their technical skills. The first module focused on the early concepts of coding and electronics. The second module taught the basic design process of taking an idea, developing it, and prototyping it using recycled materials. Finally, the third module offered basic journalism skills for them to codesign the question with the group members and interview members of their community.

A couple of weeks after our first meeting, it became clear that we needed to create a project together to collect stories and start making new memories. Why not create a video camera? It was the ideal way of exploring storytelling from the maker's perspective! It was an excellent opportunity to create accessible technology, develop storytelling skills, and explore Identity and critical thinking, all under the same project. With the video camera production in mind, I designed the rest of the electronics classes, where participants built up skills to complete the hardware. I incorporated design skills and processes, including concept development, mood-board, materials, and production.

STEAM education (Science, Technology, Engineering, Arts, and Mathematics) is a privilege (Delgado, 2020). Unfortunately, it's not accessible or affordable for marginalized communities and communities of color. This contributes to increasing the disadvantages that are already underlying in education. Creating the cameras is an exercise in bringing STEAM to these communities of color, which would otherwise not have access to it. One of the best skills gained while working with STEAM is not the technical skills in themselves, but rather the ability for problem-solving, critical thinking, and embracing failure as a way of learning. Combined with being an active and curious citizen, STEAM helps participants learn from their neighborhoods and discover where they belong. Failing helps them look at issues from different perspectives and develop problem-solving skills that are often lacking in younger generations. Learning how things work empowers the youth and makes them feel proud. They are building their learning journey based on their curiosity while gaining invaluable knowledge.

The main idea for the Tuesday workshops was to learn coding from an open-source software called Processing (Processing Foundation, n.d.). It's a user-friendly platform that promotes software and visual literacy. Coding is writing a computer program using algorithms. An algorithm is a process and a set of rules used in coding. A non-coding example of an algorithm could be boiling water. You need to create a set of rules first; you have to take a pot, fill it with water, put it on the stove, turn it on, and wait for it to boil. A code could be making pasta or rice, where both use the algorithm of boiling water. Our coding focused mainly on creating interactive stories using the Processing software based on their own experiences and knowledge. Initially, we started with the basics, then they advanced their coding skills and created poems about themselves or their family. They also brought photos of loved ones, which we manipulated using algorithms and coding.

In the coding workshop, we started with the fundamentals from an art perspective, from creating basic drawings like circles to more elaborate shapes, such as houses, cars, or robots. As the workshops advanced, I introduced interactive media. Finally, as they gained enough knowledge, I started teaching poetry and looked into coding as a form of expression.

The first class was challenging for everyone. Participants spoke other languages in the room, Creole and Spanish, as I encouraged them to feel comfortable. It is beautiful to have different languages spoken in the classroom. The diversity encourages curiosity and critical thinking from their fellow peers and creates comradery, ownership, and pride. English proficiency was not the goal. They were learning another language, after all, the language of programming. While learning to code, they were all at the same starting line, creating connections beyond their language. It was not about the differences, but about how to develop networking by problem solving and failure. Failure compels them to look at the problem from different mindsets; these differences propelled them to be creative.

The teenagers and middle school children had some ideas of what coding meant, and they were all very familiar with playing video games. They wanted results fast, which created anxiety, especially if they did not accomplish their goals. What they had imagined was not what was reflected on the screens. I encouraged the group to focus on the basics. For example, learning to locate X and Y on the grid, adding color, drawing a circle and square, etc. Going with the flow was the main mantra. I had no idea how an intergenerational workshop working with technology would go. Even though I over-prepared each session, dynamics were always hard to anticipate. Writing a line of code is not easy and making mistakes is common. A missing comma or different brackets can stop your entire code from working. When the participants achieved a difficult line of code, a bouncing ball, or changing color patterns, they were proud, which quickly created comradery.

## Tensions

Let's take a look at the issue of insecurities and fears. I started feeling considerable tension between some of the youth, particularly the first-generation youth and a particular youth who was an immigrant. There was also a sense of competition that, in this case, was not healthy. These dynamics were hard to navigate. Although I was spending time with them weekly, the trust we had created was not enough for them to share intimate feelings with me, especially not in the first few weeks. The immigrant student was not fluent in English and he struggled with directions. The other teenagers and middle schoolers did not help him initially; instead, they treated him harshly. The elder participant, Mr. B, generated respect for the teenagers and the middle schoolers with his calmness and experience, which helped maintain a safe space. I realized how important it was to have seniors in the conversation during these dynamics. It was magic! Mr. B had the best attitude while we were in the workshops. He always had a warm smile. When the tension rose in the room, he always had a beautiful story about his extended family or calmly praised the younger participants for their excellent work. He could shift the conversations with the youth, leading with memories of Hyde Park or sharing stories about his son. One of the stories he shared was his struggle as an African American moving to this mainly white community in the 1970s, how he encountered uncomfortable racist situations, and how he persisted. He now has the most beautiful and robust family, all raised in Hyde Park.

## Collaborations

As we created a beautiful, inclusive, and respectful place at the computer lab, the participants also advanced and supported each other. The teenagers brought the tenacity, the middle school children brought the energy, and the elder the wisdom and respect. Slowly I turned from a facilitator into a collaborator. The collaboration was reflected in the participatory process. While coding, the middle schoolers had ideas to create a Pacman or a computer-generated composition full of color and interactivity. However, the main issue was the lack of patience, which Mr. B had plenty of. He understood the process and helped the middle school participants to achieve it.

When it was time to start creating stories with the tools we had, I encouraged the students to bring photos that identified them. Some brought pictures of their families, others from their favorite basketball team, while others decided to bring images

**FIGURE 11.2** Interactive Mirror.

to draw and digitize. We started producing one of the first works of memories and art during the workshop series. We used the circle and color patterns to manipulate the image's original pixels. As a result, we had beautiful imagery representing a collective memory, combining the past and the future (see Figure 11.2).

The next step was to write about themselves, and surprisingly, that was harder than the first lines of code, especially for the middle schoolers! They had so many stories to tell but had a hard time bringing their narrative together. For the elder member of the team, it was easy. It came as a cascade of words. He was filled with memories of his wife, family, friends, and grandkids. On the other hand, it was hard for the Haitian teenager to find a voice in his new home in the United States, and it was reflected in his struggle with what to write compared with the other teenagers.

The end result was a small series of poems created using programing code. I provided them with a sample code to start, so they did not get stifled by technical aspects and instead would experiment, manipulate, and go deeper with their words and meaning.

## Learning Electronics

We met weekly to learn electronics and microcontrollers using Raspberry Pi on Thursdays. I remember the face of confusion of one of the middle schoolers when they realized that the kit that included a Raspberry Pi was not an edible pie! Instead, it was a collection of tiny wires, LEDs and switches, and a device that looked like a tiny computer board. Although the confusion about the Pi was a colossal disappointment to start with, they were so excited when they turned the first LED on. It was the best example of how STEAM brings wonder and exploration to education.

Connecting a wire to a breadboard and turning on an LED is a simple exercise, although it's the most uplifting part of teaching as their eyes were bright with amazement. They were proud of the work, and their age differences made no difference. Instead, they were all excited and shared the moment.

Every week, I brought up the difficulty level, from turning the light on and off to creating patterns, running motors, and rotating servos (a motor that rotates in a specific and controlled movement). Every week was a new personal challenge. Sometimes there was frustration and other days were full of accomplishment. The participants could not make the motor move without learning how to turn the LED on (see Figure 11.3). It was a learning ladder; when they moved up, they could look back onto how much they had advanced. Failing was part of the conversation, which is not easy to have. Some educational systems expect results without taking into much consideration the process. These systems don't encourage failing or critical thinking. Failure is a complex concept to grasp

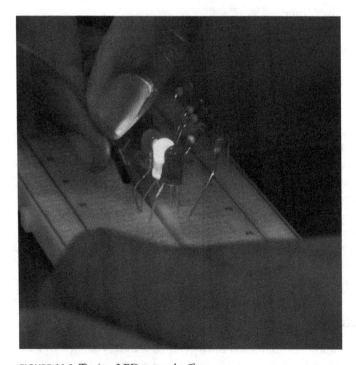

**FIGURE 11.3** Testing LED on and off.

because it means prototyping multiple times. It was more complicated for middle schoolers to review the process, pinpoint the error, and re-do it again. The fragility that frustration brought during the creative process was one of the most important aspects of ownership. It helped them recognize what does and does not work and what needs to be connected again.

The layout of the desks was essential to creating an inclusive environment too. I situated the tables in an oval shape in order to see each other. We had computers, electronics kits, and the most fundamental asset: supporting each other. My favorite part of having an intergenerational group was collaboration. Mr. B had poor eyesight, and the teenagers could help him connect the cable to the breadboard on the right inputs. The middle schoolers did not have patience, so Mr. B helped them navigate the process, and the teenagers were usually a step ahead and tutored the rest. Hence, all of the members had something to look forward to completing. It was indeed the perfect combination for a learning experience.

## Creating Cameras

For the camera body I integrated the design process. We started creating mood boards and collecting photos of different SLR and video cameras. We organized all the images together, looked at them as a group, and discussed what inspired us and what could be helpful in our camera bodies. For example, where the lens should go, how the camera's body should be created, where to grab the camera, or how to install the lenses or the microphone. We started to bring in recycled materials from our house, school, or the community center to use for the camera body. We collected them until we had a good amount of materials to choose from.

The camera bodybuilding workshop was incredible. The only tools they needed were the recycled materials, tapes, stickers, scissors, and their imagination. They were overflowing with energy during this stage. Age did not make a difference and they dove right into the assembly. The advantage of using recycled materials is that some of them already had a particular shape. This made it more challenging and exciting when trying to build, incorporating all the necessary components to be fully functional. The constraints of the compact design were mainly space for the components: microcontroller, camera lens, battery, and microphone; while being easy to carry without a tripod. The controls also needed to be secure and easy to access and operate (see Figure 11.4).

The results were outstanding. We built four different cameras, each unique, with different sizes, shapes, colors, and weights. However, the materials were the same: recycled materials and electronic components (see Figure 11.5). The groups formed organically based on their interest; the middle schoolers divided themselves into boys and girls (even though I suggested mixed-gender groups). Mr. B worked with a teenager, and one of the teenagers worked by herself. Each camera was a reflection of their style, risk-taking, and dedication. When we tried the cameras for the first time, the expectation was high. As anticipated, we ran into

**FIGURE 11.4** Building the camera.

technical issues, although the meaningful part is that all the participants were calm while trying to solve the problems.

## Interviews

At first, they had some freedom to play and get comfortable with the cameras within the BCYF building. They practiced recording their peers playing basketball or playing during the afterschool program. Then we moved to the last module, reaching out to the Hyde Park community. Again, our collective conversation was a must. I sat with the group and we created the interview questions together. What was the narrative we wanted to include? What were the highlights of the community we wanted to include? How could we re-discover the place we lived in, learning from the community members we admired? How could we build stories together to create our narratives?

Since we had middle school participants, we had to work inside the center and could not go out to the street. We could go to the Hyde Park Public Library though since it is also a city institution. Because of this, we planned the interviews at the library and in the computer lab and invited the community members to the BCYF. I contacted a friend who has been an influential art and community leader in Hyde Park for many years. Inspired by the questions created by the participants,

**FIGURE 11.5** Sample camera.

I asked him to help me develop a list of community members to interview. He was vital in identifying community leaders that influenced and participated in the community. We had musicians, community leaders, the library director, BCYF program director, after-school program staff, family members, a police officer, a former bus driver, and long-time elder residents. During the Tuesday and Thursday interviews, each group was encouraged to choose the camera's angle and decide which questions to ask. During the interview, one designated person helped lead the group.

When the final moment came, and the neighbors started to come into the building, it was fulfilling to witness how proud the participants were while interviewing their community members. Each interview was full of wonder. For example, the former bus driver was terrific with middle schoolers and teenagers. They felt connected with him. The fact that he knew the streets, the corners, the bus numbers, or even the block they lived on was an immediate bond. The police officer, a woman of color, was caring too. She was their neighbor and a wonderful friend.

One of the phrases that still resonates with me is when she said, "My super-power is the availability to bring calm when there is a lot of roughness."

The family members had a different feeling. Doing the interviews with the cameras they had created was the opportunity to show them what they had

**FIGURE 11.6** Interview.

achieved (see Figure 11.6). It was not about the stories; it was about showing how far they had come and how proud they were. It was similar to how they felt about the program director, Mr. W, whom they adored. We were able to go to his office because it was inside the building. Mr. W was their mentor and friend; his answers reflected this in the conversation, and their respect was mutual.

## Bridging Communities

Once the project wrapped up, we had to say goodbye. But there was still one more surprise for them. I coordinated with a curator to set up an exhibit of this work in a gallery in the South End. It was a final opportunity to create a bridge between communities and present the final achievement, a terrific collection of stories recorded by them as well as the outstanding work of the cameras they had created. This multigenerational and diverse group from Hyde Park shared a positive changing narrative through their stories and those of their neighbors to a very diverse community from all over Greater Boston and beyond. Using STEAM and Storytelling helped the participants to create connections, explore their history, and build their own identity.

# References

Analyze Boston. (n.d.). *BOSTON NEIGHBORHOOD DEMOGRAPHICS 1950–2010*. Retrieved from Analyze Boston: https://data.boston.gov/dataset/neighborhood-demographics/resource/7154cc09-55c4-4acd-99a5-3a233d11e699

City of Boston. (2018). *BOSTON ARTISTS-IN-RESIDENCE (AIR)*. Retrieved from Boston.gov Arts and Culture: www.boston.gov/departments/arts-and-culture/lina-giraldo

City of Boston. (n.d.). *Boston Center Youth and Family Hyde Park*. Retrieved from www.boston.gov/departments/boston-centers-youth-families/bcyf-hyde-park

Delgado, P. (2020, October 12). *Minority STEM Representation is Disappearing*. Retrieved from Institute of the Future of Education: https://observatory.tec.mx/edu-news/minority-stem-representation-is-disappearing

Giraldo, L. M. (2019). *Lina Maria Giraldo*. Retrieved from www.linamariagiraldo.com: https://linamariagiraldo.com/2021/05/22/identity-technology-storytelling/

Merchant, N. (2018, May 4). *Identity is a Fluid Social Construct*. Retrieved from Medium: https://medium.com/@nilofer/identity-is-a-fluid-social-construct-e6e81a389c7c

Processing Foundation. (n.d.). *Welcome to Processing*. Retrieved from Processing: https://processing.org/

Rasberry Pi Foundation. (n.d.). Retrieved from Rasberry Pi: www.raspberrypi.org/

# 12

# MAKING MEANING

*Terry Jenoure*

I am so many things. So many that I cannot keep count, nor can I keep track of how the many parts of me continue to shift and change. Family lore has it that when I was just three months old, my identity as an artist was revealed. It is 1953 and I am laying in a bassinette in the kitchen by my mother's side while she cooks. It is the Christmas season and my father is playing *Silent Night* on his harmonica. His rendition is slow, drawn out, and filled with emotion. Suddenly, my mouth turns downward and my eyes well up with tears. When he stops playing, I stop crying. He does this over and over to the same effect and to my mother's annoyance. My father has discovered that music creates quite a response in me. Today, I am assured that his experiments uncovered my deep connection to expressive communication, and that I have spent my life on the right path.

Although I live in Massachusetts and have for over forty years, I still consider myself a New Yorker. Born in the Bronx, I grew up on the fourteenth floor of the Bronx River Housing Authority, a gargantuan development of over one thousand apartments. Despite the enormity of the Projects, as they were known, much of who we were culturally remained insignificant in the eyes of the dominant culture. That neighborhood consisted primarily of Puerto Ricans, African Americans, and Cubans, but my parents chose to have me bussed to White schools outside our neighborhood. In the 1950s, those predominantly Jewish, Italian, and Irish schools were the highest ranking in the nation, while the Black and Brown schools were poorly funded and neglected. My family, being first-generation Americans, Puerto Ricans on my mother's side and Jamaicans on my father's, had a high regard for education and an odd dual consciousness of both public image and self-regard. Mostly, my deep learning came from family, church, and school, all of which have informed my values as well as my art practice, teaching, and leadership. I learned that the mind was capable of infinite expression, much of which

DOI: 10.4324/9781003302186-18

the world barely acknowledged. Unlike images of women I saw on TV as a child, there were powerful women in my midst. My maternal grandmother, Jesusa, spoke very little English, but we understood her and communicated seamlessly. Her fingers, gnarly but agile, understood the subtlest needs of her numerous houseplants, and she was known for her unmatched cooking skills. Although I did not have the words back then, I certainly recognized her accomplishments with plants and food as symbols of cognitive and intuitive intelligence. Most important to us was that every utterance from her conveyed care and protection for the family. My paternal grandmother, Emma, worked as a stenographer for the great Africanist Marcus Garvey. She was wise, and often visited by other women, both friends and family, for council, support, or camaraderie. The former New York governor David Paterson's grandmother, aunt Eva, was one of those women, as was Colin Powell's godmother, aunt Evadne. Needless to say, politics and ethics ruled the conversations among my father's family.

I have always identified as a Black woman. But Black comes in an array of forms. It took many years to understand that all the things I am are inimitable. They blend into one form known as me and defy categorization. So, although I am fiercely proud of my ancestry, there are environmental and experiential factors that have shaped me as much as anything. This is the richness that gives variance to race and ethnicity. There is the fact that my Puerto Rican family is from Loiza, a part of the island that commemorates its complex history of enslavement, and that I lived in Beirut, Lebanon for two years and learned colloquial Arabic. There is also my infatuation with school and my doctoral degree in Multicultural Education. That I am married to a white southern man also affects how I view the world, as does the fact that my artistic influences are rooted in the avant-garde. Yes, these are factors that make for uniqueness. Notably, my graduate school mentor, Dr. Sonia Nieto, once expressed that sentiment perfectly. One day in conversation, I told her about my 107-year-old aunt who was in a nursing home. Dr. Nieto suggested that I contact *The Caribbean Culture African Diaspora Institute* in New York City, known for its Puerto Rican historical archives, to contribute photos and information about my family migration to Spanish Harlem. I was less than enthusiastic, feeling that because my Spanish was not fluent and because I went to predominantly Jewish public schools, for these among other reasons, I did not feel like a real Puerto Rican. Sonia did not skip a beat. You are Puerto Rican *your* way! was her emphatic response.

Because I am a multi-disciplinary artist, with formal music training, and am self-taught as a visual artist and have also maintained an active writing practice, there have been countless influences on my thinking, my production, and my creative process. Improvisation is at the heart of it all. Cultural engineers within the Black Arts Movement of the 1960s set me on my journey as a young artist. Musically, these included Free Jazz improvisers such as John Coltrane in his later modal period as well as Ornette Coleman's harmolodic theory. Visually, I have always been drawn to the untrained, so-called *primitive* works by those with mental or physical challenges, Judith Scott, is a prime example, and Nigerian painter Twins Seven-Seven, whose figures have multiple appendages and heads and live in colorful villages, are among the surreal, unselfconscious artists. I have always been most attracted to those who have not only taught themselves, but those holding less regard for public acknowledgment and more for psychological freedom.

My own visual art in the form of dolls and paintings, as well as my music, which for most of my career have focused on structured improvisations are playful, whimsical, strange, biting, edgy, unpredictable, and emotionally complicated. More than anything, I would hope that these works say what I intend, which is that real beauty is found in the most unexpected forms and that spontaneous exploration, or improvisation, is a valid and valuable means to that end. For example, because I do not know where I may land when constructing a doll or painting, my myriad female watercolor figures, rarely are they attractive in traditional ways. They are fierce. They are perturbed. They are confused. They are confident. They are frightened. They are rage-filled. In all of their many phases, it is their wisdom and experience that shine through. Similarly, my music does not follow the well-worn path. It is not easy to hum and remember. My art is not intended for mass consumption. This world of improvisation is one I know like a trusted friend. And, unlike the common misconception, improvisation is not work done haphazardly, or on the fly. Moreover, even if the work is created through the combination of skill and bravery as is the case with successful improvisation, there are rules to be found beneath that treasure.

My introduction to the idea of improvisation as communication is a memorable one. It was the late theorist Dr. Roland Wiggins who taught me that Black musical forms reflect the intellectual designs of their makers. He spoke about the kinesthetics, syntax, and semantics of music. Respectively, that refers to the way actual sounds are formed, the grammatical rules (whether followed or broken) for combining those sounds, and the meanings behind the sounds. Although this is my crude interpretation, entry into this world of art as high-level communication was one that informed all of my choices going forward. Hopefully, we may be returning to our human roots, our natural birthrights, to that essential realization that sound-making and mark-making and gesture-making are not the sole propriety of those crowned as stars. No. Making art facilitates communication. Communication keeps us healthy. And, wellness ought to be our educational priority. Moreover, much like my grandmother who spoke only Spanish, while her grandchildren spoke only English, all of us firmly communicating our commitment to each other, the arts are awarded the same opportunity to speak well past any conventional notions concerning skill. The acquisition of skill should be driven by a motivation to say something meaningful. The artist, much like anyone learning a new language, may hopefully one day be identified not only by how expertly she applies paint or how perfectly she pronounces a strange new word, but more importantly by her ability to lean into those human superpowers, namely compassion, wisdom, and vision, then gird her strength, open her mouth, and *Say It Loud!*

# HEAR ME, TELL MY STORY

## Questions for Reflection and Further Applications for Practice

*Berta Rosa Berriz*

Writing is a political act! José Barreiro calls all of us to engage in literacy and language revitalization. The authors in this section on *Routes* ask us to listen as speakers negotiate meaning in a new land. Languages on the move call on us educators to open new spaces for artful critical discourse; artfully languaging our own decolonizing project and beyond.

### *Routes:* Summary of Chapters

In their relationship as student and teacher from shared Haitian cultural roots, Guy Michel Telemaque and Rocky Cotard invite us to listen to the power of homeland even as families are on the move. Chelsea Jimenez reminds us that students and their cultures, including Hip Hop, are resources for learning. As young learners make sense of the world, Ling Hao and Sally Brown urge us to use multimodal listening with scholars and the words they use in collaboration, placing value on shared meaning and collective knowledge. Charlot Lucien, Haitian Storyteller, moves with an African perspective to apply tradition to modern-day dilemmas. Bokyoung Jo and Yixuan Wang lift us through Asian Critical Race Theory and visual journals as possibilities for healing and solidarity in seeking justice. Lina Maria Giraldo builds an intergenerational learning and storytelling community through technologies. Terry Jenoure uses her megaphone to remind us that beauty is found in unexpected forms (improvisation) and making art is driven by saying something meaningful.

### Questions for Reflection

*Applying Natalie Goldberg's Rules for Freewriting[1] method consider each of the following questions and proceed to engage in a 10 minute freewrite in answer to each question.*

DOI: 10.4324/9781003302186-19

*How do you negotiate/create a bridge between your own story/traditional stories in your learning journey?*

*Making art is driven by saying something meaningful. What words come to mind that describe your compassion? How does your humanity show up in improvised communication?*

*What are the multimodal ways you listen to children's (other folks') making-meaning process? Include speech, gesture, drawing, song, dance writing stories combined. Consider ways of making this knowledge visible to your teaching/learning community.*

*Consider how these artful listening practices contribute to the possibility for healing and solidarity for social justice.*

## Applications for Practice

### Word Bowl Book Clubs

In small cooperative reading groups read and gather meaningful words from each of the six *Routes* chapters. Write the words, concepts, expressions that get at the heart of the chapter your group is reading. Throw words into a bowl. Use these words to create a poem that communicates central ideas for the chapter. *Jigsaw the groups* so that an expert on each chapter is included in the jigsaw group. Share the poem that invites others into the chapter.

Note that this approach can be used throughout K-12 schooling in a similar fashion. For example, elementary age students can read and respond to picture books from a collection of Kokopelli stories. Middle school readers can review Poetry for young people collections of Langston Hughes, or Maya Angelou poems.

*Jigsaw is a cooperative learning structure that forms new groups that include scholars from each of the word bowl groups. This allows experts from each group to represent the ideas discussed in the **word bowl** conversations.*

*Cooperative learning requires a series of skills that can help the group succeed at the task at hand. For example, helpful roles include idea-giver, encourager, or clarifier. Roles not helpful to cooperation include distractor, silent one, teaser, dominator. Two useful resources for teaching cooperative skills include Cooperative Learning, Cooperative Lives: A source book for learning activities for building a peaceful world by Nancy Schniedewind and Ellen Davidson (1987, Harcourt). Rethinking Schools also offers resources to teach cooperation:* https://rethinkingschools.org/articles/cooperative-learning-exceptional-education/

*Another resource for older students and beyond:* https://engagingschools.org/?s=Cooperation+high+school+

### Inner Circle – Outer Circle

### No Talking While Listening

Inner Circle listens and the person facing them in the outer circle tells their language story. Pause to respond to the question: *How did you know the listener was listening?* Switch roles. Outer circle listens as folks in the inner circle tell their language story. Share information about listening and details of the language stories exchanged. Follow this with small groups then the whole group exchanges ideas. A notetaker gathers new knowledge on a chart visible to all.

## Objects from Home: Tell Me Your Story

### Bring an Object from Your Home

Journal first then pair-share about your objects, ensuring both stories are heard.

What do you keep? What do you collect? What is important about the story of the chosen artifacts? What words do you use as you talk about the object? Is there evidence of a historic past in your object? Was it a gift? Is it a cultural relic related to your family?

After pair-share, silently place objects together as a collage on the floor or a table. Think of it as a creation of an installation of stories of objects of your learning/teaching community.

Time permitting, explore oral storytelling; exchange objects and retell the story of the object to another person as if it was your own. As you listen, ask clarifying questions. In small groups debrief the story that was passed on. How has it changed? What words are passed on?

## Photos from Home: Tell me Your Story

### Bring a Photo from Your Home

What do you keep? What do you collect? What is important about the story of the chosen photograph? What words do you use as you talk about the photo? Is there evidence of a historic past in your photograph? Was it a gift? Is it a cultural relic related to your family? When was the photo taken and who took the photograph? What does the composition of the visual elements reveal or imply to you?

After pair-share, silently place the photos together as a collage on the floor or a table. Think of it as a creation of an installation of stories expressed in images of your learning/teaching community.

Time permitting, explore oral storytelling; exchange photographs and retell the story of the photo to another person as if it was your own. As you listen, ask clarifying questions. In small groups debrief the story that was passed on. How has it changed? What words are passed on?

### Hope Progression

*This learning structure is an adaptation of the Arts Approach to Multicultural Education Course at Lesley University Arts in Learning Department. This learning structure is based on an activity that Dr. Priscilla Sanville first created for her third graders. I had the honor to co-teach an Arts Approach to Multicultural Education graduate level course with Dr. Priscilla Sanville for many years.*

Listen to Anna Deveavere-Smith on Hope (3 minutes)

https://bigthink.com/videos/the-future-according-to-anna-deavere-smith/

*Each person chooses a personal space for this guided imagery of hope. You may want a journal. Sit comfortably and actively listen to the reflection prompt.*

Reflect on your life now and in the past and select an environment or space where you feel connected, nurturing, safe, a place where you can reflect, be creative. If you can't think of one, then imagine one you might like to be in…where is it? When do you go there or when would you like to go there? As you see the environment, notice the time of day, the smells, sounds, textures, colors, are there people there? Or are you alone? Are there animals or plants around you? Notice how you feel? What are you doing or are you still? What are the qualities of this place that attract you and connect you to your sense of safety and comfort? What are the elements of your environment that are most important to you? Is this a public place? Is this a private place? Is this a natural place? Is this space created by people?

What **words** describe your place, your values, your culture? As you see yourself in this place ask yourself: how do I access my **hope**? What brings me hope in difficult times? Imagine symbols/words that represent this hope? If you cannot think or feel a place of hope, imagine what it might be? How does my hope nurture my activism? When you are ready, allow yourself to journal for a few minutes on what came up for you and then create a drawing that represents this space incorporating your representation or **symbol of hope**…(watch your inner critic for those of you who drawing is not in your comfort zone).

When you have completed your drawing of your symbol of hope,

then create an image with your body representing your hope, in other words strike a pose with your whole body like an action frozen in time; think of a word or phrase that captures your pose to share later with the group.

Then do the same in pairs, connecting your images in silence

Then in groups of threes,

Fours

Etc. until the entire group is in a large sculpture, or configuration of hope.

First, have everyone speak from his or her image… all together …and then all speak at the same time.

Keep repeating their phrases over and over…have each go to a large paper on the wall and put the phrases down with images on the mural paper.

*WE ARE CREATING A SPACE FOR LISTENING AND LEARNING THAT INCLUDES THE CONTEXT THAT EACH PERSON BRINGS*

As the images/collective piece is complete have **students go back to their first partner and share what was the experience like for each of them.**

Share pictures (drawings) and elements of the environment as well as all that occurred during this progression/create mural/collage on mural paper roll with all of the drawings.

Notice and reflect:

What are the similarities and differences of elements of your environment or place?

What were the words/languages that you used to describe your place?

What are the similarities and differences of your places of hope?

Were there any surprises for you?

Were your spaces public, private, communal etc.?

Who owns the space for your environment?

Why are we doing this experience? How does activism align with your hope?

What does hope have to do with listening and language revitalization?

How do you make sense of insights on hope as activism?

> *Language as culture is the collective memory bank of a peoples experience in history.*
> *Ngũgĩ Wa Thiogo*

ngugiwathiongo.com

www.ttbook.org/interview/never-write-language-colonizer

## Note

1 Goldberg, Natalie. (2005). *Writing down the bones: Freeing the writer within.* London: Shambhala.

# AFTERWORD: THE KWAKWA̲KA̲'WAKW ART OF *KOTA* – ROOTED IN CULTURAL TRADITIONS, RE-ROUTED TO LANGUAGE REAWAKENING

*Laura Ann Cranmer and Patricia A. Shaw*

## Background

We are honored with the invitation to write the closing chapter to this anthology devoted to the pressing issues and challenges of supporting the reawakening, reclamation, and resurgence of the great diversity of Indigenous and diasporic languages and cultural traditions from around the world.

To provide some of the background underlying our collaborative work together, we reflect briefly on the fact that it was our respective commitment to the powerfully centering and transformative role that "the Arts" can play in addressing complex social and cultural issues that first brought us together. To launch the University of British Columbia's (UBC) Aboriginal Languages and Literacy Institute in 2006, Pat organized a week-long Forum Theater workshop on the challenges of "Reclaiming our Aboriginal Languages" with David Diamond, the Artistic Director of Headlines Theatre (subsequently renamed "Theatre for Living"). Laura was one of 16 individuals chosen from those who had answered the Call for Participants with "lived experience" of issues related to language loss. Despite multiple diversities in the linguistic heritage of these participants (14 different First Nations languages, spread from Mi'kmaq in the Maritimes to Kwak'wala on the North West coast) and generational age (ranging from 70 to 17), what emerged in the two plays that were workshopped that week was an acute awareness of many shared struggles and a deep yearning for reclaimed language identity. Since then, we – the two authors – have worked together across a wide spectrum of academic activities: Laura's PhD dissertation, Kwak'wala language classes at UBC and University of California Santa Barbara, community-engaged research and workshops together in Alert Bay and Vancouver, collaborative conference presentations, along with many long discussions alongside community

DOI: 10.4324/9781003302186-20

**FIGURE A1.1** A painting by Bill Holm of Laura's paternal great-grandmother, A̱baya (Sarah Martin), holding up a *kota* string figure with three circles representing "Sun, Moon and Star." Integrated into the background on the left is a photo of A̱baya as a young woman in her traditional regalia as a Weather dancer. The photo on the right features A̱baya as a toddler holding her father's copper, referred to in Kwak'wala as t'łakwa, in the shape of a shield.

language advocates about policy, curriculum, and the challenges of how to effectively move forward. We have enjoyed a warm friendship and productive working relationship centering on Kwak'wala revitalization.

The now critically endangered Kwak'wala language is classified within the northern branch of the Wakashan language family. Kwak'wala is traditionally divided into five major dialects traditionally spoken in the territories that extend across the northern part and down the eastern coast of Vancouver Island, stretching eastward to the adjacent mainland of British Columbia, including the many smaller islands in between. Our work with kota has evolved primarily in consultation with community members from 'Yalis | Alert Bay, Tsax̱is | Fort Rupert, Gwa'yi | Kingcome Inlet, Ławit'sis | Turnour Island, and the Kwakwa̱ka'wakw diaspora living in Vancouver, Nanaimo, and Qualicum Beach, BC.[1]

Community-engaged research projects such as this rely on and bring together multiple networks of communities. Most fundamentally, we thank the current broadly dispersed community of fluent speakers (see footnote 1) to help us understand kota, and we are immensely grateful to their families, Band Councils, and Cultural Institutions (most especially the U'mista Cultural Society) for welcoming us onto their traditional territories and into their homes. We build on the dedicated documentation and insights of previous scholars (see especially Averkieva & Sherman, 1992; Boas, 1947; Dick,1977; Sherman, 2001). We acknowledge the academic community (the First Nations and Endangered Languages program, Faculty of Arts, UBC) for making curricular and institutional space for Indigenous language reawakening. We appreciate the community of granting agencies to financially support such work.[2]

## The Art Form: *Kota*[3]

What *is* this genre of performative art that is referred to as kota? In the rich documentation compiled in Boas's unpublished dictionary of the Kwak'wala dialect of Kwagiutl (Boas, n.d.), "kota" is translated simply as "to play with strings." Although kota did indeed function as a pastime, as a leisure activity to entertain children and adults alike in the era before radio, tv, video games, and the multitude of digital online activities that have since lured people's attention away from communal interactions centered on a repertoire of oral traditions, kota was far more than a delightful playtime distraction.

Kota is a "way of listening" to stories that have been passed down through many generations, connecting people across time and traditional territory to family life and interpersonal rivalries, to cultural traditions and responsibilities, to spiritual beliefs and practices, to transgressions and consequences that follow from unsanctioned behaviour, to survival, to persistance, to humour, and to powerful worlds of supernatural beings where creativity and imagination abound.

Kota involves a single storyteller with a single loop of string varying from four to eight feet in circumferance. The kota tradition is therefore unlike some other string figure traditions such as Cat's Cradle, which are *interactive* in that one person creates a design that another person then modifies, with this kind of turn-taking proceeding in an alternating sequence. Because kota involves just a single person executing the string figure, it engages active participatory "listening" on many levels, as multiple modalities are invoked simultaneously. Accompanying the intricate execution of each visually complex sequence of shape-shifting string images, there is characteristically an oral recitation in Kwak'wala that delivers the storyline. This Kwak'wala language component is often recited as a kind of chant. Sometimes these verses are sung, although lamentably there is no transcription of the music itself in Averkieva's fieldnotes (1930), and relatively little documentation persists of the melodies and rhythms of the original musical accompaniments. A notable and valued contribution in this domain is the collaborative compilation, transcription, translation, and musical scoring by Dick, Shaughnessy, and Wilson (1977) of 10 kota songs.

On his final trip to Kwakwa̲ka'wakw territory in 1930, Franz Boas was accompanied by Julia Averkieva, a Russian ethnographer. The extensive field notes on string games from Averkieva's trip with Boas remained unpublished for several decades until an extremely dedicated individual, Mark Sherman, tracked down Averkieva's manuscripts, and engaged in the very challenging process of deciphering (posthumously) her notes and diagrams, as well as Boas's orthography. The edited collection was published in English, by UBC Press in 1992 – over 60 years after Averkieva's fieldwork. Even at the time they were documented (1930), Averkieva reported that the figures were not played extensively. In the generations since then, the once extensive repertoire of kota has largely fallen away from practice and memory.

What is particularly exciting about Averkieva's field notes is that her documentation of 112 distinct Kwakwa̲ka'wakw kota stands as *the most comprehensive* string collection ever assembled from a single Native American cultural group. Current generations are immensely grateful for Averkieva and Sherman's (1992) rich ethnographic contextualization of the social context of the creation and the function of string figures. On a deep personal level, several of our research colleagues have a very special relationship to the woman pictured on the cover of Averkieva and Sherman's book. Her Kwakwa̲ka'wakw name is Gwa̲nti'lakw, her English name is Agnes Cranmer. She is Gloria Cranmer Webster's mother, Carrie Mortimer's great-aunt, and Laura Cranmer's paternal grandmother.

## Prologue

Subsequent to the invasion of English into people's homes through the pervasive media presence of radio and TV, which radically eroded Kwak̓wala language use in the home, the performative practice of kota came to be referred to as what "*used to be* Indian TV." Lots of social warmth and memories come with this evocative characterization. Laura's reminiscences set the context:

*The quiet living room warmed by the woodstove in the basement, A̲baya perched on the burgundy couch creates moving images with kota – her high reedy voice sings to accompany the changing images that tell a story – entertaining the baby sitting on Gwa̲nti'lakw's yellow linoleum floor. This memory of A̲baya's pure love being mirrored back to me and taking delight in my responses remains a precious touchstone in my psyche as it would not be long after when everything in my life would be completely and seemingly irrevocably altered. After four years of institutionalization in my formative years (three years at the Nanaimo Indian Hospital followed by one year at St. Michael's Residential School in Alert Bay), my character and habitus imprinted by rigid routines, lacking in familial love, I had forgotten that early precious memory of my A̲baya when she loved and entertained me as a baby. I am now A̲baya (i.e., grandmother) to my own grandchildren, and while I mastered neither fluidity in kota nor fluency in Kwak'wala, my cherished memories of the sounds and rhythms of early exposure to both have deeply enhanced my cultural understandings and my language fluency in the context of this collaborative research project.*

*Gwa̲nti'lakw, my paternal grandmother, who cared for me in my toddler years, reported that in her own childhood kota was a common pastime for children to learn both the string figures and the songs. Then there was a rich and diverse repertoire of these figures to be made. Referred to as sa̱ba̱dzo'yibidu "little movies," the sequence of string images was a mode of storytelling, with the quickly transforming string formations creating abstract three-dimensional visual configurations to be filled in with the imagination of the viewer.*

In the sections to follow, we foreground just a few of the many kota that are part of the reawakening of this performative art form, beginning with the kota depicted earlier in Figure A1.1.

**kota 1: the "Sun, Moon and Star"** (Averkieva & Sherman, 1992, p. 69)

The lyrics for Sun, Moon and Star are as follows, transliterated here into the standard U'mista orthography from the Boasian transcription system that Averkieva used in her 1930 fieldnotes. A broad English translation of each phrase is given on a separate line immediately below.

P'a̱mxsolila̱la     'I'xa̱nt'inoxw ma'luxw t'si'da̱k
*putting arms through*    *two women always menstruating*

Tła'sa̱labalis,     'ma̱ku'labilis, t'ut'ubalis
*never ending*     *like the sun, moon and star*

The continual movement through the monthly menstrual cycle – the sisterhood of women linked arm in arm – is mirrored in the daily and monthly rotations of the heavenly bodies.

In Bill Holm's painting of A̱baya holding up the Sun, Moon and Star string figure, it is as if A̱baya has the cosmos in her hands. That Bill Holm would include the photos of A̱baya as a toddler holding her father's copper and as a mature woman in her Weather Dancer regalia reveals the arc of the life of a culturally grounded powerful matriarch, despite the brutally tumultuous cultural change wrought by colonial law in A̱baya's own lifetime.

**kota 2: the "Sitting on the Roof Series"** (Averkieva & Sherman, 1992, p. 40)

Laura's voice: *As a young girl, I would visit my beloved elder Dootda (Alice Smith, who was A̱baya's sister-in-law) who would let me look at her photograph collection. I was struck by one four inch by four inch sepia-toned photo that featured a man with his forehead deeply lined, a haunted expression, looking up at the camera hunched beside a dead grizzly bear, with a .22 rifle cradled in his arm. The background was a smoke house and the setting was in Dzawadi (known in English as Knight Inlet) where the seasonal rounds of procuring food supplies included the harvest of oolichans to render into oolichan oil – a prized delicacy of the Kwakwa̱ka'wakw. Dootda reported that the man in the photo had just shot the bear from the roof of the smoke house.*

*The kota string figure titled "Sitting on the Roof Series," as explained in the Averkieva and Sherman (1992) volume, depicts a scene that is reminiscent of this photo and provides a glimpse into the seasonal round of gathering and processing of marine resources and attendant challenges. In the kota lyric, the man is on the roof and is shooing the bear away with these words in Kwak'wala, loosely translated into English underneath:*

'Nixdzo's 'nixdzo's <u>k</u>in wiyaxalisi';
*I told you, I told you, you prevent me from getting off the roof.*

D<u>a</u>xw<u>a</u>xalisi' t<del>l</del>i'bida 'w<u>a</u> 'woo
"*Go away little bear!* 'wa - 'woo"

*Although the photo I recall was of a grizzly bear [g<u>a</u>la] and not the little bear [t<del>l</del>i'] in the kota lyric, the kota string figure depicts a scene that plays out from generation to generation, following the on-going traditional seasonal cycles in Kwakw<u>aka</u>'wakw territory. The continual replaying of the scene in a kota lyric reminds us of the realities of living in these coastal lands, of circumstances related to the challenges of the co-existence of bears and Kwakw<u>aka</u>'wakw people throughout this territory, and of their mutual dependence on the wealth of marine resources (like oolichan and salmon) that they both seek out.*

## kota 3: "Lying on Back in Canoe"

Beyond the topics of land and resources, kota also reveal important cultural references underpinning what on the surface might seem to be simply playful lyrics. Carrie's thoughts on this kota (#3) and the following one (#4) provide important insights into aspects of the Kwakw<u>aka</u>'wakw worldview.

Carrie's voice: *"Lying on Back in Canoe" recounts a story of a man who is lying in his canoe on the beach and of his responses to various offers that are made to him. Although a copper is a highly prestigous symbol of wealth and standing in Kwakw<u>aka</u>'wakw culture, the man in the canoe does not respond to any of the successive offers of one box of coppers, then two, then three. However, when he is offered four boxes of fern roots, he jumps up and takes that.*

Three fundamental insights into the construct of Kwakw<u>aka</u>'wakw values appear in this kota. First, the number four is fundamentally significant. It runs pervasively through Kwakw<u>aka</u>'wakw stories and performative rituals. Secondly, this kota speaks about coppers: ownership of a copper, let alone ownership of multiple boxes of coppers, would carry considerable prestige. Significantly, one of Gloria Cranmer Webster's names is 'Wik<u>a</u>lalils<u>a</u>me'g<u>a</u>, which translates as "Copper Carrying Woman." The third culturally embedded issue relates to fern roots. Now, if a man were offered fern roots in the Big House (the community building where sacred ceremonial events take place), and they were long, the host giving the fern roots was saying to everyone who was witnessing that this was a man of standing. And conversely, if the fern roots were short, the host was communicating to the assembled witnesses that the recipient was not held in as high esteem.

## kota 4: "Two Bear Brothers' Jealousy" (Averkieva & Sherman 1992, p. 114)

This kota features a dialogue between an older brother and his younger brother, centered on family tensions of sibling rivalry and jealousies. The younger brother pleads to travel along with his older brother, who is going to gather moss. However, the younger brother is rejected because the older brother doesn't want to be slowed down by his younger brother. The string figure image and action quite dramatically ends with the younger brother jumping ahead of the older brother in order to best his older brother.

The cultural use of moss will be referenced in Gloria Cranmer Webster's section below.

**kota 5: "A Salmon"** (Averkieva & Sherman 1992, pp. 108–109)

The lyrics to this kota are built on an infectiously repetitive pattern of call and response in four stanzas:

| | |
|---|---|
| 'Wixto'las akali? | *Where are you heading jumping?* |
| Qwi'xto'lan lax Gwa'dzi. | *I'm heading for Gwa'dzi.* |
| 'Wixto'las akali? | *Where are you heading jumping?* |
| Qwi'xto'lan lax Gayuxw. | *I'm heading for Gayuxw.* |
| 'Wixto'las akali? | *Where are you heading jumping?* |
| Qwi'xto'lan lax Hanwadi. | *I'm heading for Hanwadi.* |
| 'Wixto'las akali? | *Where are you heading jumping?* |
| Qwi'xto'lan lax Dzawadi. | *I'm heading for Dzawadi.* |

In comparing the lyrics to the title, we were initially quite mystified by there being no direct reference to "salmon" in the Kwak'wala words, despite the title of the kota explicitly referencing "salmon." The answer was quite fascinating!

Kwak'wala words are characteristically comprised of many internally meaningful elements called morphemes. Consider the morphemic breakdown of the question:

| | | | | | |
|---|---|---|---|---|---|
| 'Wixto'las akali? | | | | | |
| morphemes: | 'Wix | -to | -'l | -as aka | -li |
| meanings[4] | Q.where | -LS.head | -cont | -2s | V.jump |

When Laura asked Yotu, "How do we know – apart from the title, that is – that it is a salmon that is being addressed?" Yotu answered, "Because salmon aka and people daxwa!" Both verbs translate into English as "jump," but the Kwak'wala language uses a different lexical verb [aka] to express the movement of a salmon jumping compared to how a person jumps, for which only the verb [daxwa] would be appropriate.

In making the kota itself, an intricate manipulation of the string progresses through a sequence of four distinct stages of the salmon's journey, each configuration becoming more complex as one more destination is added. Ultimately, as seen in Figure A1.2, the string figure makes a zigzag pattern that can be superimposed over the map of the actual village sites that are named – each site is aligned with a point on the string figure.

The string pattern parallels the course of the salmon's journey, following the lyrics sequentially as they are chanted or sung aloud: he jumps from Gwa'dzi to Gayuxw, then to Hanwadi, which means "place for pink salmon," and then finally up to Dzawadi, at the head of Knight Inlet.

The salmon is not only a keystone species, but also is the basis for the sacred relationship between the Kwakwaka'wakw and the salmon, as expressed in

# Salmon: Knight Inlet

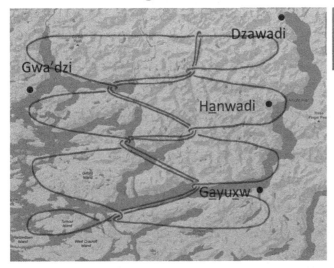

*Locations are approximate.

**FIGURE A1.2** A Salmon's journey jumping upstream through Knight Inlet, passing by major village sites.

Note: Sincere thanks to Fiona Campbell and Drew Smith for technical assistance in creating this figure.

Kwakwa̱ka'wakw origin stories, traditional songs, prayers, ceremonial dances, and names. In her keynote address, entitled "The Salmon People of the Alert Bay" (Cranmer Webster, 1998), Yotu relates an origin story of the 'Nak'waxda̱xw (one of the northern Kwagu'ł tribes) where Chief Umeł is instructed on how to get salmon for the river that he had just created to run through his village. Since twins are associated with salmon, with one twin being the head, and the other the tail, Umeł was sent to the grave of a twin to resurrect her to be his wife. She told Umeł that his people would enjoy salmon as long as her salmon tribe were treated with respect. Being a chief, Umeł promised his new wife that her people would be treated well, until he forgot his promise and became arrogant. When walking by his smokehouse and a piece of salmon bone got caught in his hair, Umeł flung the bone to the ground. Seeing this, his wife called her people and they went back into the river never to return.

The Salmon kota, a seemingly simple children's song that assumes communication between salmon and humans, reveals the sacred relationship between the Kwakwa̱ka'wakw and their knowledge of salmon, where the salmon travel to, what times of the year these annual cycles take place. The kota incorporates the Kwak'wala place names assigned to specific sites that indicate a primary home identified with a particular species of fish (e.g., Ha̱nwadi, a place of pink salmon,

Dzawadi, a place of oolichan), thus reinforcing the elemental connections between the people and the ecosystem in which they have lived for millenia.

Laura's voice: *For my part, deconstructing the song lyrics into its constituent parts of speech has greatly increased my understanding of the inner mechanics of how Kwak'wala works, and I found that my efforts to relearn Kwak'wala are cumulative and repetitive. The study of kota has helped me greatly in the singing of the songs. Although my memory of Abaya was for a time deeply buried, her singing and delight in my responses as a young one has become a precious touchstone.*

*The study of kota has become a doorway to other worlds of perception, worlds of knowing, and most importantly, a doorway to reconnection with family members, who have passed and who are living.*

## Gloria Cranmer Webster: Ways of Learning through Kota

Yotu's voice: *My great-grandfather George Hunt worked with the renowned anthropologist Franz Boas for almost 40 years, beginning in the late 1890s. On March 15, 1930, George wrote to Franz, commenting on the state of our language at that time. George said: One thing I know, they lost about two thirds of their language for there are lots of Indians comes and ask me the meaning of the words. This is the reason I say the language is disappearing.*

Yotu: *So here we are, eighty-three years later,[5] with our language in even worse shape than it was then. Mine may be the last generation with any degree of fluency in Kwak'wala. I mention this to give you some idea of the challenges we face in working with kota, or string figures. The language used in the chants is often different from that used by only a few people today. A videotape of my late mother and late aunt was made in 1986. My mother was 76 years old, my aunt was in her mid 90s. They spoke of their childhood, including learning kota from their older relatives. They would gather every evening or when the weather was bad. Both remember that the old people knew many kota. Among them, a man who was completely blind. One gets a strong sense of the closeness there was between young and old in earlier times when two or three generations of one family lived in the same house. While we can't go back to multi-generational living arrangements, we need to find a way to use kota as a way of teaching Kwak'wala and the culture in which it thrives.*

*There are so many lessons to be learned from kota. In the Two Brothers figure (see kota 4 above), children can learn about the traditional uses of moss, including its use as disposable diapers, long before white people invented them. Ours were better because they were biodegradable.*

*In learning the Man in the Canoe figure [see kota 3 above], children might ask: Why did the man choose four boxes of fern roots over four boxes of coppers? Was he boasting that he was so wealthy he didn't need any more coppers? What were coppers used for? How were our fern roots harvested, and when? Were other roots used for food? What does the number four signify?*

*A Salmon kota (see kota 5 above) is a lesson in geography with its list of place names and their meanings. When I worked at the U'mista Cultural Center, my mother and I taught Kwak'wala to a class of young parents and their children who shared a new experience. It was our most successful class. For kota to work as a teaching tool, that's where it's got to be done, and have some children learning together involving as many of the grandparents as possible. We all know about dysfunctional families in our communities, and maybe kota is a way to re-establish strong relationships between young and old.*

*Today we have to compete with TV, cell phones and all those other tech things that I don't understand and that scare me. So we better get it right.*

G̱ilakas'la. (a common word of closure, loosely translated as "thank you")]

While the general practice of kota has seemingly been obscured by the concerns of this fast paced modern life, as Yotu mentions, there are myriad ways kota can be used as a method of instruction to learn Kwak'wala and reveal lessons about familial relations (Two Bear Brothers' Jealousy), sacred resources (A Salmon), geographical lessons about the territory (A Salmon), natural life cycles (Sun, Moon and Star). Different tribes within the vast Kwakwa̱ka'wakw territory can gather together to share and teach their familial and communal versions of the different songs and string figures. For the kota whose melodies have been forgotten, the young traditional singers might be prevailed upon to create new melodies for the lyrics. Just as there are Lahal tournaments (gambling games involving diverse coastal and interior First Nations), so too could there be kota tournaments or meets between the tribes. The string figures range from the simple to the complex. Perhaps the easier string figures along with their lyrics and melodies can be introduced to the local daycare centers, on-reserve elementary schools as a practice. While the fingers learn the string figures, the ears learn the tunes and the Kwak'wala language.

## Afterword

At this point, we reflect back to the introductory address to this volume where, in recognition of the importance of our essential and over-arching oneness across all of humanity, Barreiro cites the Mohawk (Iroquois) phrase **akwe:kon** meaning "all of us," as well as the Lakota (Siouan) **mitakuye oyasin** meaning "we are all related." There is a powerful parallelism with Indigenous ontologies grounded in languages of the Pacific northwest. In hənq̓əmin̓əm̓ (Central Coast Salish), the word **nəca̓ʔmat** embraces the multiple intersecting relationships of "we are one." From the cultures along the western coast of Vancouver Island, Hereditary Chief Umeek (Atleo, 2004) clarifies how the Nuu-chah-nulth (Southern Wakashan) origin stories, life ways and experience all indicate that **heshookish tsawalk**, "everything is one." Similarly, in Kwak'wala, the word **na̱mwa̱yut**[6] conveys the deep understanding that "we are all one." One common humanity. One connected whole.

The art of kota is built simply on a string, a single string, a humble material resource accessible to everyone of every age in a community. The kota string is not a line with a beginning and an end. The "ends" of the string are neither visible nor relevant. The kota string is a circle, an iconic representation of a nonlinear, nonhierarchical, connected oneness. An embodiment of **namwayut**. The transformative power of the kota string is that this elemental single loop functions as a creative medium that can be manipulated through a sequence of hand gestures to express an infinite diversity of shapes, which – accompanied by the Kwak'wala language and song – tell stories deeply embedded in the cultural heritage of the Kwakwaka'wakw identity. The mutating shapes evolve, the fluidity of visual form and transformative movement creating a conceptual parallel to the fluidity of fluent speech, both being expressions of unique dimensions of creativity of the human mind embedded in a rich cultural heritage.

In his Opening Call foregrounding "Indigenous Creation: Literature as Historical/Cultural Recovery," Jose Barreiro invokes "… an approach to movement and creativity in the search for truth and liberation." In our closing piece for this volume, we have embraced the once-vibrant practice of kota as an approach to movement and creativity that is reawakening the critically endangered Kwak'wala language and liberating core components of Kwakwaka'wakw identity. This practice is steeped in a rich heritage of spiritual and material culture and deeply informed by ecological knowledge systems nurtured by their relationship to their traditional ancestral territories over millenia.

We are grateful to have had this opportunity to share the life-affirming, heartening, and loving aspects of learning Kwak'wala through the traditional Kwakwaka'wakw pastime known as kota.

## Notes

1 We are profoundly grateful to several Kwak'wala-speaking elders for their guidance: Gloria Cranmer Webster, Peter Matilpi, Chief Robert Joseph, Pauline Alfred, Vera Newman, Emily Aitken, and Peggy Swanvik. Our collaborative engagement with kota initially arose in the context of a Kwak'wala language class at UBC, co-instructed by Chief Robert Joseph and Patricia Shaw; classmate Julie Smith actively contributed to a foundational analysis of select kota lyrics with Laura and Carrie. In drawing on Shaw et al (2013), we particularly honour the work and words of Laura's beloved relatives Dr. Gloria Cranmer Webster (Laura's paternal aunt, affectionately known as Yotu) and Carrie Mortimer (1950–2015; also a grandaughter of Abaya), whose talent for kota and Kwak'wala language learning was a gift to us all. Both Yotu and Carrie's voices are threaded into the discussion here.

2 For support of this research, we gratefully acknowledge the Social Sciences and Humanities Research Council of Canada Aboriginal Strategic Research Grant (PI Patricia A. Shaw) entitled: Wigaxan's kwak'wale' xan's yak'anda's!
   *Let's keep our language alive!*

3 What is written as a plain "k" in the U'mista Kwak'wala orthography is a palatalized stop: "kota" is therefore pronounced (and sometimes spelled in other orthographic systems) as [k$^y$ota] or "kyota."

4 The abbreviations here stand for: Q = Question word; LS = Lexical Suffix; cont = continuative; 2s = second person singular Subject; V = verb

5 Cited from Shaw *et al*, 2013.
6 Significantly this word n<u>a</u>mw<u>a</u>yut stands as the rallying cry for the Reconciliation Canada movement, founded by the visionary Kwakw<u>a</u>k<u>a</u>'wakw leader, Chief Dr. Robert Joseph, OC, OBC, LLD, Hereditary Chief of the Gwawa'enuk First Nation. See reconciliationcanada.ca.

## References

Atleo, E. Richard. 2004. *Tsawalk: A Nuu-chah-nulth Worldview.* Vancouver: UBC Press.

Averkieva, Julia & Mark Sherman. 1992. *Kwakiutl String Figures.* Vancouver: UBC Press.

Averkieva, Julia. 1930. Unpublished fieldnotes from trip with Franz Boas to Kwakiutl territory. (The designation Kwakiutl is variously transcribed in the literature as Kwagiutł, Kwagiuł or Kwagu'ł *(inter alia)*, referencing the traditional First Nations territories and peoples around Fort Rupert/Port Hardy, BC.)

Boas, Franz. 1947. *Kwakiutl Grammar with a Glossary of the Suffixes,* Philadelphia: American Philosophical Society.

Boas, Franz. n.d. *Kwakiutl Dictionary.* Typescript ms. Edited by Helene Boas Yampolsky. *Franz Boas Collection of American Indian Linguistics,* American Philosophical Society, Philadelphia.

Cranmer Webster, Gloria. 1998. The Salmon People of Alert Bay. *Proceedings of the Twelfth International Abashiri Symposium,* Japan.

Dick, Mary (ʔənica). 1977. q̓iq̓əndəm qe da kodayu II. Songs for the Cat's Cradle II. Transcribed and translated by Freda Shaughnessy; music score by Peter Wilson. Proceedings of the 11th International Conference on Salishan Languages.

Shaw, Patricia A., Laura A. Cranmer, Carrie Mortimer, Gloria Cranmer-Webster. 2013. "Sharing Kwakw<u>a</u>k<u>a</u>'wakw Worlds of Knowledge through Kota." Presentation at the International Conference on Language Documentation and Conservation (ICLDC 3). University of Hawai'i, Manoa. [ScholarSpace, Manoa, Hawai'i: http://hdl.handle.net/10125/26128]

Sherman, Mark. 2001. Kwaguitl String Figures. DVD produced by the International String Figure Association.

# INDEX

*Note*: Endnotes are indicated by the page number followed by "n" and the note number.

9781032275468